VAN BUREN DISTRICT LIBRARY

P9-CNI-653

THE COMPLETE IDIOT'S GUIDE® TO

Getting Published

Fifth Edition

by Sheree Bykofsky and Jennifer Basye Sander

ALPHA

A member of Penguin Group (USA) Inc.

VAN BUREN DISTRICT LIBRARY
DECATUR, MICHIGAN 49045

808.02
Byk

ALPHA BOOKS

Published by the Penguin Group

Penguin Group (USA) Inc., 375 Hudson Street, New York, New York 10014, USA

Penguin Group (Canada), 90 Eglinton Avenue East, Suite 700, Toronto, Ontario M4P 2Y3, Canada (a division of Pearson Penguin Canada Inc.)

Penguin Books Ltd., 80 Strand, London WC2R 0RL, England

Penguin Ireland, 25 St. Stephen's Green, Dublin 2, Ireland (a division of Penguin Books Ltd.)

Penguin Group (Australia), 250 Camberwell Road, Camberwell, Victoria 3124, Australia (a division of Pearson Australia Group Pty. Ltd.)

Penguin Books India Pvt. Ltd., 11 Community Centre, Panchsheel Park, New Delhi—110 017, India

Penguin Group (NZ), 67 Apollo Drive, Rosedale, North Shore, Auckland 1311, New Zealand (a division of Pearson New Zealand Ltd.)

Penguin Books (South Africa) (Pty.) Ltd., 24 Sturdee Avenue, Rosebank, Johannesburg 2196, South Africa

Penguin Books Ltd., Registered Offices: 80 Strand, London WC2R 0RL, England

Copyright © 2011 by Sheree Bykofsky and Jennifer Basye Sander

All rights reserved. No part of this book shall be reproduced, stored in a retrieval system, or transmitted by any means, electronic, mechanical, photocopying, recording, or otherwise, without written permission from the publisher. No patent liability is assumed with respect to the use of the information contained herein. Although every precaution has been taken in the preparation of this book, the publisher and authors assume no responsibility for errors or omissions. Neither is any liability assumed for damages resulting from the use of information contained herein. For information, address Alpha Books, 800 East 96th Street, Indianapolis, IN 46240.

THE COMPLETE IDIOT'S GUIDE TO and Design are registered trademarks of Penguin Group (USA) Inc.

International Standard Book Number: 978-1-61564-127-7
Library of Congress Catalog Card Number: 2011905824

13 12 11   8 7 6 5 4 3 2 1

Interpretation of the printing code: The rightmost number of the first series of numbers is the year of the book's printing; the rightmost number of the second series of numbers is the number of the book's printing. For example, a printing code of 11-1 shows that the first printing occurred in 2011.

Printed in the United States of America

Note: This publication contains the opinions and ideas of its authors. It is intended to provide helpful and informative material on the subject matter covered. It is sold with the understanding that the authors and publisher are not engaged in rendering professional services in the book. If the reader requires personal assistance or advice, a competent professional should be consulted.

The authors and publisher specifically disclaim any responsibility for any liability, loss, or risk, personal or otherwise, which is incurred as a consequence, directly or indirectly, of the use and application of any of the contents of this book.

Most Alpha books are available at special quantity discounts for bulk purchases for sales promotions, premiums, fundraising, or educational use. Special books, or book excerpts, can also be created to fit specific needs.

For details, write: Special Markets, Alpha Books, 375 Hudson Street, New York, NY 10014.

Publisher: *Marie Butler-Knight*
Associate Publisher: *Mike Sanders*
Executive Managing Editor: *Billy Fields*
Senior Acquisitions Editors: *Paul Dinas, Brook Farling*
Senior Development Editor: *Christy Wagner*
Senior Production Editor: *Kayla Dugger*

Copy Editor: *Amy Lepore*
Cover Designer: *Kurt Owens*
Book Designers: *William Thomas, Rebecca Batchelor*
Indexer: *Johnna VanHoose Dinse*
Layout: *Brian Massey*
Senior Proofreader: *Laura Caddell*

Contents

Appendixes

Introduction

Books, wonderful books. It seems like such a dream that you might someday see your very own name on the cover of a book sitting proudly on a bookstore shelf or Google yourself and find a link to your book. Quit dreaming! It's high time you turned that dream into reality—*your* reality! Together, we've been in the book business for 50 plus years, and we've seen it all (or nearly all). We've been interns, editors, authors, agents, and packagers, and we've learned what works and what doesn't. Much is changing, and this is an exciting time to be in the publishing world, but much about the process remains the same.

As editors, we've evaluated thousands of projects. As authors, we've struggled to come up with ideas for books that would catch an editor's eye. As agents, we've sorted through thousands of queries in search of potential authors, and as packagers, we've tried to craft marketable books. Now we'd like to share all our hard-won knowledge with you. In the pages that follow, we explain the ever-changing book publishing process and guide you through it as smoothly as possible. You'll find yourself going from first-time writer straight through to publishing know-it-all in the time it takes to read this book.

Every writer has a reason for wanting to be published. Some of us want a forum for our ideas, some want fame, and some just flat out want fortune. No matter what your reason, to get published you'll need to convince many other folks along the way to believe in you and your writing. There's an art to doing that, and we explain it to you step by step in this book.

The book publishing business can be tough, and it can be crazy at times, but it's an exciting industry that's pretty darn fun just to be around. Although you may well experience some frustration and a disappointment or two on your way to becoming a published author, you can look forward to the satisfaction you'll feel: the pure pleasure of knowing that your ideas and your vision are being shared with the world.

How to Use This Book

The book publishing process is really a rather easy one to understand when you break it down into its five major steps:

Part 1, As You Begin to Write, explores the many reasons writers write (what's yours?) and helps you determine what the market's like for the book you want to write. What are the hot and not-so-hot topics and genres today, and how can you stay in the know?

Part 2, Submitting to Publishers, is where you find the different, sometimes bewildering methods of submitting your proposal. Here you find everything from how to avoid looking like an amateur on the page to the reasons why so many manuscripts are rejected.

Part 3, Getting a Book Contract, tackles the age-old problem that all prospective authors face: just how do you get an editor and a publisher to fall in love with your proposal and offer you a contract? Do you need an agent, and if so, how do you get a good one? How do you find editors and win them over all by yourself, if that's the route you want to take? What can you do at a writers' conference? Here's where you find out what you need to know about how publishers decide to publish. Here's also where you find out what to ask for—and what to avoid like the plague—in book contracts.

Part 4, Working with a Publisher, walks you through the actual process of being published. Now that you have a book publishing contract, a deadline, and an editor to work with, what's going to happen? Here's where you'll see the entire production process.

Part 5, Continuing Your Career as an Author, helps you develop a life that extends beyond just one book. From building yourself a career as a speaker or consultant, to learning how to supercharge the number of book projects you create, this is where you'll find out about the many ways to make money from your writing skills. We've included an overview of the sometimes bewildering world of e-books and print on demand in case you decide to explore that route to being published.

But wait, there's more. At the back of the book you'll find several handy appendixes full of resources to further you along the path to getting published. And to be sure you don't get lost in publishing lingo, we've included a glossary with all the words and terms you'll need to hold your own in conversations with agents, editors, publicists, and other book people.

But Wait! There's More!

Have you logged on to idiotsguides.com lately? If you haven't, go there now! As a bonus to the book, we've included even more information on becoming a published author you'll want to check out. Point your browser to idiotsguides.com/gettingpublished, and enjoy!

Extras

Look for these little asides and comments sprinkled throughout the chapters, extra bits of inside info we just can't resist whispering into your ear as you read:

HOT OFF THE PRESS

We've got many tales to tell about the publishing world. Some will make you wiser, and some will make you laugh out loud.

DEFINITION

Publishing terms are clearly defined here. Never again will you feel out to sea when the book talk turns technical.

SLUSH PILE

These are dire warnings, things to be avoided at all costs. They're the worst mistakes, the biggest pitfalls, and the most dangerous missteps to which writers can fall prey.

EXPERTS SAY

Here's where our friends and colleagues share their expertise. This is real advice from those involved in the book world.

Acknowledgments

Jennifer thanks her colleagues at the UC Davis Extension Arts and Humanities department and the talented women who continually inspire her at Write by the Lake. My students and retreat attendees help me remain grateful for the chance to be involved in the world of books on a daily basis. To my guys—Julian and Jonathan, you are the best. And to the fabulous Paula Munier—without her assistance, the chapters on fiction would mostly be blank.

Sheree thanks her associate Janet Rosen. Thanks to all the authors whom I represent— you are the reason I love my work. I'm grateful to all my agent and editor friends and colleagues for all their guidance, support, knowledge, and the laughs.

We'd both like to thank all the knowledgeable publishing folks who took our repeated phone calls and shared their expertise as we researched and wrote this book—and, indeed, throughout our careers. Thanks also to Development Editor Christy Wagner for superhuman development editing. Finally, thanks to Paul Dinas and his colleagues at Alpha Books for giving us this opportunity to share our knowledge with you.

Trademarks

All terms mentioned in this book that are known to be or are suspected of being trademarks or service marks have been appropriately capitalized. Alpha Books and Penguin Group (USA) Inc. cannot attest to the accuracy of this information. Use of a term in this book should not be regarded as affecting the validity of any trademark or service mark.

As You Begin to Write

You think you'd like to write—actually, you know you'd like to write. So just how do you get started? In Part 1, we take a look at the major reasons why people write. The more you know about why you want to write and what you hope to achieve, the greater your chances for doing it successfully.

We also give you an inside look at how book professionals come up with ideas for books that sell and sell. When you've mastered this end of the business, you get a close-up look at the markets for different types of books. From fiction to how-to, from steam punk to shtick lit, you learn what's hot and what's not.

Understanding how the book and publishing world works is an important step toward success for any writer, whether your goal is to see your work pubbed by a big house, or to eventually put it out on your own.

Once you learn how the categories work, you will never again wander casually through a bookstore without looking carefully to see trends and spot holes in the market. Soon, you'll be a working member of the profession!

So Why Write?

In This Chapter

- The best reasons to write
- The future of books
- The big business of book business
- Approaching publishing like trying out for a game show
- Publishers need writers—like you!

Congratulations! You've taken a big, big step. You've bought a book on getting published. And that's exactly what you'll learn in the following pages: how to get published.

Just imagine the glory and hosannas that await you as a published *author*: fat royalty checks, impressive literary awards, newspaper articles, a Huffington Post blog, speaking engagements, applause, and public recognition. Ah, life will be grand!

Well, life *might* be grand—or there's a very good chance getting published won't change your life at all. In many ways, we hope this book serves as both a cheerleader (you *can* do it!) and a reality check (that's *reality*, not *royalty* check). Take it from a couple of women who know: writing is very hard work. Getting published is very hard work. Selling books is very hard work.

But before we usher you onto the path toward a career as an author, let's step back to ask a critical question: just why do *you* want to write a book? Writing an entire book is a whole lot of work and effort. What's in it for you?

What's Your Reason?

There are as many reasons to write as there are books on a bookstore shelf. Is yours on this list?

- I'm compelled to write.
- I want the personal satisfaction of being published.
- I hope to advance my cause.
- I want to share my knowledge.
- I'd like to further my career.
- I'd like to achieve fame.
- I'd like to earn a fortune.
- All of the above.

DEFINITION

An **author** is one who writes a book or books. The word usually implies a published writer. The **royalty** is the percentage of book sales the publisher pays the author for each copy of a book sold.

I'm Compelled to Write

Some folks sit down and write because they're consumed with an inner need to write. These people must write—they can't *not* do it. They wake up in the middle of the night with the urge to jot down a few lines or even write entire pages. For these folks, writing comes naturally; it just feels right.

Have you ever heard a novelist say, "The characters are writing the book, and I'm just holding the pen" or "I've got to get these ideas on paper!" If either sounds like you, then you're someone who's *compelled* to write. Getting published may very well be your primary goal; making money would be nice, but it could be of secondary importance.

I Want the Personal Satisfaction of Being Published

Putting pen to paper (or fingers to keyboard) can be very fulfilling. And when your writing project is finished, you will have accomplished something very real. Instead of talking endlessly about how you plan to write a book *someday*, you will have done it!

Not only is the process of writing satisfying, but there are also psychological rewards to be gained from being published. The pride and satisfaction that can come from writing a book are unsurpassed. Imagine the day when you can stand in a bookstore aisle and see your name on a book. Picture typing your name into a search engine and smiling at all the results.

I Hope to Advance My Cause

Do you have a message you want to share with the world (or at least with anyone smart enough to buy your book)? You want to share your beliefs—political, philosophical, religious, or whatever—to advance a cause. More than one politician has launched his or her national campaign with a published book.

Not just wannabe pols, of course, but think also of folks like Michael Pollan of *The Omnivore's Dilemma* and the impact his book has had on the discussion about our food supply.

I Want to Share My Knowledge

You might know how to build a better mousetrap, and you think the world needs to know, too. This isn't quite the same thing as writing to advance a cause, but it's a mission to help people do something—or do something better. Perhaps you've spent 20 years underneath cars and believe you can tell car owners a better way to care for and maintain their automobiles.

The market for how-to information seems endless, and writers with useful knowledge to share can sometimes hit the big time. The old business axiom "Find a need and fill it" still holds true in today's ever-changing book market.

I'd Like to Further My Career

Publishing a book in your field can be a very powerful way to supercharge your career. Why languish in obscurity when you can gain recognition as an expert in your field? Who knows, you could build a second career as a consultant or a speaker.

There are almost as many marketing consultants in the nation as there are stockbrokers, but only one of those marketing consultants jump-started her career with a book about marketing to the group with the biggest purchasing power—moms. Maria Bailey has now written three books on the topic and is regularly quoted in the pages of *The New York Times* and *The Wall Street Journal*. Frequently hired by Fortune 100 companies, she is the acknowledged "go to" expert in this field. She built a million-dollar consulting business on books that distinguished her from her competitors.

Don't get the idea that only businesspeople can advance their careers with a book. Doctors see a huge boost in patients and endorsement deals when the medical books they've written become popular. It worked for Drs. Andrew Weil, Pamela Peeke, Christiane Northrup, and Nicholas Perricone. Almost any other type of career can be built up this way, including careers as motivational speakers, beauticians, massage therapists, and child-care providers. Could writing a book be your ticket to the top?

I'd Like to Achieve Fame

Similar to writers who hope to advance their careers, some writers hope getting published will make them famous, if only in their own neighborhoods, towns, and states or among their colleagues. The world is a celebrity-conscious place, and who wouldn't want the things that come with fame: the best table in a restaurant, a complimentary bottle of wine, your picture in *People* magazine, admiring fans, and maybe a spot on the couch at the *Today* show some morning?

Do you long to be recognized as you walk down the street? A published book might get you that. Fame is not always linked directly to fortune, however. And getting your book published may make its title but not your face (and sometimes not even your name) familiar to many. Quick, who wrote *Robert's Rules of Order?**

And some successful authors miss out on the fame part entirely. Stieg Larsson, who wrote the three-volume *Millennium* series of Swedish thrillers, died a few months before his first book, *The Girl with the Dragon Tattoo*, was even published.

Even enormously successful writers don't have the same profile as a B-list movie or television actor. You might recognize J. K. Rowling if she was at the table next to yours in a restaurant, but probably not Stephanie Meyer, author of the *Twilight* books.

**Major Henry M. Robert compiled the* Rules *in 1876.*

I'd Like to Earn a Fortune

It's by no means guaranteed, but writing a book (or writing several books) is a possible route to fortune. Rick Warren of *The Purpose-Driven Life* didn't set out to earn a fortune with his book; he was happily preaching to his big church. His book has gone on to be one of the biggest sellers in publishing history, making him "fortunate" indeed.

Making big bucks by writing books is a big goal that, quite frankly, not many achieve. But if this is what drives you, then give it all you've got. Begin by making sure your book idea has mass appeal. The smaller and more specialized the potential audience for your book, the dimmer the chances you'll make lots of money from it.

Fame doesn't always follow fortune. No doubt you recognized J. K. Rowling's and Rick Warren's names, but there are many authors whose names you'd never recognize who have, nevertheless, earned lots of money writing books. The unsung authors of popular textbooks and other books below the radar that sell year after year without ever showing up on *best-seller* lists might be unrecognized on the street, but they're very well known at the bank.

DEFINITION

The term **best-seller** is used loosely in the publishing business. Strictly speaking, it refers to a book that's appeared on a best-seller list somewhere, or sells very well in a niche. In reality, publishers and their publicity staffs attach the term to almost any book they haven't lost their shirts on!

All of the Above

Few writers have one single reason for writing. Most of us combine an emotional need to write with a secret desire for fame and a not-so-secret desire for fortune.

Why should you stop to examine the reasons you write? Because if you understand why you want to write, you can do a much better job of planning how to get published.

Is a need for inner satisfaction the only thing driving you? If so, you might be happy seeing your work published in a small literary journal. Do you have grand plans to advance your career and raise your professional profile? That calls for a specific plan of attack. Is making a fortune your primary goal? Then you'd better skip ahead to

Chapter 3 to scope out the kinds of books that are selling well. To avoid disappointment, be sure your ultimate goal and your book's sales potential match.

> **EXPERTS SAY**
>
> According to a survey taken by the Jenkins Group a few years ago, 81 percent of Americans "feel they have a book in them." The rise of print on demand and do-it-yourself e-book publishing will help many of them realize that dream.

As you embark on your publishing journey, understand that this is most often a long and slow process. If you want to write because you want to see your work available *right now*, look into some of the many other ways to be read. If you feel compelled to advance a cause or share your knowledge ASAP, blogs, print on demand (POD), e-books, e-zines, newsletters, or podcasts can help get you there faster.

Do People Still Buy Books?

"Writing a book will take me the next few years. By the time I finish, books won't even exist!" The dire prediction is everywhere: Americans don't read anymore, the book publishing industry is dead, bookstores are dead, books as we know them will soon cease to exist. So why bother writing a book?

Our well-informed and professionally stated response to those naysayers is "No way!"

Mergers and Chains

Ever since Gutenberg invented his printing press (and then quickly lost it to his creditors), the publishing industry has been evolving. Many working in publishing today like to reminisce about the bygone days during which literary editors and their beloved authors could while away the afternoon with a pitcher of martinis and a discussion of the finer points of writing, much like an episode of *Mad Men*. These days, large publishing companies are seldom run by men with martini pitchers in their offices, but rather are headed by business folks with a strong sense of the bottom line.

Even the number of large publishing houses is shrinking. (Publishing businesses are still anachronistically known as "publishing houses" after the days when most companies operated out of brownstones or townhouses that were formerly single-family dwellings.) The smaller companies are being bought up and combined into "super houses" with 10 or 20 different imprints. One editor at a major New York house likes to joke that although she's had only two different jobs, as a result of mergers, she's actually worked for seven different companies. But small and medium-size publishers all over the country are willing to take risks with topics and authors other houses might avoid. They might also have the time to linger over a glass in the afternoon, too ....

And while publishing companies merged, more bookstores struggled to stay open. The decision-making buying power was for a time concentrated in the hands of two or three large retail chains, but that is changing dramatically. The rise in book sales in nonbook outlets such as Target and Walmart helps, and even specialty retail chains like Urban Outfitters and Kitson now have large stacks of books on display. Some people are predicting the return of more locally owned bookstores and *independent booksellers*. Those that managed to stay open throughout the Borders era now have an improved outlook.

> **DEFINITION**
>
> An **independent bookseller** is a locally owned bookstore. Before the rise (and fall) of national chains such as Borders and Barnes & Noble, most towns were served by independents. Fans of independent booksellers believe the staffs there are more knowledgeable and better able to promote little-known and local authors. Some strong indie stores are Powell's in Portland, Tattered Cover in Denver, and Elliot's in Seattle.

We talk more about all the dramatic changes in the bookselling scene later, but the good news for writers is, no matter where they buy, Americans are still buying books. In fact, the U.S. Census Bureau reported that national bookstore sales came in at $16.5 billion in 2010! Those book buyers are what keep the industry going.

Online Book Sales and E-Book Sales

As further proof of the health and vibrancy of the ancient art of publishing, we need only point to the continuing strength of book sales online. Both actual books and e-books are still humming along. Amazon reported a stunning change midway through 2010: sales of books for its Kindle e-reader had overtaken the sales of hardcover books. Amazon sold 143 Kindle books for every 100 hardcovers, and the ratio is continuing to rise.

No need for authors to bemoan the switch to e-books; it's simply another book format. Hardcover, trade paperback, e-book—a book is a book, no matter what format it comes in.

Leaner and Meaner

The days when publishing was a genteel pursuit for the wealthy and authors were coddled are gone. The book business has to live in the real business world and is continually streamlining its processes. Book publishing as an industry is competently competing in the fast-paced, entertainment-driven world we now occupy. Sure, it's a tough business, but what business isn't tough?

So should you put a part of your life on hold and devote yourself to writing that book you dream of? We say, "Go for it!"

Open for Business

Now that we've convinced you that the book business is a fairly healthy one, here's your first insider's tip for success. If you learn only one thing from this book, let it be the following: *the book business is a business*. Seems simple, doesn't it? But so few authors who want to be published approach it as a business.

Product Is King

Let's forget about writing books for a moment and pretend you have an idea for a coffee company you've long dreamed of opening. What would your first step be? You'd plunge headfirst into learning everything you could about how the coffee world operates, wouldn't you? You'd spend hours sitting in Starbucks trying to figure out where its success comes from, sipping cup after cup to develop a better sense of what kind of roasted beans seem to be the most popular. You might even do a bit of travel and visit coffee plantations to see how that part of the business operates. And when you've learned everything possible, then and only then would you start to draw up the plans for your own coffee company.

Now if you decide to write a book, do you take all those same steps to achieve success? Sadly, far too few authors do. But they should!

We've said it before, but it's worth repeating: the book publishing industry is a business, just like the coffee industry, the breakfast cereal industry, or the auto industry. Product is king, and you need to learn how to approach the industry with your product. The more businesslike you are, the greater your chances for success.

HOT OFF THE PRESS

One big topic of concern for publishers has long been the decline in book reviews. Newspapers and magazines depend on advertising dollars for revenue, and as their fortunes decline, they've cut back on editorial pages. Articles about books and authors still appear on a regular basis, but the traditional book review section of a newspaper is disappearing nationwide. Blogs and tweets and other short-form mentions of books are on the rise, though, and can affect sales.

Many Happy Returns?

One major facet of the book business all authors need to understand is that unlike other retail businesses, books are 100 percent returnable merchandise. If dress shop owners buy a dress from a manufacturer and can't sell it, they mark it down until it moves. If booksellers can't sell a book, they box it up and ship it back to the publisher for full credit.

This method is a leftover from the depression era, when publishers were desperate to get more of their product into the marketplace and booksellers were tight on cash. Ever since then, publishers have tried to get this industry policy changed, but as you can imagine, booksellers like it just the way it is.

Research, Research, Research!

Start right now to learn everything you can about the book business. Become a permanent fixture in your local bookstore. Take the manager out to lunch and ask about the business. Read the trade magazine *Publishers Weekly*. Find out what the proper etiquette is when trying to get published. Learn the lingo. (Far from an admission of idiocy, buying this book was a master stroke of genius; you're on your way to learning the ropes!) Your goal is getting published, so be serious about it.

EXPERTS SAY

Trade publications in any industry aren't cheap, and the publishing business is no exception. *Publishers Weekly*, the weekly magazine dedicated to the publishing industry, runs more than $200 a year but is well worth subscribing to. You might be able to read it for free in your library (ask the reference librarian if the library subscribes) or split the cost with a fellow writer and share a subscription. Visit publishersweekly.com for current prices and to subscribe to its e-newsletters for free.

Websites geared toward writers abound. One of the best is run by the *Writer's Digest* folks at writersdigest.com. Subscriptions give you access to more professional parts of the website.

Visit publishersmarketplace.com to read about what kinds of books are being sold and who is buying them. The Publishers Marketplace folks also put out Publishers Lunch, a free daily e-zine read by everyone in the publishing business. It's filled with great info and also links to any major book-related news stories that occurred that day. You can sign up to receive it at the website. Upgrade to a paid monthly subscription, and you'll get a weekly e-mail detailing a blow-by-blow description of what book deals were done the week before. It includes info on the size of the advance, the editor who bought it, and the agent who sold it.

But I Don't Live in New York!

Although it sometimes seems that way, not all writers live in New York City. One of the great things about becoming a writer is that you can live anywhere in the country—anywhere in the world even—and still pursue a career writing books. As long as the UPS driver can find your house (or you've got a phone, fax, and Internet connection), you can deal with agents, editors, and publishers.

Co-author Sheree does live near New York City and wouldn't dream of living anywhere else, but co-author Jennifer has managed to build a book publishing career without ever having moved away from her hometown of Sacramento, California—not exactly a well-known publishing metropolis. Within a few miles' range of Jennifer live fantasy writer Peter Beagle of *The Last Unicorn*, Karen Joy Fowler of *The Jane Austen Book Club*, and best-selling legal thriller author John Lescroart.

Checking out other obscure (meaning not New York!) parts of the country, you'll find writer Deborah Sharp of the *Mace Bauer* mysteries in South Florida and best-selling author Stuart Woods on Mount Desert Island in Maine.

Don't feel left out geographically. If you're determined and professional, and if you keep at it, you can get published no matter where you live.

Think of Yourself as a Contestant

Sheree likes to encourage unpublished writers by telling them the story of how she got on the TV game show *Wheel of Fortune*. She believes that for many types of books, both publishing and game shows require similar paths to success.

"I decided that I wanted to be on *Wheel of Fortune*, and so I studied everything about the show," explains Sheree. "I learned how to dress like the contestants I'd seen every night on the show, how to talk the way the contestants talked ('Hi, my name is Sheree, and I'm a literary agent'), and in general, how to act like a contestant. So when I walked into the room filled with hundreds of other folks who wanted to be on the show, I stood out as someone who looked, sounded, and acted like a contestant. And it worked! The producers chose me." And as Jennifer was a successful contestant on *The Weakest Link*, there might be something to this theory!

Literary agents, publishers, and editors (especially those involved in popular trade books) are like the producers of a game show. They know just what they're looking for to suit their needs, and it's up to you to show them you're a contestant.

So you want to be a published author? Then learn how to walk, talk, and think like a published author. Go out of your way to meet other writers and learn what you can from them. Join writers' groups, go on writers' retreats, and buy books on writing and writers. Keep track of what authors are coming to your town to give talks, and sit front and center in the audience, soaking up what they have to say. Seek out other writers online. Ask published writers to tell you how they made it. And don't be surprised when they tell you! Everyone likes to talk about his or her own success (and maybe even about some of the disappointments). You just have to ask.

Writers Wanted!

When newspapers and magazines aren't trumpeting the downfall of the book publishing industry, they're warning readers against the avalanche of the 400,000-plus books published each year. As writers, it's all too easy to look at that figure and be discouraged. But shift your way of thinking for a second and think of what a great business this is! With more than 400,000 books published every year, that's 400,000 chances to win! Why shouldn't yours be among the chosen?

Although many (if not most) manuscripts meet with rejection, the odds that one of the published books will be yours are much better than the likelihood of hitting the Powerball lottery.

Don't ever lose sight of the fact that the book business needs writers so it can keep publishing books. Agents need authors, publishers need authors, and editors need authors—no matter what they tell you. Don't be intimidated or discouraged by your encounters with these folks because they need you to stay in business. Readers need words, publishers need words, and words come from one source—you, the writer.

If your first efforts meet with rejection, use that as an opportunity to rework and refine your ideas. Perhaps a different approach might work. In the next few chapters, you learn more about how to successfully develop an idea for a book and put together a proposal that will help catch an agent's (or editor's) eye.

So why write? Because you could get published!

The Least You Need to Know

- Writing can be a very rewarding experience emotionally or financially—or both!
- Perfectly ordinary folks have become published writers. There's no reason to be intimidated by the idea.
- Book publishing is a business, and you need to approach it in a businesslike manner.
- Americans are reading more and buying more books, and the market for books is strong and healthy.
- Yes, publishing is full of potential rejection, but it also needs writers to write books—writers like you!

Write What?

In This Chapter

- The importance of identifying your category
- Books the world *doesn't* need
- A look at the major book categories
- Good-selling categories identified

So there you are at your big family Thanksgiving dinner, seated next to your brother-in-law. "What's new with you?" he asks. "I'm writing a book," you answer proudly, eager to trump the announcement he just made about his big promotion. "Oh yeah? What kind of book are you writing?" Silence descends as you search for a way to describe your book. All eyes turn toward you as you sit there at the festive holiday table, dumbstruck by such a basic question.

What kind of book are you writing? It's a simple question but one too few first-time authors can answer with ease. What's your book about? If you can't clearly define it, you're headed for trouble every step of the way.

Start at the beginning. What book category does it fall into? Envision yourself for a moment in your local bookstore. Notice how carefully the categories are divided. Shelves are dedicated to cookbooks, health books, graphic novels, new fiction, romance, business, and more—row after row of books on all different topics. Where do you picture your book?

"What kind of a book am I writing?" you respond. "Well, it's kind of difficult to say, sort of a cross between a health book and an inspirational book, with a tiny bit of romance thrown in."

Sorry, but that won't cut it. If you can't clearly define your book, neither can an agent or a publisher—or worse yet, a bookseller. So pick a category, the closest category that fits your book, and stick with it.

What the World *Doesn't* Need

All kinds of books exist, but some topics are overpublished, and some categories have too many books in them. We checked with booksellers to find out what topics they felt are currently overpublished. Here are their top picks:

- Political bashing books
- Vampire, zombie, and ghost books
- Celebrity tell-alls
- Travel memoirs

So do we think you should steer clear of these areas? Not necessarily. However, do stay away from most of these topics unless you have some really new way of looking at them. Co-author Jennifer's long-time publishing mentor, Ben Dominitz, believes there are two good reasons to publish a book: "One, because no one has published a book on that topic, and two, because everyone has published a book on that topic."

But Enough About You

What the world hardly ever needs, however, is a book about your life story. This is harsh news to deliver so early in a book on getting published, but we want you to have a realistic idea of how personal memoirs (accounts of the events in a person's life) are viewed in the world of book publishing. Somebody's got to tell you, and it might as well be us.

Personal memoirs are a tough sell. If the story of your life is rejected, don't take it personally. This is hardly a sign that your life's worthless. It only means there aren't 10,000 or more people interested in buying a book about it! From a strict business standpoint, there's no commercial market for your story. Remember your first big lesson in Chapter 1—the book business is a business. Don't despair, however. We show you how to make it a book yourself in Chapter 25, with lots of information on how to self-publish the indie way.

When would a publisher be interested in your life story? When it's compelling and well written. When there's a core message or theme that will appeal to large numbers of people. Why would so many readers pick up a book called *Eat, Pray, Love?* Because millions of women are looking for deeper meaning in their lives and found some solace in the story.

And the Categories Are ...

You need to know your category. Publishing pros can spot a neophyte the minute you say, "What kind of a book am I writing? Well, I'm not really sure. I don't want to define myself and put my writing in a box." Pick a box. Pick a box *now*.

Before we tell you which categories are the biggies, we've got to ask you one question: are you writing *fiction* or *nonfiction?*

DEFINITION

Works of **fiction** are the products of imagination, creativity, and invention. Fiction does not claim to be true. A **nonfiction** work is one that relates actual events, facts, and information. It includes books of all types other than fiction.

Don't worry that if you decide to write in one category, you'll be stuck there forever. After writing several romance novels, Janet Evanovich says she "… ran out of sexual positions and decided to move into the mystery genre." And it looks like it worked out for her!

Fiction

Long works of fiction are called novels. Short stories are just that—shorter pieces of fiction. If your writing is fiction, you're creating your own situations and characters. Or you're taking real people, places, and/or events and weaving them into your own story—or substantially embellishing them with your own creations. Most first novels start out this way.

Fiction comes in two major classifications: literary fiction and commercial fiction. Literary fiction has a smaller, more intellectually inclined audience. These are the kinds of books you had to read in English class—books by Virginia Woolf, William Faulkner—you know the type. Commercial fiction can be broken down into more classifications, such as hardcover mainstream, and then many subcategories, or genres. These include mystery, romance, science fiction, Western, and fantasy.

Nonfiction

Nonfiction is a very broad category that runs the gamut from personal finance to travel books to car manuals and everything in between. We will cover it in just a minute.

Fiction Categories

Let's take a stroll through an imaginary bookstore and see what's on the shelf. First, we'll take a look at the major categories, or *genres*, of fiction:

- Mainstream fiction
- Westerns
- Romances
- Chick lit
- Erotica/adult books
- Mysteries
- Science fiction
- Fantasies
- Thrillers
- Faith fiction
- Horror books
- Young adult books
- Children's fiction
- Graphic novels/manga

DEFINITION

Genre fiction, usually published in paperback, refers to a particular type of fiction. This could be Western, romance, sci-fi, horror, fantasy, or the like.

Mainstream Fiction

Mainstream fiction is pretty much everything that isn't defined in another category! Usually published first in hardcover, mainstream fiction is suited for a large, general audience. Writers like John Updike, Michael Chabon, Toni Morrison, and Philip Roth all fall in this category.

Westerns

Usually published in paperback, Westerns range from classics like Zane Grey's many novels to the works of Larry McMurty or Charles Portis' *True Grit*. Westerns are—surprise!—set in the Old West and are filled with tough guys on horses, bumbling sheriffs, and saloon girls with hearts of gold.

Romances

Girl meets guy; girl hates guy; guy slowly wins over girl. The romance category is a large one, ranging from historical romances to very contemporary stories that deal with modern themes. More than half of all popular paperback fiction sales are due to this evergreen category.

Romance is the fastest-growing type of e-book—because no one needs to be seen with those cheesy covers anymore.

HOT OFF THE PRESS

The *Twilight* series for teens has sparked a whole grown-up-girls-fall-in-love-with-a-vampire/werewolf/angel genre called *paranormal romance*.

Chick Lit

This genre started with *Bridget Jones's Diary* in 1998 and has continued to grow and morph and fuel all sorts of sex-and-the-single-girl kinds of books, even though everyone complains about the condescending term.

Jennifer Weiner is a beloved chick lit writer, as is Lauren Weisberger. Weisberger invented a variation—the single woman at work in a glamorous industry—with her best-selling title *The Devil Wears Prada*.

Erotica/Adult Books

Yes, someone has to write these books (Anne Rice did for a while), and we'll bet you even know where this part of the bookstore is, don't you? Off in a hidden yet well-visited corner.

There's a definite formula to this kind of writing, and our shyness prevents us from describing it to you here. Suffice it to say, these paperback books are, uh, action oriented.

This, too, is a really, really fast-growing part of the e-book business because, yes, like romance, no one needs to know what you're reading.

Mysteries

Who dunnit, and how? Mystery novels center around a murder (or murders) and sift slowly through all the possible suspects and motives. Elizabeth George reigns in this strong category.

Mysteries are published in either hardcover or paperback. Paperback mysteries are often published as a series, with at least one recurring character with unusual sleuthing ability.

Science Fiction

Sci-fi novels take place far in the future, in imaginary worlds and on imaginary planets. Think Kim Stanley Robinson or the late Kurt Vonnegut. Vonnegut once took umbrage at being classified as a sci-fi author, claiming in a radio interview that he "didn't write for pimply faced boys." Once again, this is primarily a paperback category.

Fantasies

Also set in imaginary realms, fantasy novels are populated with elves, maidens, and animals that talk. One famous fantasy novel is J. R. R. Tolkien's *The Hobbit*. This genre is usually published in paperback (unless it's a hardcover gift edition).

The success of the movies based on the Tolkien books has given rise to a new generation of fantasy fans. Many of the young readers who devoured the *Harry Potter* books migrated to this category when they matured.

Thrillers

Thrillers are several steps above mystery novels in terms of gore and violence. Serial killers with twisted motives and determined FBI specialists on their tail might fill the plots of this genre. James Patterson has built a franchise around his Alex Cross character. Many thriller writers publish first in hardcover.

Faith Fiction

Although novels have long been written and published to appeal to a Christian audience, this category exploded into the mainstream some years back with the *Left Behind* series by Tim LeHaye and Jerry Jenkins. More recently, writers like Victoria Christopher Murray and ReShonda Tate Billingsley have arrived on the scene with their contemporary novels.

Horror Books

Stephen King. Dean Koontz. Peter Straub. Any more questions? Horror books are an extremely popular genre. The pages drip with blood, ghouls, vampires, and other unworldly creatures that will keep you awake at night.

Young Adult Books

Novels written for young teens are called young adult novels, or YA for short. For those of you dreaming of emulating J. K. Rowling's success, this is what you want to write. YA novels can fit into almost every category, including horror, romance, mystery, and others. *The Hunger Games*, a disturbing look into a future world, is sci-fi YA. One of the most successful self-published e-book authors, Amanda Hocking, writes YA paranormals.

Children's Fiction

Much of what we think of as children's books is fiction, although that seems like such an adult word to use. Winnie the Pooh wasn't real now, was he? Although we touch on the topic of children's books throughout this book, we do recommend reading our sister book, *The Complete Idiot's Guide to Publishing Children's Books*, now in its third edition.

Graphic Novels/Manga

Some folks think graphic novels are really just comic books by another name, but what they are is very, very popular. Graphic novels continue to be a fast-growing segment in publishing—sales were more than $370 million in 2009 but have dipped a bit since then. Even romance publishers are looking to graphic novels and manga as a way to expand their readership. Best-selling author Janet Evanovich's *Troublemaker* was turned into a graphic hit, as was *Twilight*.

That's it in a nutshell for fiction. Just about everything else in the bookstore is a further breakdown of the huge nonfiction category.

Nonfiction Categories

Nonfiction means you didn't make it up, so don't. The major types of nonfiction books fall into these categories:

- Biographies
- Travel books
- Self-help books
- Computer books
- Cookbooks
- Health books
- Business books
- Humor books
- Children's books
- Political controversy/current events books
- History books
- Inspirational books
- True crime books
- Poetry and belles-lettres
- Science books
- Puzzle books

Biographies

A biography is a nonfiction study of a real person, living or dead. The most successful biographies are well researched and lively accounts of someone with a bona fide place in history. When a real person writes his or her own story, it's an autobiography.

Life, by Keith Richards of The Rolling Stones, is an autobiography. A book by a music journalist about Keith Richards would be a biography.

Travel Books

Travel books can be broken down into destination guides, travel accounts, and travel guides. *Destination guides* are meant to provide information about traveling in a specific geographic location. They offer details on hotels, restaurants, and interesting sights in a particular place and have lots of phone numbers, addresses, and maps. The Frommer's and Fodor's lines are destination guides. The sales of these guides are very vulnerable to the ebb and flow of circumstance—bombings, earthquakes, and political unrest all affect travel to those areas and, hence, book sales.

Travel accounts, on the other hand, are more lyrical descriptions of a place. A travel account may contain hotels, restaurants, and interesting sights, as does a travel guide, but instead of providing short descriptive listings of such places, a travel account might devote an entire chapter to describing a good meal the author ate and the breathtaking ramble he or she took in the nearby countryside afterward.

Travel guides are nondestination travel books about how to travel.

Self-Help Books

The self-help category is another extremely large nonfiction category. Self-help includes books about improving relationships, being a good parent, managing stress, and almost anything in what's called the field of pop psychology. Self-help books are designed to help readers try to solve problems in their personal lives, like the bestseller *The Love Dare.*

Computer Books

This how-to category came into prominence in the early days of the computer age when none of us could turn on the computer without checking the manual first. The sales have been dropping year after year, but high-end programming manuals, certification guides, and other specialized books on topics like Android programming still have an audience.

Cookbooks

Everybody knows what these are—books filled with recipes. For many years, the cookbook field has been dominated by celebrity chefs with television shows like the Barefoot Contessa, Emeril Lagasse, and Rachel Ray. Noncelebs can sometimes sell cookbooks if there is a strong niche market for the topic, like raw foods.

Health Books

Health books provide helpful information about our bodies. From books by medical doctors about specific ailments to alternative health titles, the health book category stays steadily strong as the population ages.

Diet books are also included in this category—the title *Why We Get Fat* seems destined to spark a resurgence (again) in low-carb titles.

Business Books

The business books category lumps together everything from books on management techniques to books on selling real estate, from exposés of high-finance shenanigans to personal finance guides. Two very different best-selling books, *The Tipping Point* and *Rich Dad, Poor Dad*, are both, strictly speaking, business books.

Humor Books

Cartoon books, joke books, parodies, and books with humorous observations are all classified as humor. This category ranges from *Dilbert* and *Garfield* to Dave Barry. Political comedians rule the humor charts right now, with Jon Stewart and Stephen Colbert and the folks at The Onion steady at the top.

Children's Books

Nonfiction books for children abound. Some books explain science, some are biographies of important figures, and some are activity books for rainy days. An extremely popular area is that of bodily functions. A book called *Grossology* started the trend. You can imagine how delighted young children are to read all about snot!

Political Controversy/Current Events Books

Although some booksellers wish they'd see the end of these books (as they frequently run counter to the bookseller's own politics), they still sell. From Ted Kennedy's best-selling autobiography to books from former Bush administration figures like Dick Cheney and Donald Rumsfeld, these books come from both politicians and political observers. Political events also inspire instant books, like the *Tweets from Tahrir* book that was done based on the Egyptian uprising.

History Books

History books for the general audience (as opposed to textbooks) have always existed but were brought into new popularity by the works of the late Stephen Ambrose and television programs such as Ken Burns's *Civil War* on PBS, which sent readers to the bookstore.

David McCullough now dominates this category with his books *1776*, *John Adams*, and *Truman*. The stunning success of *The Autobiography of Mark Twain* (released 100 years after his death) was really fueled more by the public's interest in history than an interest in literary autobiography.

Inspirational Books

These books first appeared in the 1960s and for a time were referred to as "New Age." Well, the new age is here and is more often now referred to as "body, mind, and spirit." The inspirational category is a big one, still topped by *The Secret* by Rhonda Byrne. Her newest is *The Secret: The Power*.

True Crime Books

Ever heard of Ann Rule? This author of the Ted Bundy book *The Stranger Beside Me*—and others, including *Every Breath You Take*—has long been the queen of true crime books. True crime books deliver the heart-pounding story behind the dry newspaper headlines. Murders, terrorists, gangs of bank robbers—all real-life events are fodder for a true crime book, but with this fickle category, look for new titles on whatever chilling crime has just been committed.

Poetry and Belles-Lettres

Poetry is getting harder and harder to define. Long gone are the days when poetry was prose that rhymed. (If you're a poet, you just know it.) And belles-lettres? That's a very fancy term that refers to literary studies and writing. Extremely high-end literary works fall under this category.

Interest in poetry has risen recently due to the poetry slams that take place around the country, as well as the bequest of $100 million to *Poetry* magazine by Ruth Lilly, an heir to the Eli Lilly pharmaceutical fortune.

HOT OFF THE PRESS

Publishing poetry has never been a way to get rich; more often, it's a way to stay poor. Former Copper Canyon Press editor Sam Hamill once joked that after publishing poetry for decades, he'd only recently entered the middle class. Copper Canyon is in Port Townsend, Washington, and their author W. S. Merwin won the Pulitzer for his book *The Shadow of Sirius* as well as a National Book Award for poetry.

Science Books

Well-researched and well-written books on scientific topics do a steady business, and sometimes books about scientific figures like *Galileo's Daughter: A Historical Memoir of Science, Faith, and Love* can break out and become best-sellers. Science books are not something that can be tossed off in a matter of months, so this category demands both original thought and solid credentials. As we write this, physicist Brian Greene's *The Hidden Reality* is on *The New York Times* best-seller list.

Puzzle Books

Long a stalwart category—and the publishing foundation of at least one company, Simon & Schuster, which got its start with crossword puzzle books—puzzle books continue to sell. Every so often a new craze hits; right now it's Sudoku and KenKen. If you're a dedicated and creative puzzle person, this might be a category for you.

What Sells the Longest?

Although most would-be writers daydream about becoming wealthy novelists, in fact the books that hold records for the longest time spent on *The New York Times* best-seller list are nonfiction books. *Midnight in the Garden of Good and Evil* spent a stunning 216 weeks on the hardcover list. But wait—Malcolm Gladwell's *The Tipping Point* is currently at 332 weeks and hanging on to a number 11 spot. So maybe a career in one of these aforementioned nonfiction categories can pay off.

So what did we leave out? Gardening books, sports books, reference books—the nonfiction book category covers far more than what we've listed here. But we're not writing *The Complete Idiot's Guide to Book Categories* (which, FYI, would be categorized as a reference book). Instead of writing another 20 pages on this, we've got a better idea for you: walk out the door of your imaginary bookstore and through the door of a real one. Spend as much time as you can there. Wander the aisles. Familiarize yourself with the ways bookstores divide their sections and subsections. You might even get a job in a bookstore, if only during the holiday season, as a way to learn more about the different types of books. Sure, you can hang out in online bookstores clicking from title to title, but it's never the same as quietly soaking in what you can learn by being around real, live books.

Here's another great way to learn more: pick a book off the shelf and turn it over. On the back cover of most paperback books—and some hardcovers, too—on the very top line you will see a category printed. In the book trade, this is often called the shelf reference. This is how the publisher defines the book, and this is where the publisher hopes the bookseller will shelve it. Become familiar with these categories, and choose which category best defines your book.

> **SLUSH PILE**
>
> Don't describe your book as "a little bit of this and a little bit of that." To succeed in today's book market, you need to be very clear about the category that best describes your book. (Read more about the individual markets in Chapter 5.)

Life in the Fast Lane

Although book sales are mostly strong overall right now, it's possible to identify some categories moving faster than others. Let's take a quick look at two of them: shtick lit and the urban fantasy fiction arena.

Shtick Lit

Shtick lit? Yes, really, we aren't making this up. A "shtick" is a contrived act of some sort, and the same is true for a shtick lit book. Dream up some kooky way to spend a year or so—say, living according to the rules of the Bible, saying yes to every man who asks you out, or cooking all the recipes in a Julia Child cookbook—and write a book in which you charmingly describe your antics.

Sometimes the shtick works in a big, big way, like with *Julie & Julia*, and you also get to do a movie deal with Meryl Streep.

Urban Fantasy

Urban fantasy is a subgenre of fantasy—the books with the nymphs and fairies and elves—where the fantastical elements are all set in a large city like, say, New York, like in *The Good Fairies of New York*.

With titles like *Dead Beautiful*, *The Better Part of Darkness*, and *Four and Twenty Blackbirds*, many urban fantasy books also include song lists to create the mood while reading or are introduced to readers through book trailers on YouTube.

From Category to Specific Topic

Now that you have a better understanding of where the book category lines are drawn, is there a market for what you want to write? In the next few chapters, you discover professional tips on how to create a best-selling book idea, if you don't already have one. We also give you a solid sense of the kinds of books publishers, both big and small, are seeking—and how to find the right publishing house for your book.

The Least You Need to Know

- Your book is either fiction or nonfiction, not both.
- Countless categories and subcategories of fiction exist, from mainstream novels to mystery, from romance to science fiction, and many in between.
- Nonfiction is an even larger category that includes cookbooks, travel books, self-help books, how-to books, and so on. This category covers any book that contains true information.
- The best way to learn all the different categories and distinctions is to spend time in bookstores looking, looking, looking, ...
- Do careful research to be sure you're not trying to enter an already overpublished area or to write a book about a trend that's already passed.

If You Need an Idea, Stalk the Best-Seller List

In This Chapter

- Developing a high-concept approach
- Finding a subject need and writing to fill it
- Reading to write well
- Eavesdropping your way to the top
- The benefits of hanging out in bookstores

Most writers start with an idea and move on from there. Chances are you bought this book because you already have an idea, and you think it's a good one. So why do you have to wade through all the information in this chapter about how to come up with a good book idea? You've already got one of those.

That's great, but we want you to know how the professionals do it. We want you to have a solid understanding of how the book business works and how to succeed in that world, no matter what your main reason is for wanting to get published. Even if you don't expect to make lots of money from your book, you do want people to buy it and read it, don't you? To share your knowledge and to advance your cause, you need readers.

Publishers are taking fewer chances on books these days than in the past. If getting published is your goal, it's more important than ever for the book you're writing to work in the marketplace. The methods you'll learn about in this chapter have been used by professional writers to develop marketable ideas that sold—and sold well.

The High-Concept Approach

Have you heard the term *high concept* before? It's a movie business expression. The screenwriter pitches his idea to the producer like this: "Baby, you'll love this one! It's a cross between *Inception* and *Shakespeare in Love*. A team of dream specialists goes back in time to rescue Romeo and Juliet from certain death." In two sentences, the screenwriter paints a picture the producer can quickly understand and get a sense of its market potential. That's high concept.

To the chagrin of many traditionalists, the book business has gradually become more like the movie business. That means if you want your book to sell well, you've got to start thinking like the movie guys. Because sometimes the movie guys end up in the book business.

HOT OFF THE PRESS

A *New York Times* article about an imprint geared toward younger readers contained a quote from an editor about what was truly important: "It's not about the book, it's about the money you can make from the book." Shocked? You shouldn't be. Publishing is a business, and making money is what business is all about.

It's a fact: best-selling books become movies. Of course *The Da Vinci Code* went to film. Of course the *Harry Potter* movies ruled for a decade. Of course *Eat, Pray, Love* was made into a film.

Having your book turned into a film or television project sounds glamorous and like a guaranteed way to pocket riches. The truth is a bit disappointing, though. Many projects that are *optioned* never get developed. Jennifer's *Christmas Miracles* book has been optioned twice and never made it beyond that stage. If you get the call from Hollywood after your book comes out, don't quit your day job. Film scouts are always on the lookout for projects with potential and are continually reading the publishing trade press for early glimpses of projects, so the chances people will see a mention of your book are actually pretty good. But the chances they'll pick up the phone and call your publisher for a review copy or make an offer beyond that really aren't great.

DEFINITION

If a movie producer sees potential in your project, you might be offered an **option,** a contract that gives the producer the right to develop your work. Options are usually for a defined period of time, say 12 or 24 months. If the project isn't developed within that time frame, the option expires. Depending on what your contract says, you might get something or nothing at all if the option goes away unexercised.

Find a Need and Fill It

Granted, not all books and all reasons for publishing are conceived to appeal to a mass market. Is it even possible to sit down and consciously create a best-selling book? It has happened before, but there are no sure things in life. Many a high-stakes publishing gamble that looked like a shoo-in was a huge flop. The political novel *O* tried to mimic the success of *Primary Colors* but sank like a stone.

You can, however, set out to uncover a large potential audience and deliver a book it will buy. Let's take a look at what can make it happen.

Finding the Success Factor

So many of us are attracted to the romantic idea of the life of a writer: long mornings spent with a steaming cup of tea and a blank pad of paper or computer screen, setting the scene for the muse to come gliding in to inspire and guide us. That may be one way to write. But if you want to write and publish successful books, here is a better way: sit down with your cup of tea and a copy of *The New York Times* best-seller list, and try to analyze why each book is on that list.

> **HOT OFF THE PRESS**
>
> Sometimes publishing success is as random as choosing a seat on the subway—literally. That's what happened to author/illustrator Daniel Peddle. He saw a woman reading a young adult novel on the subway and chose the seat next to her. Striking up a conversation, it turned out that—surprise!—she was a children's book editor. She gave him her card, he followed up, and the result was a two-book contract.

It used to be the "Oprah factor" that propelled many books from her show onto the best-seller list. Now authors and their publicists vie for a seat on *The Daily Show with Jon Stewart* or Stephen Colbert's *The Colbert Report*. But what keeps a book like *The Tipping Point* on the best-seller list? It's been around for years, so the real reason isn't only the strength of the writing, but also that there's a vast audience who likes to read about these kinds of things. How can you tap into that audience?

Novels with themes that will appeal to large numbers of readers can also hit the list. Autism and Asperger's syndrome are both much-talked-about topics now, and a novel with an autistic hero, *The Curious Incident of the Dog in the Nighttime*, was a best-seller. It gave readers a fictional glimpse into the mind of a young boy and clearly struck a chord with many people wondering how these syndromes affect the mind.

Wide Appeal = Good Sales

Unless you already have your own radio or TV show, if you have your sights set on selling in big numbers, you're most likely to score by choosing a subject with wide appeal.

EXPERTS SAY

Best-seller Robert G. Allen shares this three-step formula for creating a hot book: (1) Identify a core human desire or need. (2) Find new technology for solving this. (3) Find a new way to market to this core desire/need. That's how he wrote his best-selling, no-money-down real estate books.

Audience Appeal

A big *audience?* How big? If fame and fortune are your primary goals, you need to write a book that will sell big, which means it will sell to everyone. Robert Kiyosaki did this when he wrote a book called *Rich Dad, Poor Dad.* Who wouldn't want to do what the subtitle promised—learn what rich people teach their children that poor people don't know? What about *The Purpose-Driven Life?* It clearly struck a chord with millions of readers who were feeling a lack of some kind and seeking more meaning and a deeper spirituality in their lives. Who *wouldn't* want to have more purpose in their life?

DEFINITION

A book's **audience** is the portion of the population that will be interested enough in the book's topic to buy a copy.

You must be clear eyed about how large the potential audience is for your book. Just because your mother raves about your idea doesn't guarantee it a mass audience. Even if your mother *and* your neighbor like the idea, that still isn't enough. If you're hoping for big sales, you need to uncover big topics with big appeal.

Look Around You

How do you come up with an idea for a book with a big audience? The most important trait to practice is observation. Always keep a keen eye trained on what's going on around you. What topics are in the news? On television? In magazine articles? What are your friends talking about? What kinds of concerns keep you awake at night?

To get published, you've got to work on your writing skills. But you've also got to develop your ability to create book ideas. Try the following exercise to get started.

What's Making the News?

Here's a quick exercise to start you thinking like a publishing professional. Every day, sit down with a copy of *USA Today* or visit usatoday.com. It might not be the most sophisticated newspaper in the country, but it gives lots of coverage to topics of interest to middle America. Read as much of the newspaper or the site as you can, and think of one book idea based on the articles you've read.

Perhaps there's a large article in the food section about organic farms and people who gave up their corporate careers to pursue a life of growing good produce. Or maybe you find a chart showing how many parents are home-schooling their young children instead of sending them to a troubled public school. Could you use these articles to come up with an idea for a nonfiction book or a novel that involves themes and characters that would appeal to the special interests of large audiences?

One example is a front-page story in *USA Today* with the headline "Boomer Brain Meltdown: Generation Faces More Frequent Memory Lapses." Big topic, big audience. Have there been books on memory before? Yes. Will there continue to be interest in this topic in the years to come? Yes.

Another recent story helped parents decide when their teenagers were lying. Big topic, big audience. Continuing interest!

Timing can be everything in this business, and if your proposal lands on an editor's desk the same day she just read an article on the topic, it just might do the trick.

Try, Try Again

Let's be realistic: most of the ideas you come up with using this method will be throwaways. But the more you do it, and the more you begin to think like this, the better the odds are that you'll eventually come up with a best-selling book idea. Not to mention it's a fun way to spend the morning!

Jennifer recently spotted the word *mint* in an article and spent some time ruminating on all of the meanings of the word. It gave her an idea—and she went to work packaging a book on aging gracefully called *Mint Condition*.

What's That You Said?

Eavesdropping is such a loaded word. Let's call it "heightened observation" instead. Whatever we call it, it's a critical skill for writers. Yep, we want you to listen in when other people talk. Not only can you get a great idea for a book, but you might also come up with a great idea for the title!

At a writers' conference, Jennifer was seated in the back of a large room, so far back that she couldn't clearly hear the speakers. At one point she thought she heard an inspirational writer use the phrase "romancing the soul." *Wow*, she thought, *if that isn't a book title it should be!* It wasn't … but it is now that Jennifer packaged it. It also turns out that the writer actually said something quite different. So if you can't pay attention when others talk, at least let your mind wander around the edges of what they're saying.

Jennifer's self-published travel guide *The Air Courier's Handbook* was also a product of eavesdropping. She overheard two guys in a restaurant talking about cheap courier travel—something she herself was interested in. She leaned over and introduced herself and got the phone number for a courier firm. She then went on to travel as a courier and later wrote a book about it. That's called listening for fun and profit.

Once she even eavesdropped on herself. (Yes, it's possible!) While talking to her cell phone–grasping then-6-year-old about yet another thing he wanted, she threw up her hands and said loudly, "If you give a kid a cell phone …!" Immediately a tiny bell went off in her head. Hmmm … that sounds like *If You Give a Mouse a Cookie*, a best-selling tale of a greedy mouse who wants one thing and then another and another—quite similar to what children want when it comes to high-tech toys and electronic gear. Knowing it would strike a familiar chord for parents everywhere, she sat down and wrote a proposal for a spoof book, *If You Give a Kid a Cell Phone*. True confession, the proposal didn't sell. But if you want to keep selling, you have to keep trying.

Common phrases of speech sometimes spark an idea. They can also make great book titles. Remember that *USA Today* article about memory loss we mentioned a few paragraphs ago? The perfect title for a book on preventing memory loss was right there in the story when a memory expert said, "Use it or lose it!" Doesn't that give you a perfect image for a book? And you understand exactly what the book is about.

Let the Shows Show You

Another way to find ideas for books with large audiences is to attend major industry trade shows. Trade shows are held for all types of industry: food, gardening, health, fitness, computer, interior design, cars, gift shows—you name it. If you plan to write a nonfiction book on a particular topic, check to see if there's a trade show related to it. Attending a show is a great way to learn what's hot in the industry. Prowl the aisles, pick up literature, observe merchandise and trends, and of course, eavesdrop on conversations to listen for new trends and possible titles!

Trade shows are also a prime way to find experts you can team up with to write books.

I'm Not Hanging Out—I'm Working!

"If you want to write, read," says Gary Krebs, vice president and group publisher at McGraw-Hill. What does he mean? All serious students of writing must also be serious readers. So look forward to spending lots of time in bookstores. (Yes, of course you can also hang out in online bookstores, but it really isn't the same.)

Pay very close attention to the books in the front of the store and those marked "New Releases." Get to know what's new and hot in the area of writing you're considering, and become an expert on what's available and who publishes it. After all, you can't expect to flourish in a field you don't enjoy and also aren't very familiar with.

Read everything you can get your hands on—books, magazines, newspapers, and online articles. Study what other writers are doing. The more you know about what's out there, the sooner you'll be able to spot what's not. When you find a hole, you've found yourself an opportunity!

Learn to Work the Bookstore Shelves

Here's another exercise that'll help you develop your skills. Go to a bookstore and choose a book category. Are there two, maybe three shelves devoted to that category? Are there any book *series* in your category? Spend as much time as you need familiarizing yourself with the books on the shelves. You might need to write down the titles. Now go back to the store every few days and check your section. Have new titles been added? Have many books sold? Which books? Why do you think they sold?

> **DEFINITION**
>
> A **series** is two or more books linked by a brand-name identity, such as *The Complete Idiot's Guide* or *Harry Potter* or Stieg Larsson's *The Millennium Trilogy*. Publishers are fond of series because they build awareness and momentum in the marketplace. Librarian Bron Cancilla says, "Readers like series; a good series makes everyone happy." Sometimes a series begins with a single book that sells so well the audience and the publisher come looking for more.

What Isn't Selling?

When browsing bookstores, don't skip over the bargain tables. Examine those reduced-price books very carefully. If there's a big stack of sale books on bulb gardening, that might be an area to avoid. Have several titles on yoga been marked down? Stay away. Learn from the mistakes of other writers when it comes to what doesn't sell.

I'm Not Wasting Time—I'm Working!

Just as you can legitimately spend hour after hour in a bookstore and call it work, you also can spend hour after hour online. Check out news sites like Huffington Post (huffingtonpost.com) or Salon (salon.com), women's sites, money sites, or whatever site has the biggest audience in the topic you plan to pursue. In addition, become a blog devotee in a few niche areas, and see what's going on in the minds of bloggers everywhere.

What seems to be the topic of conversation on Twitter? What kinds of posts are being retweeted? You can use the same eavesdropping techniques to try to pick up phrases or figures of speech that might make good book titles. And no one can catch you watching!

Surfing the online bookstores for information also helps you learn more about what's selling and why. And just like the remainder tables outside bookstore doors, you can tell what isn't selling online by the big, big sales ranking next to it. Anything ranked beyond 75,000 or so on Amazon.com just isn't selling in very big numbers. (In other words, the lower the number, the better the sales.)

Barnes & Noble's website (barnesandnoble.com) lets you see what the best-selling titles are in any given category. Thinking of writing a book about herb gardening? Type "herb gardening" into the search function, and once you get there select "Best Selling" in the Sort by: box, and there you have it! Instant research into how well the other titles are selling.

And just like we asked you to try to analyze *The New York Times* best-seller list and try to figure out why those books are there, check out the Top 100 books on Amazon.com and try to figure out what's making those books sell that very instant.

Sniffing Out Gaps and Niches

The more you can learn about what's available and how well it's doing, the better you'll be able to figure out what that category needs. Perhaps you'll notice there's a need for a large reference volume or maybe a small, inexpensive guidebook.

Not long after the phenomenal best-seller *The Worst-Case Scenario Survival Handbook* appeared, Workman released a book called *The Best-Case Scenario Handbook.* No, this doesn't fall into the parody category, but rather it takes the interest in one thing— how to get out of precarious situations—and transfers it to a broader, more useful category. When low-carb Atkins books were big, lots of similar books were published to fill in gaps around it. The *Harry Potter* books spawned many other nonfiction books around it like cookbooks and dictionaries.

Many a beauty and spa book has been published in the past few years, but where was the book that targeted the most stressed-out group of all—mothers! Jennifer combined her idea-creating talents with a yoga instructor and a spa owner and wrote *MomSpa: 75 Relaxing Ways to Pamper a Mother's Body, Mind, and Spirit.* A new niche in a crowded but popular field was filled.

Backlist Books: Sure and Steady

If you follow all our suggestions here—if you come up with an idea for a big topic with a big audience and then sell it to a publisher—will it become a best-seller? Perhaps.

Only 1 percent of all the books published in any given year actually make it on a national best-seller list. Your book might not be one of them, but many authors have written books that are paying the rent, and you might find yourself in their company. These authors have books with strong *backlist* sales. A book that backlists—that sells for years—can rack up impressive sales totals over its lifetime.

Keep the word *backlist* in mind when choosing a topic for a book. Look for book ideas on subjects with staying power. Here's a tip—books for writers always have a steady audience. This book, *The Complete Idiot's Guide to Getting Published,* has never been on a best-seller list but has sold and sold as a backlist title through four earlier editions.

DEFINITION

Frontlist books are those that have been published recently. Many of these are piled on tables and placed in bookstore windows. *Midlist* books are those acquired for modest advances, given modest print runs, and that have a relatively short shelf life. **Backlist** books are those that have been in stores for more than 90 days—sometimes for years. Most of the thousands of books on the shelves are classified as backlist books.

Now You Know the Game

Now we do realize you might already have your heart set on a topic for your book. We also realize that everything we've covered here sounds a bit crass and calculating. It is. Publishing is all too frequently a crass and calculating business, and we want you to understand that. Please do not dismiss it out of hand, though.

The more you know about what makes books work on a commercial level, the better you'll be able to smooth and shape the book you've already been working on. Keep reading to learn more about researching the market and gathering the information you'll need for your book proposal.

The Least You Need to Know

- Good book ideas can come from anywhere. Keep your eyes and ears open!
- Read as many print and online sources as you can, always looking for big ideas for books and titles.
- Spend as much time as you can in bookstores—they're gold mines of information. Study bookstore shelves carefully to see what's missing.
- Look for ideas with long-term staying power.

Super-Stealth Market Research Techniques

In This Chapter

- The bookstore: your number-one resource
- Checking out online catalogs
- Tips for tracking a book's printing
- Publishers, podcasts, and communities
- *Publishers Weekly,* directories, and print

Okay, now you've got an idea for a book. But how do you know if you've come up with an idea that will work? Be it nonfiction or fiction, there are good ways to test your market well in advance of even writing your proposal and sample chapter.

Let's start with the strategies to use for nonfiction. (Fiction writers, do not despair; your turn comes later in the chapter.)

Is It a Book?

The first thing you need to ask yourself is, *Does my idea have strong book potential?* What sometimes seems like a big idea for a book turns out to be only a big idea for a magazine article. Be sure you've chosen a topic with enough scope and substance to sustain a few hundred manuscript pages.

We know this is hard, but you need to put aside your subjectivity and take a good, objective look at your idea, just like the book professionals do. The more work you put into this step, the better your chances of success months from now, when your proposal is sitting on an editor's desk. It's heartbreaking to come to the conclusion that your book won't work, but think how much time and heartache you'll save yourself. We've all been there; every published author can name a book idea he or she had to reluctantly abandon. It's simply part of the professional process.

SLUSH PILE

Some topics in areas like health and beauty just can't sustain an entire book and would need tremendous padding to hit book length. If you find yourself starting to pad, you don't have a book-worthy idea. Of course, you can sell an article on the effects of suntans, but is that a whole book? Probably not. A short magazine article on what kinds of earring styles flatter which different face shapes would be interesting, but not for an entire book.

The investment will also pay you back when it comes time to write your proposal because you will have already done much of the required homework! Bonus!

Recently Jennifer heard those words—"It's really a magazine article, not a book." Her idea was a memoir-writing book called *How to Write About Your Mother.* "No" was the industry answer. Why? It appeals to a niche (writers working on a memoir) of a niche (writers in general). Not one to take rejection, Jennifer put it out herself with the *Espresso Book Machine* (more about that later) and sells it at talks.

Meeting Your Customer

When you're sure you have an idea for a book instead of a magazine article, try to picture your customer. That's right, close your eyes and try to imagine someone walking into a bookstore and asking a clerk for your book or going online and typing the topic in to a search engine. If you can't envision that happening—if your idea is too weak, too abstract, or perhaps too specialized—you need to reevaluate it.

Before working as an editor, co-author Jennifer spent several years as a book buyer for a small chain of bookstores. She met with sales reps and looked at publishers' catalogs by the hundreds. Her buying decisions were always based on one simple question: *Who will buy this book?* This is also a question she asks herself today when evaluating book projects to develop. Memorize the question and ask yourself often, *Who will buy this book?* And then ask yourself honestly, *How many of those folks are there? Are there enough to constitute a sizeable market?*

When your idea can pass these basic litmus tests (is it a book? who will buy it?), you're ready to move on to the next important step.

Sizing Up the Competition

Few books really are the first-ever ones published on their topic. You need to be clear-eyed about the books that have been done before in your area. Remember the technique in Chapter 3 about targeting a shelf in a bookstore and tracking the success of the books on that shelf? You now need to do this for the books that either compete with or complement your own book idea.

Just what do we mean by competition? Let's say you're planning to write a book on arthritis. The first step is to go to the bookstore and look under "arthritis" on the health books shelf. Are there two books? Four? Twelve? Get out your notepad or cell phone and copy down the title, author, publisher, and price of each book. Open each book and look inside the *front matter*, the front few pages of the book, to find a copyright date; it's usually on the flip side of the title page.

 DEFINITION

The **front matter** is the first few pages of the book. It typically contains, in this order, a half-title page, a title page, a copyright page, a dedication, the table of contents, sometimes a preface and/or foreword, an introduction, and the acknowledgments. Front matter pages are numbered i, ii, iii, iv, and so forth.

Now go home or have a seat in the bookstore café, and examine all this information carefully. You've got more than just some book information here—you've got clues to your own success.

The Title

Do the titles and other language on the covers make the same kinds of promises yours would? Are they clever and enticing? Or do they have a bland and general medical reference sound to them?

Let's call your imaginary book *Accurate Arthritis Answers*. A browsing book buyer would see your book and think, *Hey, accurate answers. I need accurate answers about my arthritis problem*, and reach for your book. The cleaner your proposed title is, the better.

What's missing from the shelf? Does the market need a beginner's guide, an A-to-Z reference, or a pocket guide to your topic? Maybe you could position your book to fill the gap. Could you target your book to women or seniors to make it different from the pack?

The Author

You need to know who else is writing in your chosen field. Who are these authors anyway? What are their credentials? Do they have a big-name research school behind them? Do they have television or radio shows? A zillion followers on Twitter or a popular blog?

Take a close look at your rivals' credentials and see how yours measure up. Be honest with yourself. Are yours as strong as those of the authors whose books are on the shelf? If not, get to work now to improve them. Beef up your professional contacts, create workshops or public presentations on your topic, start your own blog or Twitter persona, or write articles for industry magazines or websites. By the time you're ready to shop your book to agents or publishers, you'll be in a stronger position.

The Publisher

Finding out who published these books can be very revealing. If all the books come from major New York houses, this tells you arthritis is a hot topic and major publishers think so, too. If a book sells well for its publisher, that publisher might just be looking for more books on that topic!

But what if the topic is covered only by small publishers or by *self-publishers?* Both of those are fine and honorable ways to be published, but let's look strictly from a competitive point of view: small publishers and self-publishers don't have nearly the distribution the large houses do. If many of the books you've found on the shelves are from small publishers, you might be able to use that information to your advantage when submitting to a larger publisher.

Speaking of small publishers, there's much good to say about them. Your book is less likely to get lost in the crowd, you may get more personal attention, and you may find your editor more accessible and open to your suggestions. Keep your eyes open to the books published by thriving companies such as Chelsea Green or New World Library.

The Price

Book publishing is a price-sensitive industry. If you see four books on the shelf that are expensive hardcover books, perhaps there's a need for a small *trade paperback* on the subject. Or maybe a short and inexpensive e-book?

DEFINITION

A **self-published** book is one for which the author himself has paid the bills. Many successful authors started out as self-publishers before the big houses sat up and took notice, Benjamin Franklin included. *Mass market paperbacks* are the 4×7-inch softcover books you find in the racks at the grocery store and in airport bookstores. (They're also called rack-size paperbacks.) Any other larger paperback is called a **trade paperback.**

Your publisher ultimately determines the price of your book, but you can always pitch the project in a particular way. When you write your proposal, you'll need to show that you've done your homework about the way the competing books are priced. Tell your prospective publishers where the pricing hole in the market is and how your book could fill it.

The Publication Copyright Date

This information is critical when assessing the competition. Are all the books on the shelf a few years old? If so, the information is sure to be at least a little outdated. That might not matter for some books, such as fiction and cookbooks, but for all types of books it means the category could use a few new titles. Better yet, you'll have little competition when you try to promote your book to publishers.

Bear in mind that the publishing process moves slowly. A book with a brand-new copyright date may well have been written as long as 2 years before its publication.

SLUSH PILE

Never start a conversation with an agent or editor with the phrase "Never before has there been a book on this topic." Rather, say something like "To the best of my knowledge, this topic has never been covered quite in this way." You want to show that your idea is different from and better than the competition but not in a whole new category.

Are all the books brand new? This is also useful information to gauge. It lets you know publishers think this is a viable category and one worth pursuing (unless there are so many books the publishers consider it a saturated market).

Staying in the Know

All this information on current books is very useful, but keep in mind that it has its limitations. Maybe some books have been selling so well the store can't keep them on the shelves. At the very moment you're scrutinizing the shelves, more new books are being shipped to bookstores. When those new books arrive, some of the books on your list may be boxed up and shipped back to their publishers!

To keep current, you've got to visit bookstores regularly, and you've got to do three more things. First, you have to get your hands on the announcements issues published by *Publishers Weekly* (known as *PW* by industry insiders). Many large bookstores carry this trade magazine, and some libraries also have it on hand. Several times a year, in large round-up issues, all the publishers announce what they plan to publish in the coming season. Thankfully, the kind folks at *PW* organize these issues by topic, so it's easy for authors to keep track of what's forthcoming in, say, paperback cookbooks or hardcover biographies. It's a tremendous source of information.

The second thing you've got to do is hang around online. After you determine which publishers publish in your area, visit their websites on a regular basis. Chelsea Green, mentioned a few paragraphs back, specializes in environmentally oriented titles, so if this is your topic of choice, how could you not visit the website frequently to see what is up with it and its books? If you are writing romance, you need to spend time hanging around the Harlequin site. It even has a podcast called *Meet the Editors* that will give you insider tips on submitting.

You've done good detective work so far. Now for your third task, you need to research what is coming in the future—so head to the Internet.

Online Catalogs

To get a better sense of what publishers are bringing out in upcoming months, particularly in your subject area, get their catalogs. That's right. Like Restoration Hardware and Victoria's Secret put out catalogs, so do publishers like Simon & Schuster, Viking, Dearborn, and others. There was a time you could call and get publishers to send you a copy of their catalog, but more and more this information has migrated online to cut down on printing costs.

Identify the biggest publishers in your subject area. You already know at least some of them—you wrote down their names when doing your bookstore sleuthing. When you're checking out the websites of the publishers you hope to someday be published by, look and see if they have an online version of their catalog posted. Chelsea Green does, although some publishers keep their catalogs behind a professional firewall available only to their bookstore accounts.

The big publishers generally release information three times a year: fall, winter, and spring. Medium and small houses usually do only two: fall and spring. Publishers plan their programs according to seasons—a concept you'll read more about in Chapter 20.

How to Find 'Em

Most companies in the book business now have their own website. Just take a stab in the dark by typing in their name after the old "www" prefix and see what comes up. Or check inside a book that house recently published to see if a web address is listed. If you come up empty there, try a quick Google search.

As we mentioned a few paragraphs back, publishers' websites usually highlight their most current titles and a few big upcoming books, but they seldom list projects as far out in the future as the *PW* announcements issue or their catalog.

Get Out Your Fine-Toothed Comb

If you can access a publisher's catalog online or hustle one from a friend in the book-store business, study it carefully. It will give you a good idea of what the publisher plans to publish in the next 6 months or so.

If you find a book in your category, study it carefully, too. Does it get a full page in the catalog? If so, the publisher thinks it's a big deal. Two-page spreads mean the publisher thinks it is a *really* big deal. Are big publicity and promotional plans announced? What about an appearance on the *Today* show? Just as you did with the books you studied on the bookstore shelves, analyze these upcoming books by title, price, and the author's background and credentials.

What Are the Clubs Selling?

Here's one more great research suggestion: check out what the clubs are carrying. For example, visit the Book of the Month Club (BOMC) site at bomcclub.com to see what books it's carrying.

Why take the time to look at book club offerings? Because these people know what they're doing. Book clubs base their success on their ability to sell large numbers of books to a mainstream audience. The more you study the books they've chosen for their customers, the more you'll learn about what kinds of books sell in big quantities. Recently the BOMC cookbook section featured several books on casseroles and slow cookers. What does that mean? That mainstream America still cooks fairly down home comfort food, despite all the hoopla surrounding celebrity chefs.

You should be familiar with another kind of club—discount warehouse shopping clubs such as Sam's Club and Costco. These stores are now a big part of the book business (much to the annoyance of booksellers), and any book sold there is moving *very* swiftly.

If you don't belong to one of the discount clubs, you can sleuth through their websites to see what they're carrying. Like the old-style book clubs, the buyers for these chains are very tuned in to what sells to the mainstream. By examining the carefully edited list of what they've chosen to carry, you can avoid feeling overwhelmed by the huge selection in most bookstores or online stores. Just familiarize yourself with what's moving fast.

What Are Book Clubs Reading?

Like the Book of the Month and discount clubs that carry books, you can learn tons about what readers are interested in most by looking at another type of club: book clubs. Ask around about what book clubs in your area are reading. Talk to avid readers about what they like. Literary travel accounts of exotic places? Readable books that explain general science concepts? Novels that make history come alive?

Ask your friends and relatives who are involved in book groups, and perhaps they might also be willing to let you run your book idea by them for a quick opinion.

Cracking the Print Code

Important sales information on competing books is literally at your fingertips—but you have to know where to look.

The secret for finding out whether a book has sold well is to look at the number of printings it's gone through. When a book is first released, the number of books printed is referred to as the "first printing." When most of those books have sold, the book goes back for a second printing and hopefully a third and a fourth. You can tell just how many printings the book has gone through by checking the copyright page. You should see a series of numbers there that looks something like this:

12 11 10 09   5 4 3 2 1

These numbers are a code that tells you when that particular copy of the book was printed. The rightmost number of the first series of numbers (12, 11, 10, 09) is the year of the book's printing; the rightmost number of the second series of numbers (5, 4, 3, 2, 1) is the number of the book's printing. If you look at the preceding sample numbers, you can see that the book's first printing came out in the year 2009. That was several years ago, so if this book is still sitting on the shelf, that means it still hasn't sold out its first print run—not a swiftly moving title.

Except for hot-selling titles, most books are reprinted in steady but modest quantities. Subsequent reprintings in the 3,000- to 5,000-copy range are common. Publishers don't find it to their benefit from a business standpoint to keep large quantities of unsold books stacked in a warehouse. The spiraling cost of paper has also had an effect on the size of most reprints.

On the other hand, if you see from the code that the book is in a sixth printing, that's impressive. This book is selling.

How is this printing information useful? If you find a book that has sold in big numbers, you might wonder, *Could this be a hot topic that has room for another book?* If you find a book that hasn't gone into a second printing after having been out for some time, you might ask yourself, *Is this a dead category I should stay away from?*

To find the answers to these questions, you have to keep asking booksellers questions, reading topical newspapers and magazines, and watching this part of the marketplace closely.

Pick a Bookseller's Brain

Booksellers are tremendously helpful and knowledgeable. If you ask, they will tell. Why not approach a friendly bookseller and say, "Hey, I'm thinking of writing a book on *Topic X*. What do you think? Is that a category that sells well for you? Which book in this category sells the best?" Most booksellers, the unsung heroes of the book business, will be happy to help if you catch them when they're not too busy.

EXPERTS SAY

"I love to talk to writers about what they are working on," a young bookseller told us. "It makes me feel like I am a part of the big, wide publishing world. And that is not an easy feeling to come by when you are shelving books and answering phones." Go ahead and approach a bookstore employee! Don't be shy.

Find out who is responsible for the actual section in the bookstore where you would like to see your book. Get to know that person, and learn from him or her what works and what doesn't work in your category.

Online Sleuthing

However did we spend our time before the web? Researching anything is a breeze, and countless great online research sources are available for writers. Not only is the Internet a great place to do research, but you also can access lots of cool stuff to help you find out about the competition and the market for your book idea. Let's go over a few great sites.

The New York Times Extended Best-Seller List

Sure, you know *The New York Times* best-seller list. You check it every Sunday, don't you? But did you know there are many more books on that list than are printed in the paper? To find the top 35 best-sellers, visit the paper's website at nytimes.com and go into the "Books" section. You'll learn that, for instance, although in the newspaper you'll only see 5 slots for best-sellers in the "Advice, How-To" section, there are really 15 slots.

Amazon.com

Amazon.com, the granddaddy of online bookstores, is also a good place to do research. Amazon can offer long lists of titles on any particular subject, giving you a quick look at what has been published. It, too, has best-seller lists, but keep in mind that these only reflect the tastes of folks who are open to online shopping.

A fun way to waste an hour, though, is to go through all 100 of the Top 100 and try to figure out why each book is selling well that particular hour. The Top 100 is particularly sensitive to media; you can tell pretty quickly who was on the morning talk shows or featured on the Yahoo! home page by a sudden jump in rank.

An appearance Jennifer made for an earlier edition of this book on C-Span's *Book TV* rocketed the rankings to number 52, a number to thrill the heart of any author. Alas, a media hit like that won't sustain sales for very long, and it was back in the humdrum 1,000s within hours.

You've noticed those reviews on Amazon.com, haven't you? Sometimes they can be useful in helping you assess the strengths and weaknesses of books in your chosen category, but do read them with a jaundiced eye. You'll start to notice that many of them seem to come either from the author's close friends or the author's sworn enemies!

Barnes & Noble

Barnesandnoble.com is filled with useful info-gathering tools. The "Barnes & Noble 100" section saves you time trying to figure out just what the hottest categories in the store are, and they are updated hourly. Recently, for example, a book called *Vintage Modern Knits* ranked #8 on a cold winter day.

You can also sign up to receive quarterly e-mail updates on new releases in several categories, including Christian, Business and Money, and Lifestyle. Another function lets you sort titles by new releases and upcoming releases.

Another tool we really like at barnesandnoble.com is that you can type in a subject such as "natural health" (or whatever your topic is), and the site gives you the chance to search the top 25 best-sellers in that category. This is very helpful when analyzing markets and putting together book proposals.

Publishers Marketplace

A hardworking book packager named Michael Cader of Cader Books has developed an incredible resource for working professionals. Check out Publishers Marketplace at publishersmarketplace.com for great research features. There, you can track the sales rank of as many books as you'd like to enter, keep up with who's buying what, and even learn how to post your own available projects in the hopes of catching an agent's or editor's eye.

Some of the site is free and some is only available to subscribers, but we believe subscribing is worth it. For a modest monthly fee, you can access all manner of info about agents (including what they're looking for and how to best approach them) and learn on a daily basis what kinds of deals are selling. Cader also sends out a free daily gossip column called Publishers Lunch you should sign up for to keep abreast of the latest news.

Nielsen BookScan

This is how the big boys research book sales. BookScan is a retail tracking service for the book industry. By typing in a book's *ISBN*, you can access the total sales from the outlets that report to BookScan. Therein lies the problem, as it doesn't include large retailers such as Walmart and Sam's Club.

DEFINITION

All published books have an **ISBN,** or an International Standard Book Number, assigned by an industry publisher, R. R. Bowker. The first series of numbers always identifies the publishing house. Some older titles have ISBNs that are 10 digits long, but the system has changed to 13 digits. You can find the ISBN on a book's copyright page. Check this book's ISBN, and you'll see that Alpha Books is identified by 978-1-61564.

Many authors object to the fact that editors have been using BookScan numbers (as opposed to the longer-range and slower-moving in-house publisher's sales figures) to peg advances. BookScan is not for the general public and requires a hefty annual subscription to access. BookScan is run by Nielsen, the same people who track TV viewing numbers. Read about the service at nielsen.com. If you know someone inside a publishing house that does subscribe, you might be able to convince him or her to research the occasional title for you.

Another way to access it is through Amazon's Author Central, which offers authors the ability to track their own sales but not research other titles.

More Assigned Reading

As a serious student of the book publishing business, you need to keep up with news and trends. Read *PW*, and study the articles about what's selling. *PW* prints annual roundup articles about many of the major book categories. If you plan to write a health book, it's important that you read the health book roundup. If you plan to write a novel, be sure to read the fiction roundup.

Poets & Writers magazine does wonderful in-depth interviews with editors and agents that will give you insight into what they're looking for and why.

In addition to *PW*, also check out *The New York Times* and *The Wall Street Journal*. Both run frequent articles on books and the publishing world. Again, nytimes.com often features articles about books and publishing in addition to its best-seller list and book reviews. The free Publishers Lunch e-mail newsletter mentioned previously includes links to major publishing articles from a wide variety of sources. Start keeping a file of important articles. You never know what you'll learn there.

But I Want to Write a Novel!

Do you really have to go through all this advance work for fiction, too?

Yes. Just as a health writer should know what's already on the health books shelf, a novelist needs to know what fiction is being published and read. Be a student of the art of writing, of course, but to succeed, you must study the marketplace, too. Learn what kinds of novels are selling well (ask a bookseller) and what kinds are not (ask a bookseller). Right now the best-seller lists are dominated by thrillers and paranormals. By the time you read this, another hot trend may be selling. Make it your business to know these things. Don't bury your head in the sand (or your computer)! Get into that bookstore, and learn everything you can.

> **HOT OFF THE PRESS**
>
> Who are you writing for? Can you picture your audience? "I decided that I was writing for 'smart women on vacation,'" said Deborah Wessell, who writes the wedding planner mysteries under the name Deborah Donnelly. The better you can visualize and describe exactly who your audience is, the better you can write for them.

You know you're an absolute original and your style is unique. But if you absolutely had to name a writer or book most like yours, what would you say? You're not doing it to compare yourself with another writer, but to establish the fact that books like the one you have written have sold well.

Minimize Your Rejection Rate

Why, you might ask, are we giving you all this inside information about how to come up with a good book idea? Or about how to research the market and the competing titles? Because, as longtime agents and editors, we're tired of saying "No." It's hard to turn down proposals and manuscripts from good-intentioned, hopeful writers. It's truly heartbreaking to know how much time and effort went into a book project that, from a business standpoint, was doomed from the start.

So we figure the more time and effort we put into teaching you how to come up with a book idea that will get a "Yes!" from an agent, an editor, and a publishing company, the easier our jobs will be.

Now that that's clear, let's move on to the next chapter and get back to that critical question: what do publishers want?

The Least You Need to Know

- Be sure your topic is big enough for an entire book, not just a six-page magazine article.
- Never assume your book is the first ever on the topic. There's at least one book already for every topic ever thought of, and your job is to learn from its/their strengths and weaknesses.
- Pore over information from publishers' websites, snoop around bookstores, and find out what the book clubs are hawking and reading.
- Ask real readers and booksellers what they're looking for.
- The more time and effort you spend researching the market for your novel or nonfiction book, the better your book proposal will be.

What's Hot, What's Not

In This Chapter

- Trend spotting
- Literary and mainstream fiction
- Love 'em, thrill 'em, kill 'em
- Niche writing
- Cookbook niches
- Books for kids

Just what do publishers want? That's a tough question. And what do publishers want *right now* (for publication in 9 to 15 months)? That's an even tougher question, and possibly an irrelevant one. The awful truth is, if you sat down at this very moment and wrote a book on a topic this chapter says is hot *today*, odds are that by the time you got the finished book in your hands, the topic would have cooled down—maybe to subzero.

Let's say it takes you 6 months to write the book. That's not a very long time for anyone to write a good how-to book, much less the Great American Novel. Let's say you know somebody who knows somebody with an experienced and well-connected agent, and that agent just happens to be particularly hungry at the moment. Maybe he's going through an expensive divorce, or his biggest client just got hit by a bus.

You e-mail him your ready-to-publish manuscript. He reads it that very night and sees your book on Hot Topic X as his ticket out of mounting legal bills. The first thing the following morning, he couriers copies to the hotshot editors at his favorite publishing houses.

Twenty-four hours later, he conducts an auction. Your book sells to the highest bidder for megabucks. (Why not? After all, this is a dream.) Smelling success (and desperate to recoup the investment), your publisher rushes the manuscript into production. Nine months later, your book hits the stores amid great fanfare … and is quickly placed on the remainder table. By the time your masterpiece is published, Hot Topic X is old news, and the public now wants to read about Hot Topic Y. First the public wants books on Bernie Madoff and then they want Justin Bieber. Sarah Palin's books are selling out one minute and sitting on the shelf the next.

Sadly, you might remember that this very scenario was played out on a large scale when all the books on September 11 came out for the 1-year anniversary. Some books sold in big numbers, but most did not. Many of the Hurricane Katrina books suffered this same fate, and books by members of former political administrations sometimes hit the market a few months after the public's interest has faded.

What's In and What's Out, by Category

What's a writer to do? Now there's a question worthy of Freud. Despite the transitory and, dare we say, fickle nature of the buying public, certain trends bear watching. So with a grain of salt and an eye on how quickly the reading public can shift its interests, let's take a look at the trends affecting each of the various book categories. "Sometimes what's old is suddenly new again," says Paula Munier, director of acquisitions and innovation at Adams Media.

EXPERTS SAY

"Boomers want to stop the clock," says longtime editor Renee Wilmeth of Literary Architects. "And they will spend money on books that tell them how. As more of this group hits their 60s, you will see even more growth in the categories of health, medical fitness, and anti-aging."

Fiction

The odds for a first-time novelist are never good, but all sorts of first novels are published each year, some to great acclaim and greater profit.

The market for fiction is as good—and as bad—as it ever was. Fiction is a star-driven game; in the years we've been updating this book, the top list hasn't changed much— the John Grishams, James Pattersons, and Danielle Steels have become virtual brand names publishers can count on to drive sales. An increasing dependency on this star system has created a classic chicken-and-egg scenario: which comes first, the best-selling book or the best-selling author?

Every publisher worth its bottom line wants to publish Grishams, Pattersons, and Steels. But there are only so many of these superauthors to go around—and only so many publishers who can afford them. So everyone is looking for the *next* Grisham, the *next* Patterson, the *next* Steel. That's where you might just come in.

Every year brings with it a group of new successful novelists, of course. Sara Gruen wrote *Water for Elephants* during the NaNoWriMo contest (where you write a novel in a month; nanowrimo.org), and its success stunned everyone. Garth Stein was advised by an agent to never show anyone his manuscript about a dog and a race car driver. He got a new agent, and *The Art of Racing in the Rain* spent month after month on the best-seller list.

HOT OFF THE PRESS

The number of books a "best-seller" sells has been steadily increasing over the last few decades. Research fellow Gayle Feldman took a close look and discovered that the 1975 best-seller *Ragtime* sold 232,000 copies. Compare that to the 2000 Grisham best-seller *The Brethren,* which sold nearly 2.9 million copies. Crunch those numbers, and you'll see a staggering twelvefold increase.

As you know from Chapter 2, the fiction market is divided into two general types: literary fiction and commercial (sometimes also called mainstream or contemporary) fiction. The latter includes hardcover novels and genre fiction. Genre fiction includes mysteries, thrillers, science fiction, fantasies, romances, horror books, Westerns, and the like. What's selling in these categories? Let's take a look.

Love Is a Many-Published Thing

The romance market is booming. Take a look at these 2009 numbers from Romance Writers of America (rwa.org) about just how hot romance is:

- Romance generates more than $1.3 billion in sales.

- Romantic fiction was the largest share of the consumer book market at 13.2 percent.

But, you might think, *I couldn't write those bodice-rippers.* Well, if you think bodice-rippers are the only romances, think again. Today's romance genre is a versatile one. It encompasses many series, subgenres, and hybrids, as well as mainstream titles. Consider these subcategories, to name just a few: historical romance, time-travel romance, science-fiction romance, romantic suspense, romantic mystery, inspirational romance, multicultural romance, and young-adult romance. Then there are the new, super-sexy romances.

And if you think romance heroines are generously bosomed virgins looking for Mr. Right to carry them off into the sunset, think again. Today's romance heroines run the gamut from fresh-faced junior high school girls to divorced career women. Sometimes they even fall in love with vampires.

If you'd like to cash in on this lucrative market, you'll have to do your homework. Don't write a single word without first consulting the guidelines from the publisher you plan to target—and without reading all the romance novels you can get your hands on.

EXPERTS SAY

Not sure if your romance novel has what it takes? Join Romance Writers of America (rwa.org) and surround yourself with other romance writers who can give you valuable feedback. Active chapters are located all over the country.

Harlequin is the biggest player, and it happily provides writers with guidelines for all its series. These guidelines are jammed with information on the exact word counts for its books, definitions of style, and the level of sensuality permitted. They include lots of "absolute no-no's" and "absolute musts," as well as submission information. By following these rules, you'll save yourself lots of rewriting, and you'll greatly increase your chances of breaking into the romance field.

Dorchester also has guidelines you can access easily on its website (dorchesterpub.com). Another good source of information can be found at the Market List (marketlist.com), which bills itself as the "online source for genre fiction writers" and has submission info on most major publishers and magazines.

Love Writing About Love?

The one thing all romances have in common, from romantic suspense to mainstream historical, is that they're all stories about relationships. If you can write a love story that will move readers, this could be the field for you.

Laurie Gold puts out an e-mail newsletter about the romance writing industry that you might find useful. Check out her All About Romance site at likesbooks.com, and select "Writer's Side." And if you're in the mood for some snarky fun, check out the reviews on Smart Bitches Trashy Books (smartbitchestrashybooks.com), where Sarah Wendell really gives books the business. It's well worth reading what Laurie and Sarah say if you plan to succeed in this market.

Beyond Hot Romance

From the early days of publishing, "erotica" has always existed in some form or another, and the twenty-first century is no exception. Perhaps writing adult books is your bag? It is a hot, hot part of the e-book market. Ravenous Romance (ravenousromance.com) sells both e-books and erotic short stories and is always looking for new authors.

And like a one-night stand, who knows where it might lead … the rights to some of its e-books have been bought by bigger houses like St. Martin's Press to publish in paperback.

Thrill 'Em, Grill 'Em, and Kill 'Em

Mysteries, thrillers, suspense, and all their kin are more popular than ever—a fact that's readily confirmed by a quick glance at the best-seller list. At the time of this writing, a James Patterson (who else?) thriller tops *The New York Times* hardcover best-seller list. Such news reflects not only the immense popularity of these genres but also their versatility. The mystery and thriller genres rival the romance category in both variety and readership.

Today's market is witnessing a boom in historical mysteries, medical thrillers, techno thrillers, and legal thrillers. But whether you're writing a hard-boiled detective story or an *English cozy*, it doesn't really matter. In these genres, there's plenty of room for your novel, regardless of which category it fits. One of the oldest publishing houses around, Little Brown, has just started a new suspense imprint called Mulholland Books (mulhollandbooks.com).

DEFINITION

An **English cozy** is a type of mystery that typically takes place in England and follows a sweet old lady detective and a few of her doddering friends. They stumble onto a cold, dead body one afternoon, and the story unfolds from there. The term *cozy* comes either from the fact that you can settle in front of the fire for a cozy afternoon with one of these books, or from the tea cozy on the pot of Earl Grey you brew to drink while you read.

Nouveau Niche

The marketing types in publishing love nonfiction. Why? Because the nonfiction market is much more quantifiable—some would say more reliable—than the fiction market. Those marketers don't really know how many readers are going to want to read your coming-of-age novel, and they can't even begin to guess. But they can guess with slightly more accuracy how many of the nations millions of overweight people would be interested in *The Lean Belly Prescription* or whether fans of the shows *Mad Men* or *Glee* will buy related books. The same goes for all the trends—demographic and otherwise—reported in the media each day. Nonfiction publishers pay attention to what's hot, and (as we've told you before) if you want to succeed at nonfiction, you need to pay attention, too.

Identifying a niche in the marketplace and then publishing to that niche is called— you guessed it—niche publishing. Three of the most successful niche markets right now are alternative health, spirituality, and longevity. All these niches fill a deep need for readers.

As people grow more disenchanted with conventional medicine, they're exploring alternative therapies and lifestyles. These same folks hope to live long and healthy lives, as witnessed by the success of books like *Veganist* by Kathy Freston and *You Can Heal Your Life* by longtime best-seller Louise Hay. And look at the success of '70s sitcom star Suzanne Somers with her alternative healing titles like *Sexy Forever: How to Fight Fat After Forty*.

The same boomer group who once turned away from organized religion is now looking for spiritual guidance as they become more aware of their own mortality. A recent article in *The Wall Street Journal* noted that, in the same way boomers changed giving birth (and sold vast numbers of *What to Expect When You're Expecting*), they are now changing death.

> **HOT OFF THE PRESS**
>
> Investment books are a niche in the business book category. This is a crowded category; it can be hard to be different and stand out. *The Investment Answer* by Daniel Goldie and Gordon S. Murray stood out for a tragic reason—Murray was dying. Before it was published, the financial papers began to report the story, and the book was an immediate success.

"Fine," you say, "but I don't know St. John's wort from St. John the Baptist, and I don't know a thing about how to live forever." No problem. There are myriad trends and niches to explore, from homeschooling to women's golf, from small businesses to eBay auctions. You don't even have to be an expert—you can always team up with one.

What's Cookin' with Cookbooks?

Long a staple of nonfiction publishing, the cookbook market has disappointed many publishers over the past couple years. "The cookbook field was overpublished," admits one long-time cookbook editor, who also reveals that many cookbook editors are looking for new jobs in new fields.

Despite this recent softening of the market, some cookbooks are finding favor with the public. "Editors say to me that superstar chefs are both overpublished and still selling," says a longtime California cookbook agent.

So what is a nonsuperstar chef author to do? You can still find your niche if you work at it. The same agent suggested first-time writers could find success with "anything that ties into a product, like grilling or a panini sandwich press." Cookbooks with product or equipment ties might succeed because the publisher can persuade the manufacturer to purchase the book in bulk. A good example is the *Fix It and Forget It Cookbook*, with 2.2 million copies sold of a book that tells you what you can fix in your slow cooker.

Literary food writing is also still selling, and it is possible to build an interesting anthology or compilation book around food like the recent book featuring stories about kitchen disasters.

The Publishing House at Pooh Corner

By definition, the children's market is a perennial one. Write for children, and you can build a body of work that will enchant the little ones generation after generation. But if you think writing for children is easy, think again. To paraphrase beloved author of *A Wrinkle in Time*, Madeleine L'Engle, writing for children means writing stories too mature for adults.

L'Engle's point has been made quite clearly by the extraordinary success of the *Harry Potter* books. These enduring best-sellers made frequent appearances on both the children's *and* the adults' best-seller lists, and fans waited for years for Rowling's final book to appear. The sophisticated wordplay in the *Lemony Snicket* books also appeals to both children and adults. Rick Riordan's *Percy Jackson* books are constructed around Greek myths, informing young readers and delighting older ones at the same time.

What kind of books are working now? Annie Martin Bowler, the author of seven books, including *The Adventures of the Treasure Fleet*, says, "Editors are looking for snappy stuff. Our world is so fast nowadays and books need to move fast, too, in order to compete with video games and television for a child's attention. Snappy like the *Captain Underpants* books, that is what is working."

When you write for children, be it picture books or young adult novels, you can expect somewhat smaller advances. But with the potential of a lifetime of royalties as each generation of little folks discovers your writing, it's a much-anticipated legacy.

The children's market is as varied as the market for grown-ups. You have your pick of options, from picture books to young-adult mysteries to middle-grade nonfiction.

Picture This

Picture books have been and remain this category's biggest sellers. Picture books for young readers are also assumed to be immune to ever losing ground to e-books. Who would hold an iPad up to a baby and let them bang and drool on the pages? An actual book "involves the senses," as children's book author Renee Khatami points out.

The classic picture book is as popular as ever, but there's an increased interest in other types of picture books as well, most notably these types:

- Picture books made into baby board books (Those little books whose pages are cardboard to make turning easier for little fingers.)

- Picture books for slightly older toddlers

SLUSH PILE

Never send illustrations for your children's picture book with your manuscript unless you're a talented artist. Most publishers like to hire their own illustrators. Also, never mention the following in a query or proposal: "My niece (nephew, son, daughter, or next-door neighbor) is a wonderful artist whose work would really complete the book."

No Kidding About Kids' Fiction

Middle-grade and young-adult books also offer writers a wealth of opportunities. First *Harry Potter* and then the *Twilight* series really lit a fire in this genre. Urban fantasy and steam punk for young adults is in now, too. To really understand this category, you need to steep yourself in it and read as much as you can.

Just the Facts, Ma'am

Nonfiction for children—particularly in the areas of science, technology, and biography—are staples of this market. If your writing can entertain as well as educate, this area might be for you.

Expert Lynne Rominger observed that, although the children's market used to be thought of as a "cousin of regular adult books, not really a money-making part of the industry," this thought has long since changed. Publishers and booksellers alike recognize the fact that every 5 years they have a new crop of customers.

Market Savvy for Success

Once you develop a keener eye for what's working and what isn't, how can you put this information to use? You should be able to spot an overpublished market and avoid it. You should be able to notice a book or two on a particular topic you've never noticed before and sense that a trend is building. And you should be able to develop more marketable ideas yourself!

Still having trouble coming up with an idea? Why not spend some time brainstorming about these two popular book angles:

Devote yourself to one wacky task for a year. Remember, this is "schtick lit." It worked in a big, big way for Julie Powell, the blogger who decided to cook every single recipe in Julia Child's kitchen classic *Mastering the Art of French Cooking* and morphed her blog into the book *Julie & Julia*. The same idea worked for Maria Headley in *The Year of Yes*, in which she decided to accept a date with any man who asked her out.

Or if you can't think of an unusual way to spend a year, perhaps you could infiltrate some sort of secret society. Neil Strauss did that with his much-publicized book *The Game: Penetrating the Secret Society of Pickup Artists*.

EXPERTS SAY

For both inspiration and information, children's writer Annie Martin Bowler has turned her attentions to past winners of the Newberry Award. "I've memorized whole sections of *Charlotte's Web*," she says. What wins a Newberry? "They are always meaty topics and tend to be more serious. My goal is to win that award myself someday, so I study them as much as I can."

The Early Bird ...

Keep your ear to the ground, and you can turn today's trends into tomorrow's best-sellers. But don't dawdle; when it comes to trends, the first writer to the marketplace usually wins. Keep abreast by reading *Publishers Weekly* on a regular basis and paying careful attention to the trend articles that run interviews with editors and booksellers about what's working.

The Least You Need to Know

- Publishers' predictions can be hit or miss, but certain trends bear watching.
- The romance field has changed dramatically, and many publishers have a need for sexier manuscripts. However, if you're writing romance, get publishers' guidelines first.
- Children's books can mean small advances but long-term sales.
- Put (almost) as much effort into your market research as into your writing.

Submitting to Publishers

So you've got an idea for a book—now what? Here's where you learn the actual process of putting together a book proposal. We clue you in on the common mistakes new writers make so you can look like a pro on the page, right from the beginning!

From submitting professional queries to compiling appealing proposals, the chapters in Part 2 explain what you need to get the attention of an agent or editor. Both non-fiction and fiction proposals are covered in detail, and you learn the steps involved in either (or both!).

Start with a well-crafted query to line up interest, and move on to showcasing your work in a full-length proposal. What's the most important part of a book proposal? We tell you in Part 2, along with how to be sure your proposal contains the perfect pitch and enough compelling angles to stand out.

And thanks to the following chapters, you'll soon be able to describe your work in a way that will have eager readers waiting for the entire manuscript.

Submit What?

In This Chapter

- Understanding the submission process
- A peek at book publishing
- The top mistakes new writers make
- The correct spelling of *foreword* (that thing at the front of your book)
- Plain and simple: formatting your submissions

You've come up with an idea you think is incredible, but what now? How do you move your book idea closer to becoming the finished thing? You must begin to *submit*.

Submit, you say? *What's that?* Simply stated, the *submission* process is the one by which you let the publishing world know you have a great book available for publication.

Simply Submit

To get your book idea in front of the publishing decision-makers, you need to know how to make your way through the submissions process. This involves two important steps:

Important Step One: Write a query

Important Step Two: Write a book proposal

Why is the submission process broken down into two steps? To see how this came to be, let's peek in on a typical day in the publishing world.

A Day in the Life of Book Publishing

It's early morning in Manhattan, and unbeknownst to each other, an assistant editor and a literary agent are sitting next to each other on the subway. The doors open, and the two put away their iPads, hoist their heavy tote bags onto their shoulders, and head for the same towering black skyscraper. The elevators deposit them on two different floors. After greeting colleagues, they settle into their small offices with their first cups of weak office coffee, poured into a mug from a trade show.

For the next two hours, on two different floors, these two hard-working members of the New York publishing world lead oddly parallel lives. Both eye the fresh stack of mail perched on their desks, and both sigh when beginning the task of opening and reading the mail.

What, they still get mail? Yes. *Queries, book proposals,* finished manuscripts, editorial correspondence, newspaper clippings, promotional information—there seems to be no end to the pieces of paper that still arrive and must be read. Interrupting the ritual of reading the mail, the phone rings continuously. And then, think of the onslaught of e-mail. As a Random House editor, it was a struggle for Jennifer to simply keep up with the internal e-mail communication from her colleagues and higher-ups, let alone messages from agents and writers.

DEFINITION

The process by which a writer submits a book proposal or manuscript to a publisher is called **submission.** If the author is not using an agent, it's an *unagented submission.* The initial contact between a writer and an agent comes in the form of a **query,** which is meant to spark interest in the project and prompt its recipient to ask for more material. The packet of information about the writer's manuscript or book idea is a **book proposal.** It contains a solid description of the book's purpose, the potential market for the book, its competition, and the author's credentials. It also contains a complete table of contents, an extensive book outline, and at least one sample chapter.

This scene takes place simultaneously not only in the office of our unnamed assistant editor and faceless literary agent, but also in the offices of the senior editor, the editor in chief, the publisher, the associate editor, and even the new college intern. Let's face it—everybody wants to write a book, and everybody writes to people in publishing. So how do publishers, editors, and agents handle the volume of snail mail and e-mail?

Queries, that's how.

Quantum Query

A query is a simple, one-page letter. Whether you're sending an actual letter or an e-mail, the query is the same—the purpose of the book is described and the author makes a short case for why the world needs this book. If the contents of the query pique the recipient's interest, he or she requests a proposal. If the proposal is good and the book-to-be is deemed marketable, a publisher offers a contract.

But why can't you send your entire book? Because in most cases, the harried folks in publishing haven't met you and don't know about your project. You need to try to get their attention in the easiest and fastest way possible. A query is the correspondence equivalent of politely tapping a stranger on the shoulder and saying, "Excuse me, do you have a minute to talk?"

EXPERTS SAY

The author of eight books and counting, Candy Chand has had amazing luck in e-mailing various publishing higher-ups. Why do they read her unsolicited e-mails? "It's all about the subject line," she says. "You hook 'em with a killer subject line."

Sound intimidating? Don't worry. We show you how to write a top-notch query that will help your project stand out. We also tell you how to put together a bulletproof book proposal that will impress everyone who sees it.

But Before We Begin ...

We've seen it all. We've read thousands of queries and book proposals. Don't make the mistakes others have. Here you'll learn the things you must avoid, the no-no's that will brand you as an amateur. Read them and believe them. Commit them to memory before moving on to the next two chapters. The publishing world has rules, and you've got to follow them to get people to look at your stuff.

Co-author Jennifer once received a large package from someone she met at a writers' conference. Thankfully, it did not arrive postage due, but his letter began, "Although all the books I've read tell me to send just a query first, I've decided to take a different approach and send a complete manuscript of the book." *Arrgh!*

Not only did this fellow come off as arrogant, but he also signaled that he is not someone who follows the rules. What agent or editor wants to sign someone who clearly doesn't take direction? Not many.

And what happened to the package Jennifer received? She sent it right back, unread.

The Top Mistakes New Writers Make

If you take the following list to heart, you won't repeat the preceding faux pas or others that raise red flags. Here are a few simple no-no's that can easily undermine all your hard work:

- Letters or e-mails that contain a misspelled name
- Packages or letters with postage due
- Unsolicited material that requires a signature
- Queries that don't quickly come to the point
- Proposals that criticize other books
- Letters that are too flip or amusing in tone
- Queries that say, "All my friends think this is a great idea"
- Proposals that smell like cigarette smoke
- Queries that mention the minimum advance the writer will accept
- Proposals that arrive in a package filled with shredded paper or packing peanuts

Letters or E-Mails That Contain a Misspelled Name

How hard is it to call and check the spelling of someone's name? Why brand yourself a careless writer before the package is even open? A simple phone call helps you show you're serious about getting things right. Tell the receptionist you'd like to double-check the spelling of an editor's name, and they should be happy to help. Don't assume that what's printed in a professional directory is correct. For many years, Jennifer's name was misspelled in a major writers' guide.

In fact, any information you've plucked out of a publishing directory needs to be verified. Find out if the editor still works there and is still acquiring in the same areas. You can research so much online nowadays, but it's still worth it to pick up the phone, call the publishing company's main number, and ask to verify the spelling of an editor's name. You can also Google to see if the editor is mentioned anywhere professionally, or look on LinkedIn to see if he or she is listed, but even that's no guarantee.

Package or Letter That Arrives Postage Due

You look careless and irresponsible from the moment your material arrives if your package requires postage due. Another way to annoy your recipient is to send a package laden with little slips of paper that need to be signed to prove it arrived.

Remember, you're sending something that, under most circumstances, this person did not request. So don't make it hard for them to receive it.

Unsolicited Material That Requires a Signature or Immediate Response

Yes, we know you are anxious to know if your stuff arrived. But don't ask someone who never requested it in the first place to sign for a package they aren't expecting. It comes off as presumptuous, rude, arrogant, and so on.

Also, be patient about your e-mails. The sad fact is not every e-mail will receive a reply, so don't send e-mail after e-mail asking if your proposal or query is under consideration. Trust us, if they want to contact you, they will.

Queries That Don't Quickly Come to the Point

By "quickly," we mean in the first paragraph or two. Why is this so important? Remember our typical day in publishing? The one in which the agent's and editor's desks were piled with mail? And don't forget the blinking phone message light, the 73 unanswered e-mails, and the multiple scheduled meetings for that day. Time and attention are short. You need to get to the point.

EXPERTS SAY

"I could always spot an amateur," says former agent Martha Casselman. "Instead of trying to sell me on an idea, the letter would brag about the fact that they'd obtained a copyright for their work, and proudly give the copyright date and number. What did that mean to me? Nothing. Tell us about your book; don't tell us about your housekeeping details."

Proposals That Criticize Other Books

This is a major gripe of editors. You worked hard to put together a book proposal, and your agent spent a lot of time deciding which editors to approach with it. So why annoy the very editor you're hoping to impress?

"The author should never use the competitive analysis section to slam other books—chances are, publishers who published those books will be reading the author's proposal," a former senior editor at Hyperion advised. "Also, many times the books that are being slammed are books that were huge successes. It doesn't make sense to slam something that was a big best-seller, but many authors do."

As an editor at Prima, Jennifer has also received many a proposal that pokes fun at some of the very Prima books she's proudest of. Once again, not the way to get someone to like you and your book idea. (Chapter 8 explains how to position your book in a positive light without making enemies.)

Letters That Are Too Flip or Amusing

A query is not a letter to a friend, your mom, or a long-lost chum. This is no time to be silly. Even if friends think you're the next Jon Stewart, it's safer to write a straightforward, businesslike letter. Humor can easily work against you. So can arrogance, boasting, or conceit.

How can you impress an agent if you can't boast about your accomplishments? Be confident, not arrogant. Don't worry—you learn how to do this in Chapters 7 and 9.

Queries That Mention Your Fan Club

Don't ever write, "All my friends and relatives think this is a good idea." Book publishing is a business, and professionals in the book business aren't interested in hearing about your friends and relatives (unless they are famous friends and relatives who will be endorsing your book). They want to know about markets and demographics and national publicity.

Proposals That Smell Like Cigarette Smoke

Hey, go ahead and smoke, it's none of our business, but you'd be amazed at how the smell attaches itself to paper! Editors notice when they open a proposal that makes their eyes swim from the tobacco fumes. If you smoke, you probably don't notice it, but take our word for it: smokers send letters that smell like smoke. So just to be sure, take your manuscript to a FedEx Kinko's or a nonsmoking friend's house and print out your work in a smoke-free environment.

Does this seem like petty advice to you? Perhaps. But remember, you want these publishing people to like you and your project. You need to use every little method you can to woo them.

Queries That Mention a Minimum Advance

Queries that mention the minimum advance the writer will accept or the phrase "resources needed to complete this project" expose you as a beginner. Like writers who are paranoid that someone might steal their ideas, this is the mark of an amateur. Never mention money in a query. Never mention money in a book proposal.

When considering whether to pursue a book idea, agents and editors don't care what kind of "resources" are needed to complete your project. That's your problem, not theirs. Sooner or later, the topic of money will come up, but let them mention it first, not you.

SLUSH PILE

A big no-no when approaching an agent or editor is to be cagey about your idea, or worse yet, not reveal it at all. More than one amateur has expressed anxiety over sharing his or her surefire book idea for fear that someone will steal it. Trust us, they won't. This attitude only makes you look naive and foolish to a publishing pro. The same theory applies to asking an editor to sign a nondisclosure agreement (NDA).

Proposals That Are Buried in Shredded Paper

You want these publishing folks to be in a pleasant mood when they're reading your material. But years of experience in opening packages has taught us there is no way to open one of these types of packages without getting a lapful (or noseful) of shredded paper. Maddening! You want someone to love your project. Don't risk ticking them off before they can get to it.

Can't find a padded envelope that doesn't have that shredded paper stuff in it? If your proposal doesn't fit in a FedEx letter-size envelope, it's probably too darn long. And a query that doesn't slip right into a regular envelope is definitely too long.

Warning, Warning ...

Although this hardly ever happens, it has on occasion: a first-time writer sends off highly personal possessions along with a proposal—a grandmother's diary, baby pictures. And then what happens? It gets tossed at the publishers. Unsolicited material that isn't accompanied by a SASE (self-addressed, stamped envelope) gets tossed into the trash. So don't do it. Don't ever, ever send something you can't replace.

"I got a proposal that wasn't even a proposal exactly, it was just a scrapbook about someone remodeling their house. The original plans, scraps of fabric glued in, and lots of pictures of the progress," a how-to editor told us. "No self-addressed stamped envelope, no box we could ship it back in. It would have cost us huge money to have it packed up and sent back. So it went straight into the trash." Don't let this happen to your material.

Forward and Other Foibles

The world of book publishing is a peculiar place with peculiar rules, and it's frequently filled with peculiar people.

Even if you've learned all you can from the many books you've read, the courses and seminars you've attended, and the writers you know, there are still tiny mistakes only persnickety publishing people will notice.

Here's the big one: *forward* versus *foreword*.

Look up these two words in your dictionary. Here's what ours says:

> **forward** (adj.) directed or moving toward the front, situated in front

So if the president of the United States has agreed to write something nice for the front of your book, you think, it must be a forward. These are introductory remarks situated in front of your book, so it would seem perfectly logical. But no! The president is writing a *foreword*, not a *forward*, for your book:

> **foreword** (n.) introductory remarks at the beginning of the book, usually by someone other than the author

Even longtime authors make this mistake sometimes, and some publishing people feel very smug when they spot it.

As long as you have your dictionary out, let's tackle two more confusing words:

> **which** (adj. and pronoun) what particular one or ones of a set of things or people
>
> **that** (adj. and pronoun) the person or thing referred to or pointed to or understood

Co-author Sheree spends a great deal of her time combing through her clients' proposals changing *which* to *that*. What's the rule? If *that* works, use it.

A Great Example of a Bad Query

We stumbled on this tongue-in-cheek example of the absolute wrong approach and couldn't resist sharing it with you. It was written specifically to incorporate all the mistakes a new writer might make. Read it and weep. And then rewrite your query!

> ***Book Two of the Third Volume of the Elves from Ipanema:***
> ***Revenge of the Gas Lords: Part I***
>
> Dearest Mrs. Hurst:
>
> You may remember me from the restroom of the Writer's Conference in Bigthighs, New Jersey, in May. Actually, obviously, it was my girlfriend, Ronnette, you met—the short redhead who gave you my card and mentioned my sizzling series of fantasy novels—isn't she sassy? In any case, you told Ronnette you don't represent fantasy. Permit me to take issue with this stance. All writing is fantasy, if you just think about it, including nonfiction, which you seem to prefer. So I would maintain that you *do* represent fantasy. I checked your website, and one of your upcoming books is titled *Eat Fit and Stay Slim*. Good Lord, if that's not fantasy, what is? So sit down, take a bite of the candy bar I've enclosed, and allow me a moment to convince you of my *Elf* series merits.
>
> In the Land of Ipanema, all is not as it should be. Darkness spreads like giant bat wings over the innocent land, and the people, both large and small, are afraid. Emma Splink is a poor and impoverished pig herder who works for a cruel master in the small hamlet of Ipa.
>
> Now believe me, I would love to tell you more about the plot but then I'd have to shoot you! Just kidding. I can't tell you more because I'm only on

chapter 9, in which Emma is ensorcelled by the crone in the woods but then is rescued by her psychic sow, Gandalf.

As I mentioned, I have studied your website (congrats on your B.A. in literature way back in '61 by the way), and I notice you have an interest in chick lit. Clearly you are going to love my protagonist Emma. This girl may wear chain mail and little else, but she is intelligent, short, redheaded, sassy, and determined to rescue the world. *Gas Lords* is a sure-fire *New York Times* best-seller.

I have numerous writing credentials, including my personal blog, Craig's Funhouse, unpublished letters-to-the-editor at agentwatch.com, and a fourth-place prize in erotica from the Bigthighs Alternative Hairstyle and Writing Fair.

Gas Lords is the second novel I have written in what will be a series of 12. I must admit that the first book, *Wind from Below*, just wasn't good enough for publication. Darla, my mom, loved it. But a lot of my buddies pointed out flaws in the plot, characters, theme, and words. After two rejection letters, I put *Wind* in the desk drawer and made a vow: I will learn from this experience. Those same agents who let loose *Wind* will not pass *Gas*.

I have sent submissions to you and 50 of your top competitors. Since you haven't replied to my calls, either at your office or at your home, I would appreciate you getting back to me ASAP.

I hope you are feeling better from the stomach upset you had at the conference—Ronnette mentioned you didn't look so good.

The Blessings of Loki, Thor, and Odin Upon You,

Craig English

P.S. Hope I'm doing this right. I'm still pretty much a newcomer to the business and probably making mistakes right and left. I wasn't sure whether to include a bio and picture, so I did. I strongly urge you to run a virus scan before opening them.

Okay, which mistakes did he make? Which mistakes *didn't* he make? He is querying an agent who doesn't handle the type of fiction he is submitting, he is way too chatty and personal, and he hasn't followed any of the protocol rules. Remember, this was written tongue-in-cheek, but it's dangerously close to what some agents see every day!

Look Like a Pro on the Page

Sure, your computer is loaded with the latest design tricks. However, this is not the time to use them. Queries and book proposals are not the right place to show off your fancy fonts and graphics capability. Use a basic font, such as Times New Roman or Courier. Skip the shaded boxes, cartoons, and artistic borders. Keep it plain.

Plain is also the order of the day for paper. Don't send off a query on scented paper, fancy marbled paper, or anything other than plain white, businesslike stock. And don't get fancy with the inks. Use plain black ink, please.

Likewise, when sending an e-mail query, keep it businesslike in appearance. No fancy colors or type and, need we say it, no emoticons please. ☺

Now Where Should I Send It?

With all this talk of submitting, to whom shall you submit? It's a reasonable question. Sometimes writers submit their stuff to an agent, who then decides to represent them. The agent submits the writer's material to an editor. Other times, a writer just goes ahead and submits to an editor. So what do we think you should do?

If you plan to write a book with broad national appeal, we think you should first try to get an agent. (You'll learn more about agents in the following chapters—particularly Chapter 10.) If that doesn't work, you should try to submit directly.

In the next three chapters, we discuss queries and book proposals. It's our aim to help you prepare these materials in such a way to interest an agent. And if you can't? We'll cross that bridge when we come to it, in Chapter 13.

The Least You Need to Know

- There is a well-defined process for submitting your materials: submit a query and then, if requested, a book proposal.
- Follow the rules, or you risk looking like an amateur—or worse, a difficult author to work with.
- Careless errors in queries or book proposals can undermine your other efforts.
- If you're writing a book with a large potential audience, first try to get an agent to represent you.
- Be businesslike. Don't try to be clever or witty. And don't use scented paper or fancy typestyles. No emoticons in your e-mails either.

Queries That Sell Nonfiction

In This Chapter

- What's a query?
- Editing yourself
- Tips on hooking 'em
- Playing by the rules, and playing nice
- Dealing with rejection

Now that we've frightened you into thinking your entire publishing career rests on a single piece of correspondence, how can we calm you down? By telling you this: the formula for writing successful queries can be learned, and your lessons begin now.

This chapter tackles querying for nonfiction books. Novelists, your turn comes up in Chapter 9. We do, however, urge you to keep reading this chapter.

Although you learned the basic idea behind a query in Chapter 6, it bears repeating: the query is your first contact with either an agent or an editor. It is your calling card, your way of introducing yourself and your book idea to the publishing world at large.

Query? What's That?

A successful query should contain the following items:

- A brief description of the book
- A brief description of the market for the book
- A brief description of the author

Brief? Just how brief are we talking here? One page, that's how brief. Your query should never, ever be longer than one page. You need to distill your brilliance, your wisdom, and your expertise into one potent, page-long brew that will leave a reader reeling from its power.

Here's a quick exercise to help you distill that brew:

1. Sit down with one blank page of paper.

2. Write out a two-paragraph description of the book.

3. Write out a two-paragraph description of the market for the book.

4. Write out a two-paragraph description of yourself, the author of the book.

Okay, now pretend you're Ernest Hemingway. No, you don't have to run in front of a herd of bulls; all we want you to do is simplify your writing. Take a hard look at what you've written and start cutting out extra words. Make two long sentences into one medium-length sentence. Get rid of adjectives. Turn two wordy paragraphs into one punchy one.

Let's look at some Hemingway-esque transformations.

About the Author, Take 1

This is the first draft of the bio:

> Jennifer Basye Sander entered publishing as a way to escape a failed career in California politics. Her first book project was *The Sacramento Women's Yellow Pages*, a directory of woman-owned businesses. She worked for several years as a book buyer for a small, independent, northern California bookstore chain before becoming an acquisitions editor for a nonfiction publisher.

> As an editor, Jennifer worked with many best-selling authors, including Mary Kay Ash of Mary Kay Cosmetics, and award-winning writers such as the James Beard and IACP Award–winning food writer Elaine Corn. As an author, Jennifer's own books range in topic from travel (*The Air Courier's Handbook*) to small business (*Niche and Grow Rich*) to inspiration (*Christmas Miracles*). Her book *Christmas Miracles* was a *New York Times* best-seller. Formerly a senior editor at the Prima Publishing division of Random House, Jennifer also operates her own book packaging company, Big City Books Group, in Granite Bay, California, and runs a writers' retreat in Lake Tahoe, Write by the Lake.

About the Author, Take 2

After a short consultation with Mr. Hemingway, we now give you the revised paragraph:

> Jennifer Basye Sander first entered publishing with *The Sacramento Women's Yellow Pages.* Her early success with that book led to a career in publishing that includes both a short stint as a book buyer and many years as an acquisitions editor. She worked with several best-selling authors and has herself authored many books, including the holiday best-seller *Christmas Miracles.* A former Random House editor, she is now a book packager and writing retreat leader in Granite Bay, California.

Get the idea? Write as much as you want and then go back and delete most of it. (Don't really throw it away, though; you'll need the long stuff for your proposal.) Keep the good stuff that sells you and your book.

About the Book, Take 1

Let's see how this works with a description of a book. Here's a two-paragraph description of our imaginary book, *Accurate Arthritis Answers:*

> *Accurate Arthritis Answers* is a unique idea. Instead of relying on the advice of just one arthritis doctor, I plan to seek out advice from top arthritis experts around the world. Research schools, government studies, health websites, blogs, magazine and newspaper articles, and medical journals will all be scoured to cull the latest information on arthritis. Arthritis sufferers will learn about cutting-edge medical treatments, the dramatic difference that exercise can have, and the effects of nutrition upon their affliction. Special attention will be paid to recent discoveries in alternative treatments, such as herbal therapy.

> The book itself is divided into four different sections: Traditional Medicine, Nutrition, Exercise, and Alternative Therapies. Each section is written by a top expert in the field. Organized in an easy-to-understand style, *Accurate Arthritis Answers* will also contain colorful charts, illustrations, and a useful medical glossary. At 175 pages, the book will be a small and handy size for the lay reader.

About the Book, Take 2

Okay, how do we say that in one short, punchy paragraph? Like this:

> *Accurate Arthritis Answers* fills a real need in the marketplace. Unlike other large medical books, it is a short, easy-to-read book for the general reader. Instead of relying on the knowledge of just one doctor, it brings together the expertise of a wide range of international experts in the field. All types of treatments are examined, from the traditional medical approach to the latest research in herbal and other nontraditional remedies. Arthritis sufferers will now be able to turn to one single source for all the latest information.

Writer, Edit Thyself

Go ahead, give this exercise a try. Start writing long descriptions of your book, your market, and yourself. Then shrink them down to query size. You'll quickly learn to spot what needs to stay and what needs to go.

A one-page query does have more than three paragraphs sometimes. What is your strongest area? Your credentials, your book idea, or the potential market? Choose your strength, and devote two entire paragraphs to it.

Why does your query have to be perfect? A well-written query is your best shot at seeing your book published. So work on it, over and over again, until it looks right to you. This is not the time to write a hasty and flip message. This is the time to set aside a week to perfect your query.

EXPERTS SAY

Writer Candy Chand has her queries down to a sweet science. "Every one of my queries is just a few paragraphs long," she told us. "In the first paragraph, I introduce myself and my other published projects. I spend two paragraphs describing my new project and then close with one paragraph thanking them for considering it." Does it work? She's sold several projects that way, including *The Twelve Prayers of Christmas* to HarperCollins.

If you're sending an e-mail query, don't just sit down and dash off a little something the way you would ordinarily. No, craft and hone that e-mail; work it over exactly the same way as you would any piece of professional correspondence. You only get one shot, so don't blow it.

What *Not* to Say

Here are four things agents don't want you to put in your query:

- That this is an exclusive submission if it really isn't. (Don't lie.)

- Asking after their health and happiness. (They want to know more about you.)

- Stating how well you can write. (*Show* them how well you can write.)

- Stating that if an editor doesn't want this particular project, you'd be happy to write anything he or she wants. (You're writing to demonstrate your knowledge and your talent, not your flexibility.)

Hook 'Em Early

The best queries have a strong hook in the first two lines. What's a strong hook? Something that grabs the readers' attention and keeps them reading. Let's look at a good example, the query Candy Chand used to land her book contract for *The Twelve Prayers of Christmas:*

Dear Editor:

As a published author, with my sixth book in the works, I always look forward to new and exciting projects. Therefore, at this time, I'd like to share with you a manuscript dear to my heart—a holiday picture book titled *The Twelve Prayers of Christmas.*

This festive work of flowing prose is designed to share the Christmas miracle from the POV of each of the individuals present on that holiest of nights: the donkey, the innkeeper, Mary, Joseph, the star, the lamb, the angel, the shepherd boy, each of the three wise men, and, of course, the Christ child Himself.

Upon your request, I'd be happy to send you the completed manuscript. Thank you for considering this project. I'm looking forward to hearing from you soon.

Best regards,
Candy Chand

Candy heard from an editor the very next day. Why? Let's take a closer look at this query.

Right away, Candy identifies herself as a published author working on her sixth book. Any agent or editor would keep reading. If you can't describe yourself this way, it's best to focus in the first one or two lines on the potential size of the audience for your topic. Candy could have described the enduring popularity of Christmas-themed gift books or the built-in marketing angles.

In addition, she describes the book itself in one short paragraph.

Finally, she offers to send the completed manuscript upon request. Remember, in a query, you're just describing the idea, not sending along your whole body of work.

This information all pulls together into a very effective query that grabbed an editor's attention. "After about a year or more of several editorial bites but no cigars," Candy explains, "I sent it to the editor at HarperCollins Children's. The next morning, I received a reply requesting the material. So I sent the manuscript via e-mail. The editorial director e-mailed me back the next day after to ask if she could call me. She did call and told me she loved it and would take it to committee. Two weeks later, she called with the news that it sold."

EXPERTS SAY

"Can they write? That's what I look at first in a query letter," says agent Andrea Hurst. "Does it draw me in? Do I want to read more? With nonfiction, I ask myself: Is this a unique and timely idea? Does it fit in with my agency? Does this author have a strong platform and a sense of the marketing that is involved?" Andrea sums it up this way: concise, well written, marketable, and unique. For fiction, the author's voice must carry through into the letter or e-mail and draw her into the book.

Another Approach

Here's another good approach for a short query to an agent:

Every Halloween, news stories warn us about strangers intent on poisoning our children's candy. Every Thanksgiving, we hear how turkey makes us sleepy. We all know that we use only 10 percent of our brains, we should drink at least 8 glasses of water a day, and cell phones are dangerous in hospitals. Unfortunately, none of these things are true.

People have access to more medical information than ever before, yet they continue to harbor false beliefs about their bodies and health. *Eight Glasses of Water a Day: Mistakes, Half-Truths, and Outright Lies About Your Body and Health* identifies such myths and provides detailed, well-documented explanations as to why they are mistaken. A number of books have been published on "medical myths," and some have sold quite successfully. However, our book differs in the depth in which we cover each belief, with well-documented evidence. It is an amalgam of *Freakonomics* and *Why Do Men Have Nipples?* We include lighthearted myths and describe the research disproving them, while also delving into more complicated or controversial areas, such as vaccine safety and drug costs.

Originally conceived as a lighthearted reminder to doctors about the myths "even they believe," a very short version of this concept will be published as an article in the *British Medical Journal* in late 2007. We expect the book to have even broader appeal because these myths are so pervasive in our media and collective subconscious. The next few months will be an opportune time to promote an upcoming book because we are already scheduled for radio interviews and will issue press releases about our manuscript through the University media offices.

The strength of this book lies in the expertise and capabilities of its physician authors. Aaron E. Carroll, M.D., M.S., is a graduate of Amherst College, the University of Pennsylvania School of Medicine, and the University of Washington School of Public Health. He is now Assistant Professor of Pediatrics at Indiana University School of Medicine. Rachel C. Vreeman, M.D., is a graduate of Cornell University and the Michigan State University College of Human Medicine; she is now a health services research fellow. Both are accomplished researchers who have been published many times in scientific literature and in newspaper editorials. Moreover, both are skilled in describing complicated nuances of medical research and policy in ways that are easily accessible to the general public, as shown in their previous print, radio, and television interviews.

We would be pleased to send you a book proposal if you are interested. If you have any questions, please feel free to contact us at any time.

Sincerely,

Aaron E. Carroll, M.D., M.S., and Rachel C. Vreeman, M.D.

They've got a great hook in the first few sentences because we all know those rumors about Halloween and Thanksgiving. The authors then quickly describe the book and the theory and establish that this is a popular topic and they are well qualified to write on this topic. But did it work? Yes, the literary agent Janet Rosen of Sheree Bykofsky Associates, Inc., plucked it out of a slush pile and sold it under the name *Don't Swallow Your Gum!*

Write a Good One and Then Let It Be

Go ahead and write that query. Make it as perfect as you can make it. But after you drop it in the mail or hit "send," leave it alone. Believe it or not, many authors can't leave it alone even after sending one off.

Agents and editors have all received them—the letters and e-mails that begin, "Please disregard the query I mailed to you on January 22 and replace it with this version, which I think more accurately captures the essence of my book." Or "This information should be added to the proposal I sent to you last week. Please remove pages 4 through 8 and replace them with these new pages." Crazy but true.

Do not, under any circumstances, attempt to do this! When your query disappears through the slot in the mailbox, when your e-mail provider says the e-mail has gone through, move on to something else in your life. Don't lie awake at night wondering how you might have done it differently. It will just drive you nuts.

E-Mail Etiquette

The query tradition grew up in the era of snail mail, and much of the etiquette derives from the same era. For some years, many agents were reluctant to make the switch to e-mail, but now it is a rare agent who does not work that way. Some agencies have gone totally green—witness this statement from Upstart Crow Literary Agency:

> Upstart Crow Literary is an entirely green company, and we accept submissions only via e-mail. **We do not accept submissions via hard copy and the U.S. Mail. Mailed submissions will be tossed unread into the recycle bin.** (Is this because we're eco-conscious? Or because we hate messing about with giant stacks of paper and letter openers and having to lick envelopes and stick stamps and make frequent trips to the post office? Perhaps it is for *both* reasons.)
>
> We not only prefer e-mail, we ask that you not send us anything on paper unless you clear it with us first.

Each agent has his or her own policy, of course. The major guides to agents, such as *Jeff Herman's Guide to Book Publishers, Editors, and Literary Agents,* list agency websites, and you should check there first to see what the policy is.

> **SLUSH PILE**
>
> Should you e-mail attachments? No, particularly if you're sending off an unsolicited query. Editors and agents are just as reluctant as you are to open attachments from people they don't know. Once you have established contact, let them tell you how to send more material.

Back in the postal era, the query process was slow and nerve-wracking. E-mail has made it a bit less so now. With an e-mail query, you won't have to worry about choosing the wrong kind of envelope! Candy Chand has had wonderful success in e-mailing queries. "Don't be afraid to try; the worst thing you will hear is 'no.'" E-mail queries can also get a response in minutes—Candy has sometimes heard back almost instantly. Sure beats checking the mail every day for some kind of sign your package got through.

E-mail queries can also take a long time or go unacknowledged all together. Remember how many e-mails those editors and agents get? Be polite in how often you check in. If you send an unsolicited e-mail query on a Monday, don't send another one on Wednesday asking if the first one was received. Give publishing people some breathing room. After a week and a half you can send another e-mail, but if that one doesn't get a response, move on to the next name on your list. Don't become an e-mail stalker.

SASEs and Other Ways to Hear Back

Remember the definition of *unsolicited submission?* It's one the agent did not ask you to send. Because you're sending something that wasn't requested, it's up to you to cover the cost of getting a reply. Always include a *SASE* with your correspondence so the agent can easily reply.

> **DEFINITION**
>
> **SASE** is short for "self-addressed, stamped envelope." Never send a query or proposal without one. The publishing industry would go broke if editors had to pay to return all the unsolicited material they receive. If you haven't included a SASE and the agent or editor isn't interested, you will never hear an answer, and your stuff goes straight into the recycling bin.

If you want to know whether your query arrived at its destination, include a small, self-addressed and stamped postcard the agent can just pop into the mail. On it, write something like this:

> Yes, the attached query was received in my office on _____.

If you are sending a real letter rather than an e-mail, you can also send it via FedEx or UPS. This is more expensive than the good old U.S. mail, but it also lets you track your letter and ease your mind about whether it ever arrived. (Two-day express mail is considerably less costly than next-day air.)

Do not call an agent's office to ask whether your query arrived. You will appear anxious and unprofessional.

But They Asked for It!

You met an agent at a writers' summer camp who encouraged you to send your proposal? Congratulations! But please don't assume the agent remembers the invitation. Put in the first line of your query, or in the subject line of your e-mail, "We met at the Mendocino Writers' Conference, and you asked that I send the following proposal." An agent might meet a hundred writers at conferences throughout the year—and talk to another hundred on the phone. So don't be hurt if he or she doesn't remember you or your book.

And don't forget to include a SASE with your query if you are mailing it.

Voicemail

If you're anxious about a query you've sent off to an agent or editor, should you ever—*gasp*—call them to check up? Try not to. We understand the impulse, but for unsolicited queries, the protocol still revolves around written correspondence. If you do break down and place a call to check up, please leave a pleasant message. Sheree has received more than one hostile voicemail message from anxious writers demanding to know if a package has arrived or when they might hear a response. The folks who left those messages received their rejections swiftly!

Remember, your early contacts are all about establishing a good working relationship, and if you are a pain in the neck from day one, there's a good chance your writing won't ever see a bookstore shelf. Harsh advice but true.

The Rules

Now that we've given you the rules, please believe us when we say it's in your best interest to follow them. If you try to get around them, if you try things you think are clever or devious, it can backfire. At the very least, an agent might think you're annoying. In the worst-case scenario, you could come off as a nut—and agents aren't very eager to sign up nuts! Let them know you've done your homework, you know how the routine works, and you will follow the rules.

Having said that, we must confess that sometimes people do break the rules and succeed because of it. And sometimes people win the lottery. But as a first-time writer, you improve your chances tremendously by playing it straight.

A Few Words on Rejection

We've all been there. Rejected. It doesn't feel good, but it is a big part of the business. Agent Jeff Kleinman of FolioLit has this good advice to share with writers about how best to deal with it:

"It helps to know why publishing folk reject most manuscripts. We agents, for example, generally reject manuscripts for one (or more) of three reasons:

1. "The writing simply isn't strong enough. This is the most common reason, especially for fiction. You all have heard, I know, that fiction is often a tough sell, but a lot of agents and editors are certainly looking for the next great novel. I'd say about 90 percent of the fiction projects that cross my desk, though, get rejected because the author hasn't quite taken the time to really hone his/her writing skills—really learning how to write great characters, or use dialogue, or create resonating descriptions, and so forth.

2. "The author's platform is not large enough. This is especially true for nonfiction but also critical with fiction projects that are iffy. 'Platform' means the author's visibility within his/her target readership community—so media coverage, speaking engagements, and so forth all factor in.

3. "The project is not big enough. I'm not talking word count here—I'm talking book sales. So if the concept seems run-of-the mill ['oh, great, another coming-of-age novel—what's really special about this one that will make it stand out in such a crowded marketplace?'] or something that will appeal only to a smallish audience [Salt Lake City's monuments, for example—this could be a very useful book, but it's probably not going to appeal to folks outside the Salt Lake City area]. This is another easy reason to reject a manuscript."

So Jeff has come up with a concrete plan he encourages authors to follow when they've met with a "no" or two. Test the waters a bit, and adjust accordingly:

"Now that you know why books are often rejected, see where your book fits in. Try the following as you approach agents and/or editors: send out 10 queries. Do *not* think of the rejection letters as being letters telling you the recipient wasn't interested in your stuff. Look *only* at the form of the letter itself.

1. "If you get 10 form rejections in response, then something may very well be problematic in Step #1 (i.e., rewrite, build your platform, or revise your book's concept).

2. "If you get one or two 'real' letters—either written on your cover letter, on the agency's form letter, or an actual addressed letter or an e-mail that is clearly from a real person about your own project—then you're probably on the right track, so submit another 10 to 20. If, after about 30 rejects, you're still not getting the offers, seriously consider going back to Step #1 as well.

3. "The more real letters and actual e-mail responses you get, the more you should think you're on the right track.

"The trick is, of course, not to take the rejection personally. Use them as a tool to work your way through the publishing maze—you're wandering around in the dark, so think of rejection letters as the walls you bump into as you go down the hall. Don't hate the wall, or get overly discouraged because you keep banging your nose—use the wall to guide you along the way."

As hard as it is to deal with rejection, Jeff's method can go a long way toward helping you process the information and move on toward success.

The Least You Need to Know

- Queries should be one page long and should contain a brief description of the book, the market, and the author. E-mails should be about the same length.
- Practice being brief by editing your writing to one powerful paragraph.
- Don't use a query to air your grievances with anyone.
- Unless you include a SASE with your query, you might never hear an answer. E-mails may or may not get a response.
- A good query states its purpose up front in the first paragraph.

Bulletproof Nonfiction Book Proposals

Chapter 8

In This Chapter

- Building a book proposal step by step
- Selling your idea
- Selling your market
- Selling yourself as an author
- Choosing your best sample chapter

Congratulations! You crafted a great query, and an agent or editor has asked to see your book proposal!

Um, now what do you do?

The Art of Proposal Writing

In a book proposal, you're proposing an idea for a book. You *propose* to do it because, in most cases, you haven't actually written the book yet!

I Don't Have to Write the Book First?

We'd like to let you in on an industry secret. Here's how most professional nonfiction writers work, in this order:

1. They come up with an idea for a book.

2. They write a book proposal 10 to 20 or so pages long.

3. They send it off to their agent and wait.

If a publisher decides to publish the book, the writer sits down in front of the computer and writes the book by the agreed-upon deadline. But if there are no takers, the professional writer files away that idea and comes up with another one and starts the process over again.

That's right: to sell a nonfiction book and get a contract from a publisher, you don't really have to write the book first. You can write it later. First, however, you have to write a good proposal.

Some proposals are long and some are short, but Jennifer thinks she wrote the smallest one ever—on a mini-sticky note. Many years ago she'd written up a long list of personal goals, one of which was a reminder to "wear more cashmere." Jennifer liked the way that phrase sounded so much she wrote it on the tiny yellow note and stuck it to the side of her computer.

Years later, an editor who'd seen that note on her computer years before called and asked her to turn the idea into a book! *Wear More Cashmere: 101 Luxurious Ways to Pamper Your Inner Princess* (Fair Winds) spawned a whole series of indulgence-themed gift books that kept Jennifer in cashmere for years. So remember, always write down your clever ideas!

When Should I Start the Proposal?

Don't even think about querying agents or editors or spending money to attend a writers' conference until you've written at least some portion of your book proposal. Not only will it give you a more solid sense of what you're doing (and help you distill it into a good query), but it also cuts down on the lag time between when an agent or editor says, "I'd love to see your stuff," and when you can actually send it. So get a jump on things and start now.

Working on your proposal will also help you sort out your ideas about the book and help you find out quickly if you have enough material for an entire book. You'll then have a quick answer if an agent or editor says, "Sounds interesting. Give me an *overview*."

DEFINITION

An **overview** is another term for summary. In the movie business, it's called a "take-away." What will your reader take away with him after reading your book? Write it out in one succinct sentence.

Building a Book Proposal

Here's a short list of what you should include in your book proposal. Read through this list once and then sit down and begin to write your own version. A book proposal should develop before your very eyes.

What Makes Up a Proposal?

The parts of a book proposal are as follows:

- A cover page with the title, your name, your address, and your phone number
- A three- to five-part pitch
- A detailed table of contents
- A sample chapter of the book
- Attachments such as recent media coverage about the topic or the author—you!

We offer a longer description of each key element in the sections that follow. If you have trouble understanding any elements, don't panic. We've included sample book proposals for you to read in Appendix D.

Electronic Book Proposals

Does anyone still send out a real printed book proposal? "You should see my office," says Paula Munier of Adams Media. "Yes, they do. I have stacks of proposals every-where!" But what about an electronic book proposal, one that you can e-mail the minute an agent or editor asks to see it? Of course, it will be exactly as described in the following sections, but you will need to build it in such a way that all attached articles are either scanned into PDFs or contain live links to the exact web address you want.

Anyone with computer skills can do it this way, but please do take the extra step of printing out a version before you send it off to make sure that if an editor prints one out (and they will to take it to meetings) it all turns out the way you planned with no kooky pages.

SLUSH PILE

Remember from Chapter 7 how businesslike your queries should be? A book proposal should be equally businesslike in appearance—no fancy graphics, colored paper, or elaborate typestyles. Your writing skills are on display here, nothing else. An electronic version should also be businesslike when viewed on the screen or printed out.

The Cover Page

This is a great first step. It takes only about 5 minutes to do it, and after you've made a cover page, you can consider yourself on the road to building a book proposal. Simply create a page that—in pretty big type—has the book title and subtitle, as well as your name, address, and contact info.

If you're sending off the proposal to an agent who requested it, put your name and address on the cover page. When you have an agent and she's shopping your book to editors, she'll put her own name and address on your proposal's cover page.

After you've made a cover page, print it out and hang it on the wall next to your computer. Whenever you're feeling discouraged, glance up and see your title and your name in large type! Jennifer's office walls are covered with title pages, all designed to guilt-trip her into finishing her projects. As a technique, it really does work.

It's important to note that we just mean a plain cover page for your proposal, not a fancy, highly designed idea for your future book. As you'll learn in later chapters, authors (and even editors!) have little control over the actual cover, so you should not invest time, energy, or money into this part of the proposal. In fact, a heavily designed proposed book cover in a proposal tips off the editor that the sender is a newbie.

The Pitch

You know the sales term *pitch*. In a book proposal, you're trying to do the exact same thing—pitch a book idea (and hopefully make a sale!). The pitch section of the proposal can be broken down into five smaller parts:

- The idea
- The market
- The competition

- The publicity and promotion potential
- The author

Remember all that work you did while writing your query? Those long paragraphs describing the book idea, the market, and the author? Pull them out now and see what you can use.

EXPERTS SAY

Robert Kosberg (moviepitch.com) is known as Hollywood's "Mr. Pitch" because he pitches 20 to 50 ideas a year to studio heads. What can you learn from him for your book pitch? This: "Ask yourself if your idea can be boiled down to two power-packed sentences that generate excitement."

Does your pitch have a professional tone? Why not read a few book pitches from the pros to find out. At Michael Cader's Publishers Marketplace (publishersmarketplace.com), you can read actual book pitches made by literary agents as well as a few unrepresented writers. Click on "rights postings" to read what's being pitched and how.

What a Great Idea!

First, describe the idea behind the book. What kind of a book is it? What kind of information will it contain? Describe your book in one tight sentence and then elaborate on the idea for several paragraphs. Co-author Sheree tells her clients that this is their chance to describe the contents of their book "enticingly and thoroughly."

Off to Market

Now describe the market for your book. Who are the millions of potential readers? Why will they be interested in your book? The market section should contain as much hard data about *demographics*, trends, and other facts as you can get your hands on. Remember to avoid using the sentence, "Everyone should read this book."

DEFINITION

Publishers love **demographics.** Publishing is an inexact science, and the more a nonfiction author can cite demographics about population statistics, the size of an age group, or personal-income levels when describing the potential audience for his book, the better the agent, editor, and publisher can sleep at night, knowing there's a market for the book.

The market section of your proposal could also contain information about possible nonbookstore outlets for your book. Where will these millions of potential readers be found? In gardening stores, lingerie shops, niche websites, or hospitals? Let the publisher know if specialized sources of distribution can target these folks.

Compete with the Best

The competition section is an easy one to write. As a matter of fact, you've already done much of the work. You've spent hours wandering the aisles of your local bookstore or clicking from page to page at an online source. At last you get to display the knowledge you've gained!

To create the competition section, list all the books already published with which your book will compete. The purpose of this section is to establish that you know what else has been done in your area and that you believe your book fills an existing need. Describe these books at length, but also be fair and balanced in assessing what you perceive to be their weaknesses. Do not attack. Remember the advice from Chapter 6? Never use the competition section to slam other books. You never know who will end up reading your book proposal!

A secondary purpose of the competition section is to highlight books that, instead of competing with your proposed book, complement it. Complementary books can help you establish that a book like yours will succeed. Check out the sample proposals in Appendix D to see how they describe other books on the topic. This helps you use the success of other books to build your case.

This is also a good place to point out how your book could cross over and succeed in two markets at once. Publishers love the dazzling idea that one book might sell to two different types of people—for example, that a novel like *The Art of Racing in the Rain* will appeal not only to fiction lovers but to dog lovers and auto racing fans, or that a money workbook for couples could work in the finance niche as well as in the relationship section.

Be sure to also include examples of similar books that are deep in reprinting (remember that research skill from Chapter 4?) to show there's a healthy public appetite for the topic.

La Publicité

The publicity and promotion section is of critical importance in today's publishing market. All publishers want to know how hard you plan to work, how many media contacts you already have, whether 10,000 people follow you on Twitter, and whether this topic lends itself to *publicity* and *promotion*. So the more you can supply here, the better.

> **DEFINITION**
>
> What's the difference between **publicity** and **promotion?** The two words some-times seem to be interchangeable. The bottom line is—the bottom line! Publicity is free. Promotion (which can mean advertising) usually costs money.

How do you find out this stuff? By paying attention to how often the media writes about your topic or about the audience your book targets.

Publicity Opportunities

Using *Accurate Arthritis Answers* as an example, quickly come up with some of the different places this book could get publicity:

- National magazines targeted to older Americans (such as AARP's various magazines), the national network of small newspapers for seniors, and health websites geared toward an older population

- The morning news shows, such as *Today* and *Good Morning America*, which frequently devote time to health issues

- Nationally syndicated radio health shows and podcasts, which are growing in popularity

- Health editors at all major media

- Newsletters in retirement communities, such as the various Sun City communities around the country

We'd like to pass along a request from tired editors at this point: "Please advise writers that a real tendency to oversell in the publicity and marketing section has become apparent," said one editor who wished to hide behind the curtain of anonymity. "Everyone used to claim they and their book were a [shoo-in] to be booked on *Oprah,* and everyone claims that they will market endlessly—it starts to read like every writer went to the same seminar about book marketing and is parroting what they learned there." What does this mean to you? Be realistic in what you say you can and will do for your book.

Is It Especially Timely?

Are there special times of the year when your book could be promoted? Talk about the potential for gift or seasonal promotions. Are there any major events (such as an upcoming election or a hot new movie) that your book ties into? If so, mention it.

Bear in mind how long it takes to publish a book, though. Don't mention events that are happening in the next few months. Don't claim that a book you're proposing in July will be tied to an election a few short months later in November.

Bulk Sales?

This is also a good place to mention any possibilities you see for large sales of the book to groups, businesses, and organizations. Publishers are very interested in pursuing large, nonreturnable sales, and the special sales department is always looking for product to move. Using the arthritis book again, here's how you could say it in a proposal:

> The pharmaceutical manufacturer behind one of the major drugs used to treat arthritis has expressed a willingness to purchase 2,500 copies of *Accurate Arthritis Answers* to use as a premium. The author also intends to seek out other large group purchases for the book.

If you already have a solid commitment for a large buy for your book, be sure to mention it. If you plan to buy a large number of the books yourself (to give away to clients or sell at speeches), mention that also. Publishers are interested in protecting their investment, and this kind of information could help tip the balance in your favor.

A Stamp of Approval

Finally, have you approached any big-name authors or professionals who are willing to give you endorsements for your book? Let the publishers know who you plan to approach and if you have existing ties with these folks. Michael Chabon lives down the street? Malcolm Gladwell is your cousin? Write it down!

If you do have close personal or professional ties to big-name folks, approach them now. It's even better to have an endorsement in hand when you're in the proposal stage. This, too, could help tip the balance in your favor.

Let's Hear About You!

Finally, you'll need to include information about you, the author. Here's where you can really let loose and brag about what you've accomplished in life: awards, honors, education, experience—pile it on. Let everyone know about your writing experience, publishing history (if you have one), and professional success. Do you have local, statewide, or national recognition in your field? Talk about it here. Try to position yourself as someone uniquely qualified to write this book.

Are you a skilled public speaker or presenter? Do you hold seminars or classes that relate to your book? The publisher needs to be reassured that you're not only a qualified author, but that you can also be an effective public image for the book. If you have professional photos on hand, include them. But don't send candid snapshots that would undermine your authority.

What about your online presence? No one is interested in how many friends you have on Facebook, but if you tweet on the topic of your book and have an impressive Twitter following, put it in. A popular blog on your topic? An e-zine that goes out weekly to tons of people?

Now that you understand everything that goes into the pitch section of your proposal, you're ready to move on to the other sections.

Do You Need a Partner?

While working on this section of your proposal, please take the time to seriously consider how strong your credentials will look to the editor who is considering them. Are they as strong as they should be or could be? Might you have a better chance at selling this book if you teamed up with another expert in the field? Keep an open mind to the possibility, as that might well help you sell the project. A major best-selling economics book (perhaps the only best-selling economics book?), *Freakonomics*, was the result of a newspaper reporter teaming up with an academic. Neither could have written the book on his own!

Best-selling author James Patterson seems to publish constantly, and he does. How can he put out five books a year? He teams up with other writers. "I found that it is rare that you get a craftsman and an idea person in the same body. With me, I struggle like crazy. I can do the craft at an acceptable level, but the ideas are what I like." Patterson believes he is more proficient at creating the story than executing it. Why not use his method to form a writing team and increase your own chances for success?

Detailed Table of Contents

That's right, you'll need to include a detailed table of contents. Not only should you list each and every chapter, you also should include a short paragraph to describe each chapter or section. This is sometimes referred to as a chapter summary. Describe not only the purpose of each chapter but also some of the content.

Sample Chapters

We've told you not to write a book until the proposal is accepted, but that doesn't mean you shouldn't write at all. A good proposal contains some good sample chapters, so get to work on a few.

Including a good representative sample chapter is important. Not only is the writing itself important, but so is the topic. A well-chosen sample chapter can be a powerful thing. Just as the query was a way of introducing yourself to a stranger (and presenting yourself in the best possible light), so, too, is the sample chapter. It gives you the opportunity to influence the way you're perceived.

It's important that the chapter you include is representative of the rest of the book in style, content, and length. It's not unusual to include Chapter 1, but if Chapter 1 is not representative, send in one that is. Better yet, include Chapter 1 plus a later representative chapter.

Write What They'd Enjoy Reading

When we were trying to get the contract to write the first edition of this very book, *The Complete Idiot's Guide to Getting Published*, we needed to write and submit a sample chapter. With all the possible aspects of getting published to choose from, which do you think we chose? Publicity.

We wrote a sample chapter about book publicity and how important it is for authors to work hard to publicize their books. We included lots of information about how hardworking authors can make a big difference in the sales success of their books.

Send an Upbeat Message

Why did we choose that topic? Because we wanted to send a positive message to the publisher: that these two women, Sheree Bykofsky and Jennifer Basye Sander, know what they're doing. They understand how to make a book sell. They will work their tails off to make this book succeed.

Why choose a chapter with a negative tone—like one that talks about the high rate of book returns or the changes afoot in the publishing business—when we could do something positive? Not only was the chapter on an upbeat topic, but it positioned us as go-getters. Hey, we got the contract, didn't we?

So what should you choose for your sample chapter? Choose something that will help the reader. And the reader, in this case, is not the general reading public but the agent or editor reading your proposal. Give that person a sample chapter that will make him feel great or learn something new. Don't choose a chapter that will leave him depressed and reaching for a box of tissues. Here is an excellent opportunity to make him feel good about you and your ideas. Look at your material and see if any section will get the editor or agent nodding his head in recognition or agreement. Help him say "yes" to you!

The Kitchen Sink

The very last thing that goes into your proposal is important: evidence of your and your book's credibility. Here is an opportunity to include all the media attention you and/or your topic have gotten and that you've been saving up. With an impressive bundle of clippings, you can establish yourself as an expert, and you can establish your topic as big.

HOT OFF THE PRESS

Creating a successful book proposal is a lot of work. Here is some good news, though: once you're a successfully published writer with an agent and an established reputation, you can write shorter proposals. Some authors only e-mail an idea to their editor and end up with a contract!

Website, Magazine, and Newspaper Articles

Did we say *recent* articles? It's important to include only articles from the last 5 years. If all your clips date from years ago, an agent or editor will wonder what happened to your career in the meantime.

It's also important that the articles you include about your topic be recent. If you include dated material, it might appear that the topic itself is old news and that the book wouldn't sell.

Be careful about the quality of the clippings you send. Ripped, smudged, or messy-looking clippings will do you no good. Copies of articles on websites that are so small they can't be easily read aren't helpful. You are a professional, and you need to look like one. Be sure you include only clear copies that are readable, neatly presented, and of a reasonable length. It's better to send nice new copies rather than large original clippings from a newspaper. And because you'll be making many copies of your proposal, making photocopies is cheaper than buying up 20 copies of the newspaper with your article in it.

If you're putting together an electronic proposal, remember that you need to triple-check your embedded links.

Video Clips

Videos, whether on a disc or a link to YouTube, of you being interviewed on a major television program are great to include in your proposal. Short pieces are best, though, so don't go overboard—agents and editors will rarely watch an hour-long video. A professionally edited and labeled video clip is best, one that strings together several short pieces with professional-looking titles in between. Worst is sending the wrong video, like the one of your children in the bathtub. Be sure to label your disc clearly with your name and address in case it gets separated from your proposal.

Has all this proposal talk left you feeling overwhelmed? In Chapter 11, we fill you in on some folks who can help: *proposal doctors* and *book doctors*.

DEFINITION

You can hire a **proposal doctor** or **book doctor** to help you write your proposal. They are mostly former editors or longtime writers. You'll see their advertisements in the back of writers' magazines, or you might also ask an agent for a recommendation.

Proposing Your Self-Published Book

If you have a self-published book you're now trying to sell to a publisher, you must include a copy along with your proposal. Also include a brutally honest description of the sales and distribution of your self-published book. Did we say "brutally honest"? We mean it. Be sure to specify not only how well your own edition sold, but where and how you sold it—whether out of the trunk of your car or at Barnes & Noble.

Under no circumstances should you fudge, puff up, or exaggerate how well it sold. Trust us—if you lie, you will be caught. And that will be the end of your chances of selling the book.

It may work to your advantage if your book sold well to a limited audience (for example, through your own speeches or a targeted website) but never made it to the major bookstore chains. That way, if a publisher *does* release your book, it will appear fresh to a bookstore buyer and not seem like old news.

And here is some harsh advice—all publishing folks are hip to the way many self-published authors try to game the list at Amazon.com (by sending out lots of e-mails to friends and contacts asking them to all buy on the same day to drive the number down). So please don't brag about being a "#1 Amazon.com best-seller" if it was only for a day. Seth Godin, the author of 12 books, recently shared this about the sales ranking game:

> Like theatrical producers on Broadway, staying up all night at Sardi's, waiting for the reviews, pub day has always been an important (and dramatic) event for book publishers. The Internet has only made it more so because it's so easy to frontload your promotion, jack up your first-day sales, manipulate the best-seller lists, and generally create a kerfuffle.

> In the 1960s, it wasn't unusual for a book to spend a year on the best-seller lists. Today, in books, music, and movies, it's been compressed. A movie has a hit weekend, maybe three. A song hits the radio for a few days. And books—books are in and then they're out.

> I'm personally exhausted from this rollercoaster. I don't think it does service to the books or to their readers. Now that online noise has crescendoed, the upside of short-term sales manipulation is diminished, and the best books don't really reach everyone they should.

More than one self-published book has sold successfully to a major publisher. Two big examples are Robert Kiyosaki's *Rich Dad/Poor Dad* and Richard Paul Evans's first book, *The Christmas Box*. Both were self-published originally and then picked up by major houses. Kiyosaki's book has been on *The New York Times* best-seller list for more than five straight years, and Evans has produced six best-selling novels since his first effort.

SLUSH PILE

Don't send any gimmicky presents with your proposal unless they relate to the book itself. A proposal for a book on chocolate truffles probably won't be harmed by sending along a box of samples. But don't send a box of truffles with your proposal for a book about world peace.

Do you have a handle on what exactly a book proposal is now? It might seem daunting at first, but we know you'll get the hang of it. So what are you waiting for? Get to work!

The Least You Need to Know

- A book proposal is a 10- to 20-page description of the book with supporting information.
- Professional nonfiction writers write a book proposal first; if it sells, then they write the book. You can do the same.
- The more compelling the information you provide about the market, the greater your chances of finding a publisher.
- Choose a sample chapter on a topic that will leave the reader (the editor or agent) with a good feeling.
- Include clean copies of recent media about yourself and your topic.
- Do not send gifts or attention-getters with your proposal.

Fun with Fiction

In This Chapter

- You've got to write the whole book first!
- Query, query, query
- Writing a novel synopsis
- Now you've got an agent on the line!
- Summarizing your novel

When writing nonfiction, you can sell your book before you write it. No such luck with fiction. Fiction is a different ball game with a more complex set of rules. It's harder to play and harder to win—but the rewards are enormous. The most successful novelists become, in effect, the brand names of the book business: King, Grisham, Rice, Roberts, Patterson, Steel …. Although Jennifer and Sheree have been updating this book every few years, the names of the biggest fiction writers really haven't changed much. Okay, Anne Rice switched from writing about vampires to writing about Jesus and then announced she is no longer Christian, but that's about it.

As the late best-selling author James Michener used to say, "You can't make a living [writing novels] but you can make a killing." Win in the very competitive field of fiction, and you can win big. How big? According to recent speculation, James Patterson makes $70 million a year. *Seventy million.* Is that big enough for you? Following behind, Stephen King makes around $34 million a year just off backlist titles, and Nora Roberts comes in at around $28 million a year.

In this chapter, we tell you how to write queries and book proposals for fiction. But before we do, let's look more in-depth at the wide world of fiction.

So I Have to Write the Whole Book First?

Yes, to sell a work of fiction, you have to write the entire book first. Why? Because fiction requires more craftsmanship.

To write nonfiction, you need to know how to organize information in a clear and entertaining way. But writing fiction requires a mastery of myriad techniques. From pacing to character, plotting to dialogue, more skill is required to pull it off. Moreover, a novel has a beginning, a middle, and an end—and lots of complications along the way. Publishers can't tell from an outline and a sample chapter alone if you can sustain a narrative and keep readers turning the pages for 250, 500, or maybe even 1,000 pages. The late Stieg Larsson, for example, wrote all three books in his trilogy before even trying to publish *The Girl with the Dragon Tattoo*.

You have to supply them with proof, which is in the completed manuscript. You need to have written an entire novel before you can approach an agent to represent you. Agents, like publishers, need to know you can keep it up for hundreds of pages. Then with your masterpiece in hand, you can prove you've written a page-turner. You might become the successful novelist you—and your mother—always dreamed you could be.

Want Support? Mingle with Other Writers

Writing may be a lonely business, but getting published doesn't have to be. Join a writers' organization so you can keep abreast of new markets and trends and make valuable contacts with agents and editors. We've mentioned Publishers Lunch a few times (publishersmarketplace.com). By subscribing to this free online newsletter, you'll feel like you're part of the publishing and writing world.

If you're completely antisocial, don't despair. Many writers' organizations have online chapters you can join. (See Appendix C for some good resources to pursue.) You can cybernetwork without leaving the privacy of your own computer. Horror writers, check out the Horror Writers Association (horror.org) when you're feeling the need for community.

You can also sign up for a writing class at your local college, which will help you make friends and contacts even as you polish your writing skills. Here again, you don't have to leave home if you don't want to; a number of writing classes and seminars are available online, run by writing organizations, local universities, and online "distance learning" centers such as Education To Go (ed2go.com).

HOT OFF THE PRESS

Getting involved with NaNoWriMo (National Novel Writing Month) is a cool way to not only spur yourself to write a lot very quickly (the goal is to write a 50,000-word novel in the month of November), but also to socialize: in many cities, groups form and meet frequently to write together. So if you feel like you're out there alone, check out what's going on at nanowrimo.org.

And Then I Have to Write the Whole Book *Again?*

You and your mother aren't alone. Agents and publishers like nothing better than successful novelists. Like the Energizer Bunny, successful novelists just keep on going and going and going. They sell, sell, sell. New York literary agent Ethan Ellenberg, who represents fiction writers in all genres, puts it this way: "A successful novelist can write 10 or 20 books over 10 or 20 years."

That's the long haul, and the long haul is what publishers are looking for when it comes to fiction. It takes time and money to build an audience for a new novelist. Publishers are willing to spend that time and money when they believe they're building a new brand name for their house. Brand names attract a huge audience whose loyalty sustains through book after book after book.

Once that audience exists, though, the sky's the limit. People who read fiction read their favorite writers like they purchase their favorite brand of products. And when they find a new favorite writer, they read everything that writer ever wrote—as well as everything he or she goes on to write in the future. They also like to tell their friends and recommend the book to book clubs they belong to. This makes successful novelists an excellent investment for publishers. It more than makes up for the initial investment required to build an author's name.

That's why it's not enough to show the publishing world you can write one great novel. You have to convince them you can do it over and over and over. Show them you, too, are in it for the long haul and you can keep them turning pages through 10 or 20 books over 10 or 20 years.

Most importantly, you have to convince them you aren't just a good writer, but you're also a good *storyteller.*

The Never-Ending Story

Literary agent Don Maass, author of many novels as well as *The Career Novelist: A Literary Agent Offers Strategies for Success*, advises aspiring novelists to make the distinction between good writing and good storytelling. Artful language does not make good storytelling. Conflict does.

"John Grisham is not known as a great stylist, but he's a great storyteller," says Maass. "Take the opening scene of *The Firm*. It's just a job interview, but it's riveting because of the conflict. In a Grisham novel, there's conflict on every page, and conflict keeps readers turning the page."

Forget Dickens!

According to Maass, the biggest mistake many fiction writers make is to rely on nineteenth-century storytelling techniques—techniques that no longer engage today's fiction readers. "I see so many manuscripts that begin with long, rambling descriptions, descriptions that would be great in a novel published in 1890, but not in a novel published in this era," says Maass.

What works today is the novel that's written cinematically. Film and TV storytelling have become the vernacular for audiences the world over. Not only does cinematic storytelling resonate with your readers, it also attracts film and TV interest, which increases your appeal to prospective publishers and ultimately increases your potential audience exponentially.

Elmore Leonard, author of dozens of best-selling novels over more than 30 years, admits it was the film version of his novel *Get Shorty* in 1995 that made him truly famous. "When I meet somebody and I tell them I'm a writer, and they've never heard of me—I ask them if they've seen *Get Shorty*. 'Oh, yeah,' they'll say, 'great movie.'"

With the success of the movie *Get Shorty* and then the book and movie sequel *Be Cool*, Elmore Leonard won a new audience—an audience far greater than the book audience. The movie also brought Leonard more readers, making him a bigger brand-name author than ever. Years later, he's still at it, both with novels and scripts—the FX series *Justified* is his project.

Writing in a cinematic way helps you get your start in the book business and sets the stage for crossing over into other media as well.

Read, Read, Read

So where do you go to learn twenty-first-century storytelling techniques? Surprise! Go to a bookstore.

"The best course is also the least expensive," says Maass. He advises his clients to study today's great storytellers. "Read, study, and analyze. Then write your own powerful stories—stories with conflict on every page. Tell the best damn stories that you can."

We'll take Maass's advice one step further: read books about writing written by writers you admire. We like Barbara Shoup and Margaret Love Denman's *Novel Ideas: Contemporary Authors Share the Creative Process.* Now in its second edition, it includes long interviews with best-selling authors such as Jane Smiley, Ha Jin, and Richard Ford and goes into great detail about plot, dialogue, developing characters, and of course, dealing with editors!

Writing Is Rewriting

Joyce Carol Oates likens writing the first draft of a novel to "building a house." The second draft, she says, is when "you decorate it." As she writes and publishes with blinding speed and shows no signs of slowing down, her metaphor is worth adopting as your credo.

Just as a house is not a home until you've moved in, furnished it, invited friends and family over, and poured them a drink, a manuscript is not a novel ready for public viewing until you've rewritten it. Be prepared to do at least three drafts:

- A first draft to get the story down
- A second draft to refine the story, capitalize on its strengths, eliminate its weaknesses, and layer meaning and theme
- A final polish for language and style

As we've noted, writing good fiction isn't easy. Don't panic if you know your work needs revising but have no clue where or how to begin. People out there can help you figure out what you need to do to make your story shine.

Take It to the Next Level

The days of Maxwell Perkins—the famously nurturing and hands-on editor at Scribner's for Ernest Hemingway, Thomas Wolfe, F. Scott Fitzgerald, and others—are gone. Gone are the editors who discover a diamond in the rough in the *slush pile* and then spend months, even years helping the writer rewrite until the manuscript is ready for publication. Editors today don't have the time or the energy for the sort of intensive editorial work their predecessors such as Perkins gave to such raw young luminaries as Fitzgerald, Wolfe, and Marjorie Kinnan Rawlings.

> **DEFINITION**
>
> The **slush pile** is where all the unsolicited manuscripts are piled, waiting to be read, and then discarded if postage was not included.

If you're thinking agents have taken over where editors have left off, think again. While it's true that some agents do develop close working editorial relationships with their authors, most do not. Agents are first and foremost salespeople; their job is to sell your work, not edit and revise it. Remember, they don't make money until they make a sale, so you need to give them something that's ready to sell.

Still, you can find professionals who can help you be sure your manuscript is publisher-ready before you send it out the door. Find an experienced editor who will critique your work, suggest revisions, and help polish your prose.

Ask your writing friends and any publishing professionals you may know in the book business for referrals; you can also look online and in industry publications. Be sure to choose an editor who has experience in your genre. Remember that word-of-mouth is the usually best recommendation, but still ask for references. Rates vary, but you'll find ballpark ranges for editing fees in the *Writer's Market* or at the National Writers Union (nwu.org). Also check out Appendix C, which lists lots of good resources.

Ready, Set, Query

Okay, so you, the great storyteller, have written a great novel with an engaging protagonist. You've included conflict on every page. The ending not only satisfies your readers, it leaves them screaming for a sequel. You've pounded out several hundred pages readers won't be able to turn fast enough—and rewritten those pages until they sing.

Congratulations! You wrote a novel. Now take that 12-pound doorstop and put it away where you can't see it (and the dog can't eat it).

What? After we insist you write the whole novel first, now we tell you to put it away?

Exactly. The last thing anyone in publishing wants to do is read a 12-pound manuscript from an unknown writer. Agents and editors are drowning in them. All those publishing cartoons you've seen in *The New Yorker*, the ones with the editor sitting behind a desk mounded high with papers, are true. You have to sell these people on the idea of reading your hefty tome. That's where your query comes in.

Targeting your queries should reveal better results than the shotgun approach. Seek out those editors and agents most likely to appreciate your story, and query them first. You'll find their names on the acknowledgments page of your favorite books and/or the books most like your own. You can also find them in industry publications such as *Publishers Weekly* and the online Publishers Lunch, both of which feature deals made in the fiction business. Find out who's representing/buying novels like your own—and put them at the top of your to-be-queried list.

Did you read Chapters 7 and 8? They were good introductions to what comes next, especially for you. (If you didn't, go read them now.)

Introducing the Mighty You

Your query is your major sales tool. It's a one-pager that sells an agent on taking a chance on you. Your query must convince your quarry to invest several minutes, hours, and even days evaluating your novel—all this on the off chance that the time invested will pay off.

SLUSH PILE

Remember, agents don't earn a salary. They invest hundreds of hours looking at stuff in the hopes that they can find a writer who will someday bring in the dough via royalties.

All that in one page, huh? It can be done. The trick is to keep the query simple, sweet, and sell, sell, sell. Here's how you break it down.

Paragraph 1: What Kind of Book You've Written

You've written a 55,000-word mystery set in Jamaica at a Club Med titled *Dead Men Don't Date*. Skip the cute introductions; get straight to the point by describing the genre, your concept, and a sentence or two about the plot.

The only exception is if you've met the agent at a writers' conference or you've been referred by a mutual friend or colleague. If so, mention that first. As with every business, publishing is a business of people. Any kind of personal connection counts.

Paragraph 2: What Your Book Is About

Dead Men Don't Date is a story about young, unpublished romance novelist Melissa Manhattan, who escapes the cold, slushy, January streets of her native New York City in search of sun, sex, and a multibook contract at a writers' conference in Jamaica—only to wake up and find the publishing industry's leading sleaze-bag agent dead in her king-size Club Med bed. Through a combination of wits, pluck, and an uncommon knowledge of deadly voodoo poisons, our girl Melissa solves the murder, saves the life of the biggest independent romance publisher in the business, and lands a six-figure contract as well as a very attractive and well-connected publicist—not to mention bringing the murderer (a disturbed ghostwriter driven to the edge after years of putting his sexy prose into lesser writers' mouths) to justice.

Paragraph 3: Why Only You Could Write This

You grew up in New York, where your mother worked as a secretary at a big publishing house. You spent your summers in the Caribbean helping your father with his life's work, the cataloging and classifying of voodoo poisons. You have met a sleaze-bag agent and personally know two ghostwriters committed to mental institutions for the foreseeable future.

Paragraph 4: Other Impressive Stuff

You studied creative writing in college and wrote your Master's thesis on "The Importance of Poisons in Agatha Christie's Poirot Novels." After school, you worked for a couple years as a reporter for the *Bronx Cheer*. You've published a number of short stories in mystery magazines, both print and online. You serve as president of your local Sisters in Crime chapter. You are already hard at work on book two of the Melissa Manhattan series, *Dead Men Don't Call You Back*.

Paragraph 5: How to Reach You

You would be happy to send a copy of the manuscript for review; the agent should feel free to contact you at home or at work anytime. If you are sending actual mail, you have also enclosed a SASE as well as your cell phone number and e-mail address. You look forward to hearing from him or her.

> **SLUSH PILE**
>
> You won't make it very far if you do any of the following: hand-write your query, fail to send it to an agent who represents fiction, spell the agent's name wrong, or spell anything wrong. And please, don't say "fiction novel." It's repetitively redundant.

How Hard Can That Be?

Writing an effective query ultimately depends on salesmanship. For some reason, many people who can write great novels cannot write a decent sales letter. So if you feel your efforts to sell yourself and your work on paper fall flat, don't despair. Enlist the help of a copywriter friend or colleague to help you punch up your pitch. If you don't know anyone with that skill, hire someone. Look at the freelancers on Guru. com (guru.com) for advertising copywriters.

Remember, this short come-on is your foot in the door. It's worth investing more than a little time and money on perfecting your query. So when the door opens up a crack, you want to slip in a Gucci loafer, not those old sneakers you wore to paint the front room.

An Invitation for a Proposal!

You glance down and spot an unfamiliar number on your ringing phone. Might be a bill collector or … could this be *the call?* Has your query hooked an agent?

"I'd really like to see more," the agent says. "Can you send me a proposal?"

A proposal for a novel? If you read the chapter on nonfiction proposals (Chapter 8), you now know all the different types of information that go into one of those. But what on Earth do you put into a fiction proposal?

Very little, actually. Here's what goes into a fiction proposal:

- A *synopsis* of the novel
- The first 50 pages of the novel, or the first 3 chapters, whichever is longer
- Information about the author

DEFINITION

Before an agent or editor will read your whole novel, he will want to read your **synopsis,** a 10-page summary of your novel, written in the present tense and in the third person. It spells out the plot of your novel in an effective and readable way.

Unlike a nonfiction proposal, you won't have to spend countless hours analyzing the competing titles. Novels are generally understood to stand on their own, not to compete directly with similar novels on similar themes. You won't have to do research and include data on the market for the novel. The market is understood—it's people who read fiction.

So let's see how to put together a synopsis.

Summarize, Please

Why do you need to write a synopsis if you've already written the whole novel? Here again, it's a question of time. Agents and editors aren't going to plow through your 12-pound manuscript to see if your plot is full of holes. They can figure it out by skimming a 1- to 10-page synopsis. They also don't have room in those cluttered offices for an extra 30 chapters when they can tell in 50 pages or fewer that your characters play like cardboard cutouts and that your pacing is wildly uneven.

Like the query, writing a synopsis is an art all its own, with its own set of rules.

Hook 'Em Again?

Entertaining and scintillating? How can you condense an entire novel into a few pages, much less be entertaining and scintillating? Granted, it's not easy to breathe life into such a stilted narrative, but it can be done. Many writers spice up their synopses with snippets of dialogue and small bits of scenes. Whatever you can think of doing to add flair to your synopsis, do it.

Approach the writing of your synopsis as if you were writing a treatment for the movie adaptation of your novel. Not only will a cinematic style ensure that your synopsis is engaging and compelling, it will make it that much easier to sell the film rights later.

Sample Synopses

Did you join the local writers' group for your genre? Do you attend workshops as part of a romance writers group or a mystery writers group? Or do you meet with a group of local writers at the Starbucks down the street to swap tales? Ask your friends if they have sample synopses you could see. Study these synopses and then write one for your book that outshines them all!

If they're interested, some agents, such as co-author Sheree, will request the whole manuscript in lieu of a proposal. Even then, it's necessary to include at least a one-page synopsis and bio.

Sheree likes to request the whole book for several reasons:

- So she can finish the book while it's still fresh in her mind if it's got her hooked after Chapter 3

- So she can be sure the novel is complete

- So she can be sure the novel keeps her attention through the end

Exclusivity

There's a lot of confusion about this topic. When an agent asks for exclusivity, it means she wants to be the only agent currently considering your manuscript (see Chapter 11). If an agent does ask for exclusivity, be sure she gives you a reasonable time frame for a response. Ask exactly what she expects, and be sure you understand her terms, as each one might be different. Sheree usually offers a 4-week turnaround for a proposal or manuscript in exchange for an exclusive first look at a manuscript. So go ahead and e-mail the entire file once you have a clear idea of how long the exclusive period is.

Giving an agent exclusivity does not mean you are then required to use that agent if the agent likes your manuscript. She is still going to have to click with you. The agent should show some passion for your project, offer you terms for representation that you find reasonable, be able to give you references, and be able to do whatever is reasonably necessary to make you comfortable that he or she is the best agent for you. If not, move on to the next one!

The Least You Need to Know

- With fiction, you must write the entire novel before trying to get an agent or a publisher.
- Be sure to rewrite and polish your manuscript before sending it out. If you need professional help to take your first draft to the next level, hire an experienced editor to advise you on the rewrite.
- Write your novel in a cinematic way to increase its marketability.
- Never send the entire manuscript unsolicited; try first with a short query.
- Your query should include a short description of your novel.
- Your proposal should include a 1- to 10-page summary of the novel and either the first 50 pages of the manuscript or 3 complete chapters.

Getting a Book Contract

Whether your goal is to find an agent first or go directly to a publisher yourself, the information is all here in Part 3. Here you find great tips on how to locate agents and even how to get agents to find you! But if that doesn't work, you learn the protocol for approaching publishers without an agent. Whether children's publishers, university publishers, or even the swiftly changing world of indie publishing, you have lots to learn about the different styles of publishing books.

We also help you understand two critical areas of the publishing process: what goes on in an editorial meeting and what goes into a standard publishing contract.

Never again will you feel out of the loop about what's happening with your proposal as it goes to an editorial meeting. And never again will your head spin with confusion over publishing terms and conditions. Soon, you'll be dazzling dinner companions with your in-depth knowledge of royalties and copyright!

What's an Agent for, Anyway?

Chapter 10

In This Chapter

- Why writers need agents
- Why agents and editors "do lunch"
- How agents negotiate contracts
- Some common contract pitfalls
- How agents help you stay on the publisher's good side

You've written a tantalizing query, and your bulletproof book proposal is put together. The outline for the book (or the entire novel itself) is solid and waiting for a buyer. You're ready to go. But wait! You worked darn hard on all this—why should you cut an agent in on the deal now? Because writers write, and agents sell.

Whether you write fiction or nonfiction, it's hard enough going about the business of writing without also having to deal with the actual business end of it. Very few writers are really equipped to both let their imaginations soar on the blank page and at the same time concentrate on trying to market their work.

Here are a few quick reasons why writers use agents:

- Contacts
- Contracts
- Money
- Guidance
- Subrights
- Business savvy

Friends in High Places

Agents devote much of their time to cultivating contacts with editors and publishers. They do lunch; they circulate at book parties; they attend conferences; they share cabs. Agents make it their business to get to know *acquisitions editors* at all the major publishing houses. Agents learn what kinds of books each and every editor likes and, more importantly, just what kind of book each editor never wants to see again!

DEFINITION

The editors who are responsible for bringing in new books are called **acquisitions editors.** They're often called senior editors, but they may also be editors or editors at large. The titles vary from house to house and generally depend on the level of responsibility or the amount of experience an editor has.

Each publishing house has its specialties. Some large houses publish a vast array of books on a vast array of topics. Random House, for instance, has a mind-boggling number of imprints, each with a different personality and focus. A smaller publisher such as New World Library, on the other hand, is known for spiritual and personal-growth titles. Agents keep track of who publishes what, who went out of business, and even which publishing companies seem to be nicer to their authors than others. This is the sort of specialized knowledge an agent can use to sell your book to the right publisher.

Editors do jump ship a lot. They change jobs, change careers, go on maternity leave, and quit to write their own books. A good agent tracks the circulation patterns of all the editors while remaining a constant contact for the author.

Agents and Editors "Doing Lunch"

Lucky for agents—particularly poor, starving agents—this is the only business around where the buyer wines and dines the seller. This expensive practice alone should help convince you of the important role agents play in the publishing business.

Publishers value the knowledge, judgment, and wisdom of agents enough to ply them with meals. Just as authors can't effectively do their job of writing while also being their own agents, publishers can't do their jobs of acquiring and editing while at the same time screening a million writers and projects.

When an editor agrees to take a look at a project an agent is representing, he knows this is a professional project worth considering. The editor is relying on the fact that an agent is not likely to take on a project (investing hours of her own time, office help, and supplies) she doesn't believe to be of the highest quality. Editors rely on agents to do quite a bit of the screening and selecting for them.

What do they find to talk about during these long publishing lunches? That is where all your hard homework, all the information you dug up about the audience, the market, and the potential for your book comes in. The agent works to sell the editor on the potential of your book, combining her knowledge with the information you've supplied. In the publishing business, unwritten books are the stuff of dreams. Who knows where the next big thing will come from? Every agent, every editor, and every publisher hopes she has found it.

You might wonder how, if agents and editors are friends, they can negotiate contracts. Agents and editors share a love of books and the arts in general, so it's natural that they would become friends outside of work. While there's always an understanding of professionalism when it comes to negotiating contracts and acquiring projects, it can benefit the author if the agent and editor are friends. The agent really learns what the editor likes and can try to match the author with the right person for the project.

Here's a snippet from a rejection letter Jennifer's agent got for her novel. Note the final message:

> Thank you for sharing [the novel] by Jennifer Basye Sander with me … I just didn't completely click with the voice here, and I really wanted to … She has a great platform and a lot of wonderful credits to her name, so I do hope you find the perfect home for [the novel]. I'm sorry it's not with me, but I hope to see more novels from you in the future.
>
> All my best,
>
> P.S.: How about a lunch in the new year? A mid-Jan postholiday one? Let me know if you're up for it.

A Hope and a Prayer

Does a book have an intrinsic value? Well, no. The value of an *intellectual property* is determined purely by taste (the editor's) and perceived need. It isn't like a diamond or a vacuum cleaner, something that has an expected value in the marketplace.

DEFINITION

What is an **intellectual property?** A house owned by a college professor? No, it's a legal term for, according to the *Random House Legal Dictionary*, "copyrights, patents, and other rights in creations of the mind; also, the creations themselves, such as a literary work, painting, or computer program."

A book is more like an autographed baseball or a piece of twentieth-century art: it's worth whatever someone is willing to pay. So over lunch, agents get editors excited about the books they have for sale. Agents also listen closely as the editor describes the kinds of books he or she hopes to find.

"Is That the Best You Can Do?"

Well, the lunch meeting between your agent and the prospective editor was a great success. The agent sends over the proposal, the editor reads it, and eventually the editor calls your agent to make an offer. This doesn't happen that same afternoon, however. Not all sales pitches are made over lunch, of course. Agents spend plenty of time working the phones and firing off e-mails to gauge interest and solicit requests for proposals and projects.

Profit or Loss?

In Chapter 14, you'll get an inside look at what happens during editorial meetings. But before then, we'll just say that the editor needs to get the support and approval of a whole bunch of other folks—and to do what's known as a *P&L* (profit and loss statement)—before he or she makes that call to your agent.

DEFINITION

P&L stands for a profit and loss statement, which takes into account all the money that must be spent on a book, balanced against the money that can be expected from potential sales. A publisher hopes the P column outweighs the L column by a desired profit margin.

The profit and loss statement is used to estimate in advance what a publisher can expect to earn from the publication of a book.

Any Other Takers?

Agents often meet and talk with several editors from several publishers to raise interest in a project. Let's pretend your agent has submitted your brilliant proposal to editors A, B, and C. Editors C and B are polite, but editor A is the only one who calls the agent with an offer. Editor A wants to be sure he's not "bidding against himself." If only one bid is on the table, the agent doesn't have much leverage to get it raised. Agents do have a trick or two up their sleeves, however, to try to maximize the publishers' offers and get the best possible deal for their author. This process is referred to as an auction and can take place over the course of an afternoon or a few tense days.

Let's not forget that an agent's work is done on "spec"—her income is solely based on *commission*. No sale, no commission; low sale, low commission. Your agent earns no money at all from representing you until your book is sold to a publisher. Then depending on your agreement, she receives anywhere from 10 to 15 percent of your royalties and 15 percent of your advance. (More on your advance later in the chapter.) So it's possible for an agent to work long and hard, only to earn nothing if your book isn't sold. You can see why an agent will always try to get the best deal possible for you, the author—because at the same time, it's her deal, too.

DEFINITION

Literary agents work solely on **commission,** a percentage of the book's income.

Money, Money, Money

So the editor wants your book. Great! You get the call from your agent and begin dancing around the room shouting, "Show me the money!" Just how much money can you expect? This is a sticky subject. Sadly, most American writers have rather small average yearly incomes. Around $10,000 a year is typical, and that may reflect a number of different income sources (web content creation, magazine and newspaper articles, freelance copywriting, etc.) in addition to book royalties.

How much money you can expect depends on many factors. We've seen first-time advances for nonfiction books range anywhere from as low as $5,000 to as high as $100,000. You may only hear about the mega-advances, but that might be because they're so unusual that it makes them news.

At a single meeting, a major publishing house might allocate $2 million to acquire 5 books—with $1.9 million going to a single title. A smaller publishing company might allocate as much as $50,000 to acquire 5 or more titles. If you really have a great background—a platform that includes a large speaking schedule, a huge Twitter following, a newspaper column, a high-profile name, or a tremendous idea—the number will reflect that.

> **EXPERTS SAY**
>
> In *Merchants of Culture*, a book about the publishing business, author John Thompson describes the "web of collective belief" that builds up prior to the publication of a book, the hope that it will achieve big sales. The seeds for that collective belief are often sown by the agent's enthusiasm. "In the absence of anything solid, nothing is more persuasive than the expressed enthusiasm of trusted others …."

Megamarkets

The size of your *advance* could also be higher if you establish a ready market for your book. With *Christmas Miracles*, co-author Jennifer was able to establish how well Christmas books sold, how well books on miracles sold, and how well inspirational short-story books such as *Chicken Soup for the Soul* sold. All that research paid off—as did the passionate pitch her agent, Sheree, made at a Women in Publishing Christmas party.

> **DEFINITION**
>
> The money paid to an author upon signing a contract is called an *advance against future royalties*, or simply, an **advance.** That's money up front that will have to be earned back once the book is available for sale. An author's royalty account starts as a negative figure that reflects the advance. When the royalties earned surpass the amount advanced, an author begins to receive more money.

Advances for Fiction

Advances for first-time novelists are generally on the low side, but if your book is perceived as a best-seller candidate and an auction ensues, the advance could go off the charts. From time to time, an unknown writer hits the million-dollar jackpot. It happens.

Double Indemnity

When agents negotiate contracts, the size of the advance is just one of many complicated issues. In Chapter 15, we'll walk you through a typical publishing contract piece by piece.

Rely on Your Agent

Although agents negotiate contracts on behalf of the author, the agent does not sign the contract. The author does. But you shouldn't sign the contract until the agent is happy with it, until you have read it completely, and until you understand it. Your agent is there to explain the quirks of the contract. Don't be afraid to ask about any and all details.

Publishing agreements are sticky wickets, but thankfully (for agents and authors), they're all pretty much the same. An experienced agent is aware of the traditional traps and loopholes. Nobody, including most lawyers, knows publishing contracts like an agent. Agents know just when to push and when to back off.

Let's Do Another One, Just Like the Other One

Agents sometimes maintain "boilerplate" contracts with the publishing houses with which they do business. What does this mean to you? On other contracts, the agent has already gotten the house to agree to more free copies, a better royalty rate on special sales, or a bigger cut of e-book royalties (a huge hot-button issue these days), or she's eliminated the option clause (which ties up the first look at your next book). The agent then has a boilerplate she can use with that house for future contracts.

EXPERTS SAY

Author and former lawyer Tim Perrin says that whenever you receive a first offer from a publisher, you should always say, "Oh? Is that all? I was thinking more like …." Then name a figure substantially higher than what you've just been offered. "It's never failed for me," says Perrin. "I don't often get double or triple the amount first offered, but I always get a substantial increase. I make more money in those 10 seconds than I do in any part of writing."

After the Deal Is Done

So your contract has been negotiated and signed, and you and your editor have a direct relationship. Your editor will now guide you through the publishing process. Is your agent's job finished? Not by a long shot.

An agent is an experienced publishing player. She can help you learn the ropes so you, too, will be an experienced player. After the contract is filed in a drawer, the agent takes on these tasks:

- Getting the most from the publicity department
- Examining your royalty statements
- Ensuring you get paid properly
- Selling subrights and licenses for your book
- Assisting you and the editor in solving any major problems that might arise in revising or finishing the manuscript
- Being your book's greatest advocate

Good Cop/Bad Cop

The best part of all is that your agent can be the bad guy. As an author, you want your editor to love you. You want to shy away from any kind of behavior that could damage your relationship with your editor. (More on this later in Chapter 19.) But what if you aren't happy?

Your agent can do the job! Call and tell him your concern, and ask him to speak on your behalf. You can sit back and let your agent air your complaints in such a way that you don't jeopardize your relationship with your publisher. Your agent is the bad cop. The agent can do the yelling (about the crummy cover design, the lack of a publicity campaign, missing e-book sales, or the slow royalty checks) while you sit back and bat your eyelashes.

Publishers are people, too. Even if your book is the best thing since *Gone with the Wind*, those with the power to help you will not put forth their best efforts if you alienate them. At any given time, a publishing house has lots of different books to peddle, so don't give it a reason to spend less time on yours. Your second most important job as a writer (after writing the best book you can) is to make the publisher love you and your book. Be as pleasant as you can. Let your agent do the unpleasant things.

> **SLUSH PILE**
>
> Don't ever pick up the phone and call the editor directly about a contract issue. This will make both your editor and your agent angry. Relax, and let your agent do her job.

Substance in Subrights

When an agent places a book with a publisher on behalf of an author, the most basic right the publisher acquires is the right to publish the manuscript in book form in the English language. Every other right associated with the book is considered a subright. Some typical subrights associated with the book are audio, video, book club, movie, and—most important to an author with an agent—foreign rights.

Most agents maintain subagents in territories outside the United States for foreign sales and subagents in Hollywood for movie sales. When an agent withholds foreign or movie rights from the publisher, this means that—with or without the help of her subagents—the agent can license those rights directly to foreign publishers and movie studios.

If the agent and her subagents share a 20 percent commission for such sales, as is typical, this puts 80 percent of each sale (less taxes) directly into the author's pocket. When publishers keep movie, foreign, and other subrights, they may keep 25 to 50 percent of the sale and apply any proceeds against the author's unearned royalty account, thus depriving the author of additional monies for valuable subrights. Occasionally, it's to the author's advantage to allow the publisher to control subrights, such as, for example, when the publisher gives the author a fair percentage and aggressively goes after those sales.

Understand that these sums are usually on the low side. But if your book sells in 20 countries, those small sums will begin to add up.

Should You Get an Agent?

Now you know the full story. An agent's role goes far beyond brokering a profitable deal with a publisher.

We're not saying you need an agent because co-author Sheree is one. (And we're not saying that because Sheree is Jennifer's agent either!) We're both writers, and we know a lot of other writers. We've seen all that can happen to writers in the rough-and-tumble world of book publishing. Get yourself a good agent, and you will have less to worry about.

Even in-house editors, like Jennifer, who know the ins and outs of the publishing business, use agents when they become authors.

How the heck do you find an agent? Move on to the next chapter, and we'll show you where they hang out!

The Least You Need to Know

- Agents do many things, from negotiating a contract to guiding you through the publishing maze.
- Agents get to know editors and what kinds of books they want to publish so the agent will better know who to market your book to.
- Books are intellectual properties and are worth what the highest bidder will pay. An agent is better equipped to handle the bidding.
- Standard boilerplate publishing contracts favor the publisher, not the author. An agent knows the ins and outs.
- Agents can help you maintain a good relationship with your editor and publisher.
- When an agent controls the subrights, the author is likely to make more money.

Finding and Working with an Agent

In This Chapter

- Where do agents hide?
- Tips on choosing the best agent for you
- Fiction or nonfiction?
- Agent etiquette
- Landing a live one!

With any luck, we convinced you in Chapter 10 that you need an agent, particularly if you're a first-time author and want to sell your book idea to a large national publisher. If you've decided an agent is the way to go, read on. In this chapter, we tell you how to find a good one.

Members of the Club

So how do you tell if an agent is the real thing? A large percentage of established agents in the business are members of the Association of Authors' Representatives (AAR), the largest professional association of literary and dramatic agents for authors. To get a list of all its members or to search for an agent by name or interests, visit the association's free website at aar-online.org.

What does this list tell you? That the agents listed are what they say they are: experienced literary agents. To become a member of the AAR, you must be a well-established agent with several contracts negotiated on behalf of authors with major publishing houses. In addition, you must pass a rigorous application and screening process and agree to abide by the AAR's strict Canon of Ethics.

In their Canon of Ethics, the members of AAR pledge loyal service to their clients' needs. A member's accounts must be open to the client at all times with respect to the client's transactions, and members promise not to represent both buyer and seller in the same transaction. The AAR believes that the practice of agents charging clients or potential clients for reading and evaluating literary works (including outlines, proposals, and manuscripts) is subject to serious abuse that reflects adversely on the profession. Current and future members may not charge for reading and evaluating literary works and may not benefit from the charging of such fees by any other person or entity.

Just How Much Is This Gonna Cost?

It costs nothing to have an agent who's a member of AAR read your material. Other agents may charge reading fees. Most of the reference books that list agents note whether they charge a reading fee, and if so, how much.

Reading Fees? No

The fact that an agent charges a reading fee does not necessarily mean he or she is taking advantage of you. In fact, if you ever got a glimpse at the gobs of unsolicited material that flood into agents' offices every day, you might understand the idea behind a reading fee. Remember, agents don't make any money at all until they sell your project.

But the AAR believes that reading fees can easily lead to corrupt practices like charging for books they might never read, or charging for needless editing or ghostwriting on a book they knew was not salable. So do try to stay away from paying a reading fee.

Rather than paying reading fees to an agent, hire yourself an independent editor or sign up for a writing class if you want your writing evaluated. Agents either represent you or do not represent you. We don't think you need to pay someone to evaluate your work in exchange for representation. And by all means, do not pay an agent a fee to represent you or to place your manuscript with a publisher. Agents collect commissions, not fees.

They're Agents, Not Readers

Not only do most literary agents not charge reading fees, they also don't provide "reader's reports." An agent will simply tell you whether your manuscript is suited to his agency. If the manuscript doesn't interest him enough to represent it, he certainly won't take the time to tell you what he thinks is wrong with it. But if he does want to represent your book, he will take the time to help you make it better.

The hard truth is this: if all the agents you approach who don't charge fees turn down you and your project, it's pretty likely that the publishers are going to have the same reaction. So if this happens, spend your money on a good book doctor, a writing class or seminar, or an independent editor. All these will help you improve your work and its chances of someday being published.

Where to Find Help

Many good book doctors and freelance editors can help you with your proposal, and agents sometimes can give you the names of such people. So might members of local writers' groups.

EXPERTS SAY

"Book doctors should respect your confidentiality," says book doctor Jerry Gross. If you use a book doctor, no one needs to know about it. Other than the confidentiality question, what else should you ask a book doctor before hiring one? First and foremost, be sure she's skilled in your area. "If you are writing a sci-fi novel, be sure the book doctor critiques or edits sci-fi novels, too. You don't want someone with an expertise in romance novels." And always be suspicious of someone who "guarantees" that if you work with her, she will get you an agent or a publisher. Jerry Gross is a member and co-founder of the Independent Editors Group. His website, bookdocs.com, lists more than a dozen book docs for hire.

Then there's the Editorial Freelance Association (EFA), a nonprofit organization whose members are all freelance editors. Check out EFA's website at the-efa.org, or call 212-929-5425.

Screening Agents

Are all good agents members of the AAR? Are all members of the AAR good agents? Many good agents are not members of the AAR and don't charge fees. But evaluating them may prove difficult without checking with an association.

After an agent has offered to represent you, but before you sign up, feel free to ask for names and phone numbers of other clients. The agent should happily let you speak to some of his clients to get a better sense of who they are. If an agent is reluctant to hook you up with any other clients, take this as a red flag.

Not sure what kinds of questions you should ask an agent before agreeing to let him represent you? Here are a few questions that will help you sound him out:

- How long have you been in business as an agent?
- Do you have specialists at your agency who handle television and movie rights?
- Do you represent other authors in my area of interest?
- What is your commission?
- Do you issue 1099 (nonemployee) tax forms at the end of the year?
- What kinds of books have you sold lately?

You owe it to yourself and your book to be rigorous in your evaluation of a potential agent. Do most of your early research through books, online, and via any personal sources you might have. Don't call and ask agents for their biographies or the names of potential clients until they've offered to represent you. After they've offered to represent you, it's perfectly proper to ask such questions.

Where to Look for Agents

So where else do they hide, these agents? Co-author Sheree would like to say that all the good agents are close to New York City (guess where she has an office?), but she would be lying. New York–area agents might have an easier time accessing New York editors face to face, but excellent agents live all around the country. Agents outside the Big Apple make frequent trips to New York. They pack their appetites in their carry-ons and schedule their breakfasts, lunches, dinners, drinks, and coffee dates with as many publishers as they can.

Besides checking the membership list of the AAR, you can find agents several other ways.

EXPERTS SAY

Agent Gordon Warnock advises writers to follow agents on Twitter. "Especially when we are reading submissions, that is when we tend to get ranty and give out all sorts of unsolicited advice in an effort to prevent specific errors in future submissions." You can follow Gordon at @gordonwarnock.

Look in a Book

Three great books list agents: *Literary Market Place (LMP)*; *Jeff Herman's Guide to Book Publishers, Editors, and Literary Agents*; and *The Writer's Digest Guide to Literary Agents*.

The *Literary Market Place* is a very good but very expensive professional reference. Although it's full of information, only one of the many sections in it is devoted to agents, so unless you plan to dive into the publishing business full time, you're better off with the more commercial books for writers.

Jeff Herman's Guide to Book Publishers, Editors, and Literary Agents is put together by literary agent Jeff Herman. He's been doing it forever it seems, and he includes lots of personal and professional information about the agents he lists. Each agent listing includes the agent's description of the type of book he or she likes to represent and the type of book he or she never wants to see again. If you're just beginning your search for an agent, Herman's book is great. Be sure to get the most current edition available because the listings change every year.

The Writer's Digest Guide to Literary Agents lists more than 750 agents who "sell what you write." It's concise, is kept up to date, and is an excellent resource not just for finding agents, but also for learning about the publishing industry. Buying a copy also gives you access to all their online information.

Face to Face

A great way to find an agent is through a recommendation from a friend or colleague, particularly a published friend or colleague. But what if you don't know any other writers? Get thee to a writers' conference!

In any given month, somewhere around the country, a writers' conference is being held. Most organizers of writers' conferences arrange to have a few agents on hand for potential authors to meet. These meetings are invaluable. Not only do they give you a chance to shake a live agent's hand, but you also can often arrange for personal appointments with agents to discuss your project. This is time you wouldn't be able to get from them on the phone with a cold call.

If you're serious about writing, writers' conferences are never a waste of time. They're especially useful for authors who write in a particular genre, as some conferences specialize in genres, such as mystery, romance, and sci-fi. The Guide to Writers' Conferences & Workshops at shawguides.com is a fabulous resource for writers. It provides more than 600 detailed conference and workshop descriptions, including upcoming dates, faculty, and programs.

Making the Most of Writers' Conferences

All writers' conferences are not created equal. Many are large affairs with lots of writing craft workshops and keynote speakers. Many exist for the simple purpose of introducing prospective authors to lots of agents. Whatever their purpose, there's much to be gained from almost every conference. At the very least, it's a place where authors can learn about the writing and publishing process and meet other authors at different stages in the process.

The important thing to remember when attending a conference where agents are present is not to rush yourself to the point where you think you need to finish the novel you started last Thursday or write a book proposal in one day just because you'll have the opportunity to discuss it with an agent. Agents are used to getting follow-up contacts long after the conference is a distant memory. If they're not in business that long, you'd be wise to select another agent anyway.

Frequently conferences present authors with a chance to pitch their work to agents. Please keep in mind that pitching your work is not necessary, though. The purpose of the pitch is to see if the agent wants to see your proposal or manuscript. It's important to be concise. Just say enough to achieve that goal. So many times, Sheree says, an author will start off with a wonderful pitch and then ramble on and on long after Sheree exhibited enthusiasm and requested the material. If an agent requests your material, stop pitching and just find out where to send the material, how they want to receive it, and what to expect in terms of a response.

HOT OFF THE PRESS

Meeting an agent at a writers' conference can be like speed dating, in which you have a limited amount of time to make a good impression. Most appointments are for 15 or 30 minutes, and you should arrive with your best material in hand and a well-practiced speech about your project and why it should be published. Like a speed date, this is not the time to go into heavy background on your life; rather, stick to what will sell your project and you as a potential client. It also gives you a chance to see agents up close and get a feel for who you'd most like to work with.

You may be great at queries and your book may be fabulous, but if you tend to get tongue-tied in a one-on-one, skip the pitch and absorb information. You don't have to pitch anyone at all. Most books that end up in bookstores are the result of a written query or proposal and never got verbally pitched by anyone.

And if editors from publishing houses are present at the conference, listen to whatever they have to say but don't pitch your books to them. Before approaching editors, learn about the publishing process and try to find the perfect agent who will do the pitching for you.

Not Cheap Though ...

Writers' conferences are wonderful things, and they can bring you into the world of publishing like nothing else. But ... they are also very expensive, and you need to be clear about why you're spending your money.

Are you really ready to pitch agents? Are you just going to dip your toes into the scene and check it all out? Are you hoping to be discovered? Try to be realistic about why you're going and whether or not this is the right time in your career to spend the money to go. We have both seen writers' conference "junkies" who seem to pop up at every conference and are always, always working on something that isn't quite ready yet ....

"I'd Like to Thank My Agent ..."

Don't know any writers? Can't get to a writers' conference? Well, you can open a book, right? That's a great place to find agents! Take a book, any book, off the shelf. Open it to the acknowledgments page. (Not all books have such a page, but many if not most do.) This is where the author thanks his family for their patience, his editor for her guidance, and his agent for all those lunches.

Looking in the acknowledgments is a great tactic for finding an agent, particularly when you need to find one who represents books in your area. Writing a health book? Look inside the health books you admire. Writing a romance novel? Check out recently published romances. This method helps you find the agent who might be open to your type of writing.

Does the author thank everyone in the world but her agent? Hmmm … must have been an oversight.

Eeny, Meeny, Miney, Mo

So you've looked inside your favorite books. You checked out the AAR site, and you met eight great agents at a writers' conference last weekend. You've highlighted, cross-checked, and pondered the selections. You know which agents represent your area. Do you have to just choose one? No! You're in luck. It's perfectly acceptable to send *multiple queries*, or queries to more than one agent at one time.

> **DEFINITION**
>
> When authors write to a number of agents at one time, this is called a **multiple query.** You're approaching a number of agents at once to try to get them interested in requesting your proposal, chapters, or manuscript. This is an accepted practice in publishing.

Still, you want to be somewhat selective about whom you send your precious queries to. What if they all responded at once and they all said "Yes"? Select your hottest prospects first.

Exclusive Territory

When an agent does respond and requests more material from you, she might also ask for an *exclusive* for a limited amount of time; 3 or 4 weeks is standard. (See the "You Hooked One!" section later in this chapter for more on exclusives.) What does an exclusive mean? It means that for the next 3 or 4 weeks, she can study your material closely and not have to worry that you might be swiped out from under her by another agent.

> **DEFINITION**
>
> When only one agent is considering your proposal, this is called an **exclusive** submission. If an agent asks for an exclusive submission, be sure to set a time limit. Three or four weeks is reasonable. Sometimes you can get a faster answer and special attention from an agent when you grant her an exclusive.

If an agent chooses you, do you have to choose her? No. But realistically, if someone does want to represent you and offers you a reasonable author/agent agreement (and if she doesn't seem obnoxious), well, why not? Don't try to interest an agent you really don't want. You will waste both your time and hers.

The Good Agent

The best things to look for in an agent include the following:

- An established reputation
- A reputation for selling books in your field
- Accessibility (after she's become your agent)
- A manner that lends itself to comfortable communication
- A passion about her work—and about yours

If you can't find all these qualities in an agent who responds to you, move down your list until you do.

Are You Really Ready?

How do you know when you're ready to begin querying agents? You're ready if you have two things: a well-written query and a polished proposal for nonfiction or a polished manuscript for fiction. If these elements are in place, get started!

Fiction

If you're writing fiction, don't even think about querying agents until you're satisfied that your novel is the best it can be. You'll hear from time to time about first-time novelists selling a novel for a million dollars. It happens, but rarely. What you might not realize, though, is that although this is the first book that writer has sold, it's probably not the first book he's written. Many writers write 2, 3, or 10 novels before selling one.

Novelists write and write, regardless of whether they'll get published. True novelists usually get published, eventually. But don't send something to an agent just because you worked hard on it or are sick of looking at it! Send it because it's good. Don't ask an agent to decide whether it's good; ask discriminating colleagues, teachers, and editors for their honest opinions first. Take praise from family and friends (who may be biased or who don't want to hurt your feelings) with a large grain of salt.

 SLUSH PILE

No matter how brilliant you think your book idea is, if you don't have the written material to back it up, you will fail. Do not approach an agent or a publisher with an idea for a book until you have something in writing—your writing!

Sometimes novelists need to put their novels aside and let them sit for a while. Then they go back to them with a fresh perspective and reevaluate them. Very often authors come back to their first novels years later and say, "Oh my gosh, what was I thinking?"

Nonfiction

For nonfiction, you can submit before you've got the entire book written. As you learned in Chapter 8, nonfiction is usually sold on the basis of a book proposal, a table of contents, and a representative sample chapter. If a publishing house likes what it sees in a proposal and decides to publish it, you have a deal.

There are several models for paying out advances. Some publishers pay half the advance upon signing a contract and half upon receipt of an acceptable manuscript. Others might break that up into smaller sums for milestones such as a third on signing, a third on completion of the first half of the book, and a third upon delivery of the manuscript. A manuscript is deemed acceptable when it matches the promises in your proposal, as reflected in the contract description.

When you have a good nonfiction proposal together, go ahead and start querying agents. If you haven't yet started your sample chapter, don't worry. Start it soon, but don't let it hold you back. If an agent is interested in your query and then asks to see more, you don't want her to have to wait too long. She might forget you!

> **SLUSH PILE**
>
> Although most nonfiction books require only a book proposal, there is one instance in which you will need more. Creative nonfiction books that are literary memoirs (such as Jeanette Walls's *The Glass Castle*) require a more fictionlike approach. You can't sell creative nonfiction with a bare-bones nonfiction proposal. Like a novel, you might need to write the whole book or a substantial portion first.

Big Name, Superb Credentials

You might not have to wait until a proposal is done before querying agents. If you have superb professional credentials, such as a recognizable name, you might not have to wait. Write a strong query and see what kind of reaction you get from agents. It might be that an agent will be able to link you with a co-writer for the project. The agent might also be able to guide you in the proposal process.

Return to Sender

If you're opting for snail mail (and check the agent's website to see if he or she still accepts actual mail because some don't), please don't send your unsolicited query via certified or registered mail. The agent will think he's being sued! Seriously, you don't want to look overcautious or paranoid. Portray yourself like the professional you are.

Once again, we remind you of the importance of including a self-addressed, stamped envelope (SASE) with your correspondence to agents. This simple step can make all the difference in hearing back. If you leave out the SASE, the agent might assume you need no reply if the agent isn't interested. If that's the case, it's better to say so than to look sloppy.

Remember that unsolicited queries via e-mail sometimes get answered quickly, sometimes slowly, and sometimes not at all. At least with the old snail mail/SASE you would get some kind of closure, which is sometimes in short supply today.

Hold My Calls, Please

Unless (and until) you have an agent/author agreement with an agent, do not try to call a prospective agent on the phone. It will backfire. Approach agents the way they want to be approached: with a query.

Agents need to evaluate your writing, not your speaking. So give them what they need and more: a great query that will pique their interest right away. Sheree's phone used to ring off the hook with all manner of phone calls, but she and all other agents appreciate the relative silence now that so much of the business is conducted via e-mail. Words, that's all that really matters.

You Hooked One!

An agent received your query, read it, and e-mailed or called you! Hurrah! This is a good sign. But don't jump the gun and start writing your Pulitzer acceptance speech yet. When an agent is intrigued by your query, she might call you to find out more about the project. She might also be calling to learn more about you as a person.

If the agent does want to go further, she might ask for an exclusive. Remember, this is when you assure her that she is the only one considering your project for a particular length of time. It's hard to say no to an agent on the phone, and that's why it's so important for you to have done your research before deciding which agents to query. You don't want to go to the dance with the wrong partner!

Another Darn SASE?

When an agent responds to your query and asks to see more material, if you're sending out hard copy you once again need to include a SASE with your proposal. There's more at stake here, in fact. You're sending a lot of material, and you want it back if the agent decides to pass. To be sure your package was received, send it via an express service such as FedEx or UPS. You can track it by phone or online without calling the literary agent and looking anxious. The good old U.S. mail is just fine, too. According to statistics, 99.9999 percent of all mail is delivered properly.

For packages that weigh more than 1 pound, include return postage, either loose stamps for the proper postage or a check to cover the cost of an express service. If you're e-mailing files, just think how much cheaper it is to be a writer nowadays than when 100 percent of the business was done through the mail! In fact, agent Jeff Kleinman of Folio Literary Management says the only time he even sees a printed manuscript or proposal anymore is when he's dealing with foreign rights sales with overseas agents.

Try, Try Again

What if an agent looks at your proposal and tells you it still needs more work? She might tell you exactly where she thinks it's weak and how to improve it. Or she might think your proposal is so weak that you need to hire help and suggest that you work with a book doctor. (See more on book doctors earlier in this chapter and also in Chapter 8.)

Shopping Yourself

If you decide to try to place your book first without an agent, don't shop the project to all the publishers in town and then try to find an agent after you have a stack of rejection letters in hand, no matter how good your project is. Agents can't go back to the same publishers; if a publisher has passed on a project already, an agent will feel awfully foolish when the editor points it out—and it will come back to haunt you. Come clean with agents about which publishers have already seen the project and decided to pass.

SLUSH PILE

If you use a book doctor or other kind of professional in preparing your proposal, and the book finds a publisher, you need to be sure your finished book does not disappoint the publisher. If the publisher bought your project based on a proposal that had help, be extra sure your book meets or exceeds the expectations set in that proposal. Don't promise one thing and deliver another. Many publishers have been burned by books that didn't match the quality or content of the proposal. In cases of extreme differences in the quality of writing between the proposal and the finished manuscript, the publisher has the right to hire a book doctor to fix it and charge the cost to you.

The Least You Need to Know

- Members of the Association of Author's Representatives (AAR) abide by a professional code of ethics and don't charge a reading fee.
- Find an agent through the membership of AAR, directories that list agents, or writers' conferences.

- Looking in the acknowledgments section of books you admire in your genre could lead you to a great agent, too.
- With nonfiction, query agents when your proposal is finished. With fiction, query when your novel is finished.
- Always include a self-addressed, stamped envelope (SASE) with any correspondence to an agent.

What You Can Expect from an Agent

In This Chapter

- When an agent calls to represent you, what's next?
- The agency/author agreement
- When it's okay to call
- Dealing with rejection letters
- Every author's first question
- How agents sell books

Was that a dream? Did an agent actually call and say, "I want to represent you"? You wrote a good query and you have a great idea, so stop pinching yourself!

Right about now you might want to run to your agent's office and pop open a bottle of champagne, but you and your agent both have more work to do.

A Day in the Life of an Agent

What exactly do agents do all day? Let's peek in on Sheree's typical day:

An agent has to like doing a lot of things and doing them all at once. In the course of a day, I play many roles as an agent: editor, salesperson, social worker, and much more. On any given day, I may evaluate writers' works, call editors and pitch new projects, follow up on pending proposals publishers are considering, talk to a writer who is upset her editor is quitting the business, receive an offer or two and haggle for more money and/or better terms, and negotiate the fine points of a contract already in the works. I do this all while the e-mails and the phones bring a new, never-ending stream of demands. Fortunately, I enjoy being busy.

Today was a typical day. It started out with a pile of papers on my desk and phone calls from yesterday that needed to be returned. When the mail arrived, I paused to see if there was anything particularly interesting, and yes, I struck pay dirt—literally. Right on top was the telling envelope that revealed an acceptance check for a book I thought would never see the light of day—a book on astrology. I rubbed my eyes in disbelief.

The author had died tragically just before the book was due, with only three chapters to go. After many complications, the publisher had hired a writer (for a flat fee) to complete the last few chapters. She understood the author's idiosyncratic voice and the editor had expertise in the area, so they were able to complete it so it would seem as if the author herself had done it. It was a sad and unusual situation, but it was still gratifying that the book would finally be published after everyone's hard work.

No time for reverie, though. Publishers called to ask questions about projects and register their interest; others called to make offers (my favorite calls). As Tim Perrin wisely advises, whatever they offer, pause and say, "Is that all?" There were a few contracts to negotiate and a few authors with requests ("Where are my contracts?" "Should I hire a publicist?" "Did you see that horrible cover?" and the ever popular, "When is the publisher sending the *[expletive deleted]* money?").

One thing I love about being an agent is successfully troubleshooting—well, in hindsight, anyway. It's extremely rewarding to save books from the cutting-room floor and keep authors and publishers from shooting each other.

One of the pleasures of being an agent is the chance to come up with an idea, seek out an expert, and bring that idea to readers in book form. I've done it over and over again—with a famous disc jockey, with a well-known movie reviewer, with an artist whose work I saw in a museum, and many others. Most agents are continually on the lookout for high-profile folks they can approach with an idea.

Sometimes I have to step in and help find solutions, either for the author or the publisher. I once saved a project for both my author and the publisher (they weren't happy with the work as it had been turned in) in 24 hours' time by coming up with a solution that pleased both parties. Those are the moments I truly relish.

As usual, several editors called with a shopping list of titles in search of authors. I am so pleased they think of me when they have such projects. I have placed more than 30 great authors with series books at the request of the publisher. Many, if not most, series titles (like the one you're reading!) come to fruition this way.

After I looked through the mail for more checks, read some queries and rejections, and glanced at some requested manuscripts, I fired up the computer to check my e-mail. There they were: the usual 100 e-mails of which only a small portion could be deleted out of hand.

Here's something interesting: my Chinese agent is asking if we'd like to accept two offers from Chinese publishers for two of my authors. Hmmm … we just double-checked and saw that these two authors had already published with this agent in China. What's up? It turns out that there are at least two languages in China, and the rights are sold separately. So we are, happily, free to accept these offers. What do you know? A book can be sold in 10 countries and in 11 languages (at least).

As you might guess, my to-do list (I'm a Virgo) is miles long and the phone is ringing. Remember, every day my day looks like this, and so does the typical day of other agents in the business.

That's pretty much what happens in a day in the life of an agent. Whew! But remember we said *you both* have work to do. So put down your champagne glass because you have some things to take care of as well.

99 Percent Ready

It's rare that the manuscript or book proposal you sent in is 100 percent ready to go. Chances are, the agent will want to discuss some fine-tuning and changes.

At the very least, you'll need to change the cover page to your manuscript or proposal. Remember, it has your name and address on the bottom. Now that you've got an agent, you'll need to drop your own information and add his or hers.

"I Really Like It, but …"

Fixing the cover page—that's no problem. But is this agent passionate about your project? Does he or she believe in your book? It's imperative that the person who is going to represent you to publishers feels confident about your book's prospects. If the agent has any doubts going in, you want to know about it.

Let's say your agent loves your project, but maybe she also has some changes she needs you to make before sending your book out to publishers. After all, what an agent sends out is her calling card. She must maintain a good reputation with publishers to stay active in the business. You must make your work as perfect as possible.

SLUSH PILE

Spelling mistakes are unacceptable under any circumstances. With the advent of spell check, there's just no excuse for misspelled words in your manuscript or book proposal. But be careful—even spell checkers can work incorrectly. Read your manuscript for spelling and usage first—and then use spell check.

On your proposal, your agent might feel the competition section needs work. This might mean you need to strengthen your facts or do a quick double-check to be sure you haven't left out major titles. She might also feel that you've been too hard on the competing titles and might risk alienating the publishers of those books you've maligned (who might have otherwise become your publisher).

Your new agent might also make recommendations on your author bio section. Perhaps you've been too humble about your accomplishments. Or perhaps you've been a touch arrogant and need to tone it down. Perhaps she wants you to beef up your credentials with a blog or more professional endorsements.

Whatever the agent suggests, feel free to discuss it with her. This is very important: discuss all changes. If an agent makes suggestions to your manuscript (about combining chapters, say, or dropping a section), you don't have to agree. Do not make any changes to your work you don't feel 100 percent good about. If you can't get the agent to see things your way, or vice versa, perhaps this is not the agent for you. True, you've both wasted your time, but thank heaven you discovered it early.

On the other hand, the agent does have quite a bit of experience in this area. Do try to be open-minded and understand what your agent's suggesting (and why). The agent has your best interests in mind and is trying to make your project as salable as possible because you really have only one shot at it. Remember from Chapter 7 agent Janet Rosen's client whose book idea sold after the title was changed from *Eight Glasses of Water* to *Don't Swallow Your Gum*. That kind of suggestion gets made all the time.

If the agent sends out a project that wasn't quite ready to go and everyone who sees it turns it down, that's the end of the road. Publishers seldom want to see the same project twice.

Love at First Sight

Now let's say you and your agent are completely simpatico. You see eye to eye about the book and agree on what's necessary to touch it up and make it ready. The conversation you had about your book energized both of you. You like the agent's manner. You can talk to her. She listens. Great, so what's next?

The agent might suggest that you call one or two of her other clients for a reference. This is a great way to learn more about what the agent is like to work with on a long-term basis. Take the numbers; it wouldn't hurt to call. In fact, if the agent doesn't offer this, you should bring it up.

This is also a great time to find out more about how the agent works. Ask the agent to describe how she plans to sell your book. What's the process? And what more does she need from you? Here are a number of good questions to ask your agent:

- Will I need to make copies of the proposal or manuscript, or will you just send it electronically?

- How many publishers do you plan to contact?

- Will I get copies of the rejection letters?

- Do you e-mail editors to test their interest or call the publishers to let them know my proposal is coming?

- Do you plan to submit to several publishers at once or only one at a time (exclusively)?

- Have you sold many books in this category?

Are there any wrong answers to these questions? Not really. But it's better to ask in advance about how the agent works than to grumble about it later.

The Agent/Author Agreement

The answers to "who does what?" might be found in the agent/author contract. This is an agreement the agent sends to you after you have agreed that she may represent your book.

Most times, the agent/author agreement covers just the one book. Ideally, an author hopes that one perfect agent will represent him forever. Just as ideally, agents long for clients whom they can represent profitably forever. But at this stage of the game, take it one book at a time.

SLUSH PILE

In many ways, this is a trial run with an agent—an engagement, not a marriage. Maybe you're really just dating for a while. Hopefully, the relationship will turn out well—the agent will sell your book, and you two will get along famously. But continue to monitor the relationship after your book is successfully sold. Is the agent still communicating? Is she still passing along information as she receives it? If not, maybe the relationship should end.

Examine the agent/author agreement carefully before you sign it. Be sure you understand all the terms and that they are acceptable to you.

One of the things you might notice is that there's typically a charge for expenses such as postage, messengers, copying, and other office expenses. Most agents require that the author pay for these expenses. This charge is not to be confused with the reading fees discussed in Chapter 11. Some agents put a cap on such expenses. For instance, co-author Sheree caps these fees at $150 per book. Realistically, however, it could cost an agent several hundred dollars to sell a single book.

How are these fees collected? If your agent sells your book and receives an advance check from the publisher, the office fees are deducted (along with the agent's commission) before a check is sent to you. And if an agent hasn't had any luck selling your book after trying for a year or so, don't be surprised if you receive a bill for expenses in the mail one day.

So be sure you know what the fees could be. If the agreement doesn't mention office fees, ask. These costs have dropped considerably with the universal acceptance of electronic submissions, but you should still be aware of the possibility.

"Hello, It's Your Author!"

You shouldn't call agents during the query process, but now that it's official, go ahead and call. You have a right to expect reasonable access to your agent, not to just shoot the breeze, but to be kept informed of everything the agent does on your behalf. Expect progress reports from time to time.

Your agent will be pleased if you respect his time. Call only when you need to, and try to group your questions. Better yet, e-mail all your questions, and ask your agent to call you.

Do we make agents sound scary? They aren't really. But they are busy people who, like us all, have developed particular ways of working. You will get along nicely with your agent if you just accept that fact.

What's Going On?

Up to this point in your writing career, you have been in control. But from the time an agent starts to try to sell your project, the agent is now pretty much in control of what happens.

Here's what you hope is happening: the agent is calling editors to pitch your book. He's talking up you and your book as he lunches with editors. Throwing humility to the wind, he has all the top editors clamoring to see what you've written. He has written a glowing cover letter, which accompanies your proposal as it goes out to publishers that request it.

How long does the process take? Well, it's not a fast one. It takes several weeks for editors to respond. The cover letter your agent sent along with your material might have requested a response within a certain time period. Sometimes agents include a sentence similar to this: "I'd like to have all offers in by January 30." But even with a clock ticking, editors tend to move slowly. (In Chapter 14, you'll get a glimpse at the inner workings of a publishing house to better understand the process.)

What is your agent doing while the days slip by without an answer? Making follow-up calls to check that the proposal arrived. The real purpose of the phone calls is to remind editors of their early interest in the project, of course. But so as not to appear pushy, they employ more subtle tactics.

Ante Up

If a publisher calls to express an interest in acquiring your book, the agent once again works the phones. Calls are placed to all the publishers that received the proposal, and the agent says: "Publisher X is interested in that book you liked so much, and I wondered if your house was still interested." This way, the editors are once again prodded into action.

Such news might result in a larger offer because the second (or third or fourth) bidder has to beat what's already on the table.

The Rejection Blues

Realistically, most responses will be in the form of *rejection letters*. Even the best writers get rejection letters, so if it's any consolation, you're in fine company. Your rejection might be a curt "not for us" e-mail sent to your agent or a lengthy treatise on just why the editor isn't going to buy it. But either way, it means no, and that hurts.

DEFINITION

When an editor declines to pursue a book project, she sends out a **rejection letter.** Rejection letters sent directly to authors say little more than "no thanks." But rejection letters sent to agents might contain more information about why the editor turned it down.

Plain and simple, those letters hurt. They hurt you as the author, and no matter how many rejection letters your agent has seen in her career, they hurt her, too. Talk about it with your agent. She can help you overcome the sting of rejection letters.

Should you even see your rejection letters? Yes. Here's what you can learn from them:

- How many publishers have seen your work

- Which publishers have seen your work

- What kind of a relationship your agent has with publishers

- What kinds of criticism your project is receiving

All this information will help you get better and will help increase your chances of getting published in the future. Are all the letters saying the same thing? If all the editors say they don't see a market for your book, that might tell you something. If all the editors say there are too many similar titles already out there, that, too, might be sending you a message.

One of Sheree's clients once asked for the original copies of two of his rejection letters. In one, the publisher said the proposed book was "too specific." In the other, the publisher said that the book was "too general." The author framed the letters side by side in his office. You'll be pleased to know this story has a happy ending: another publisher thought his proposal was just right, and his book was published!

No matter what you wind up doing with them, try to learn from those letters—and learn to deal with rejection. Consider it a personal growth experience.

 SLUSH PILE

Don't respond to rejection letters with a rebuttal in writing or a nasty phone message. You can easily make enemies in the publishing world with such loose-cannon behavior. Your agent will not be pleased, and editors will not be pleased. Pin your rejections up on the wall and toss darts at them instead.

Going Once, Going Twice, ... Sold!

What if several publishers let your agent know they plan to make an offer for your book? To get the best price for it (in other words, the biggest advance), your agent will plan an *auction*.

Here's how an auction works:

- Your agent chooses a date and alerts the interested publishers.

- Your agent may establish a *floor*, a minimum bid, or reserve the right to decline unacceptable bids.

- On the day of the auction, your agent calls the editors for their bids. (Not all editors will end up bidding.)

- As the number rises, the agent continues to call editors and inform them of the latest price.

- At the end of the day (or days), the editor with the highest bid gets your book.

DEFINITION

When an agent has all interested publishers submit their bids on the same day, it's called an **auction.** This is the best way to get a high advance. The agent might also specify a minimum bid, called a **floor.**

An auction day can be very exciting for both the agent and the author. You'll find it hard not to call your agent every few minutes to check on things. Let your agent call you, though. She needs to keep her phone clear for editors with big checkbooks!

"How Much Can I Expect?"

This is the dreaded first question every new author asks an agent, and it's a question that's impossible to answer. The size of an advance depends entirely on the perceived size of the book's audience. It depends on how much the publishing house loves your book. It depends on how unique your book is. It depends on how many publishers are interested in your book. It depends on the timing of your book and how many competing titles are out there.

Other factors that can affect the size of an advance include whether the publishing industry is on an upswing or a downswing. The size and power of the publishing house that wants to buy your book figures in, too. Another factor may be whether that publishing house had a good year or a bad year. It may also make a difference if the publisher had a fight with his spouse or whether it's raining outside. Who knows?

No doubt you've been keeping an eye on the publishing business and have read many dire warnings. Yes, advances are indeed getting smaller. Some houses have floated the idea of "profit sharing," which is code for paying a smaller advance up front and sharing a bigger slice of profits later on (if there are profits later on). The HarperStudio imprint tried skipping advances and going to a profit sharing model, but pulled the plug on the experiment fairly quickly.

Nibbles

If an editor is interested in your book, chances are she'll call your agent before making a formal offer. This lets the agent know you've hooked at least one fish!

We filled Chapter 14 with information on how editors pull together information before making an offer, but in this chapter, let's just say that the first offer is never the best offer. Your agent works hard to try to get the offer increased.

Reeling 'Em In

As the author, you should be included in the action surrounding your book. Your agent will want to keep you abreast of interest, offers forthcoming or on the table, and any anticipated closing date. You should definitely be included in the conversation about money.

This does not mean that you, too, will talk to the editor. Money talk goes on between an agent and an editor; it does not include the author unless the editor has specifically requested a chance to talk to you before bidding. But you do get to approve the final deal—congratulations!

Breaking Up

You worked hard to get yourself an agent, and you got one! Now that agent has sold one or two of your books, and you're feeling … well, feeling like maybe you want to get a new agent. Like any relationship in life, dealings between writers and agents don't always work out smoothly forever. So can you change agents?

Yes, you can change agents. Most relationships between writers and agents go from book to book. If you want to change in between books, it should be fine. However, changing agents while a deal is being negotiated is verboten. And even if you've changed agents, the publisher will continue to send monies through the agent of record for a book as long as that book is in print.

The Least You Need to Know

- Know what you can expect from an agent who wants to represent you.
- Familiarize yourself with an agent/author agreement.
- An agent might ask you to make changes to your work, but you don't have to agree.
- Rejections sometimes have much useful information you can learn from.
- The size of an advance is totally unpredictable, but what is certain is that your agent will work to get you as large an advance as possible.

Submitting Directly to Editors

Chapter 13

In This Chapter

- Working without an agent
- University presses, small publishers, and niche publishing
- The world of children's books
- Basic submission guidelines
- Should you self-publish?
- Tips for publishing electronically

What do you do if you can't get an agent? Or what if you simply don't want to use one? Can you try to work directly with a publisher without the extra layer of an agent? Sometimes. In this chapter, you discover how to work with an editor one-on-one. We also explain some of the specialized situations in which agents aren't required. You learn how to make a professional submission without an agent, too.

It's entirely possible to get published without the help of an agent. Many writers have done it. In fact, in some areas of the publishing business, agents rarely, if ever, are used. Where? At university presses, scholarly publishers, regional publishers, some small presses, midlist nonfiction, and many children's publishers. Are these the only areas in which you can try without an agent? No, you can try to approach anyone on your own, but these are the areas of the business that might be most open to you working alone.

Let's take a quick look at the world of academia first.

The Ivy Leagues

University presses are a world unto their own, with specialized methods of editorial selection and approval. Acquisitions editors who work for university presses crisscross the country attending professional conferences and reading scholarly journals of all sorts—literary, anthropological, medical, sociological, and the like—to stay on top of what the current issues are and who's tops in the field. They familiarize themselves with the leading scholars in their field of publishing specialty and cultivate relationships with them in the hopes that these experts will someday write for them. To put it bluntly: in most cases, you don't call such editors—they call you.

EXPERTS SAY

Planning to turn your dissertation into a book? Then you need to buy a copy of *Revising Your Dissertation* (UC Press, 2002), which will guide you through the process of turning your dull, dry academic treatment into a lively read for the general public. The expert folks at UC Press in California know a thing or two about both academic and trade publishing.

Can you submit without being "summoned"? Yes. First, send an e-mail query to the acquisitions editor describing yourself and your book and then wait for the editor to respond. All the same rules for writing queries (that you learned in Chapter 7) apply.

University presses have even less money than other publishers and surely cannot afford to pay the return postage on all the unsolicited material they receive, so if you're going snail mail, remember your SASE.

Curriculum Vitae

An editor at a university press will take a long, hard look at your educational and scholarly credentials. If you don't have the right ones to back up your book, the chances are slim that a university press will take you on.

If an acquisitions editor does respond to your query, he or she might ask you to send in a "prospectus." Don't panic—that's just a book proposal by another name. Why the world of scholarly presses uses that term is unclear; perhaps it just sounds more scholarly.

Readers and Referees

Unlike a trade publisher with its pub board and editorial meetings, folks outside the university press primarily judge the early fate of a proposal.

If the editor likes what he or she sees in your prospectus, and if your credentials are up to snuff, your material is then sent to a *reader*, or a *referee*. These well-known professors and other experts are qualified to judge your material from a professional standpoint. Because the editor is seldom academically qualified to pass judgment on a manuscript, readers perform this critical task.

> **DEFINITION**
>
> University presses use **readers,** or **referees,** to help with the acquisitions process. These folks review and evaluate manuscripts written in their fields of expertise. They're either paid a fee or paid in kind with free books from the press.

How many readers or referees will see your material? Perhaps only one or maybe as many as three or four. It depends on the topic and the input from the first reader. Readers might sometimes recommend your book "with reservations." The editor then comes back to you and asks for changes or a response to the reservations.

Read More About It

The average print run from university presses is lower than what a trade publisher would do, but you might find that university presses have a longer-term commitment to keeping their books in print.

An excellent way to learn more about the world of university presses is through a book published by the Modern Language Association (MLA). The *MLA Style Manual and Guide to Scholarly Publishing* is the standard guide for graduate students preparing theses. Over the years, it has grown to include information on how to get published. Check to be sure you've got the most current edition.

Year after year at the annual MLA conference, many in the academic world decry the difficulty of having their scholarly work published. Do fewer presses, fewer opportunities to publish, and yet the same "publish or perish" atmosphere exist on campuses? Is academic publishing on the verge of disappearing, as so many at the conference fear? Not likely, but it is a specialized industry in which it is very difficult to succeed.

University presses sometimes venture into trade publishing territory. A recent example is *The Autobiography of Mark Twain*, published by the University of California Press, which spent weeks on the best-seller lists.

Small Can Be Good

Some of the success stories coming out of *small publishing* companies show that small can indeed be beautiful. Thriving presses exist all over the country, from Tennessee and Louisiana to Washington and Vermont, from New Mexico to Colorado. New York is less and less the only place where book publishing gets done.

Great small presses like Sasquatch in Seattle and McSweeney's in San Francisco are still willing to read unsolicited, unagented submissions. Here's what the website for McSweeney's, run by best-selling author Dave Eggers, says about submissions:

> We are happy to consider book submissions from anyone, regardless of publication history, agent, or spelling. However, one effect of this policy is that we tend to fall behind very quickly; we apologize in advance for our very slow response.

Mini-majors refers to independently owned publishers such as Running Press in Philadelphia, Chronicle Books in San Francisco, and Workman Publishing in New York. They're not big publishers with sales of hundreds of millions of dollars, but they're independently owned, medium-size companies with solid sales in the $20 million to $50 million range.

DEFINITION

How small is small? Instead, ask how large is small, as the case may sometimes be. The term **small publisher,** or *small press,* is used loosely but generally is applied to publishing houses with sales of less than $10 million a year. **Mini-majors** are publishers with $10 million to $50 million in annual sales.

Small publishers and the mini-majors are generally more open to dealing directly with authors than the New York houses are, and they can be somewhat less intimidating for a first-time author. Many a big-name author (including Deepak Chopra) got started with a small publisher before achieving fame with a larger house (much to the chagrin of the smaller publisher, which took a chance on an unknown).

When you work with a publisher that has a small staff, you can sometimes have a closer relationship with the editor, publicist, and other people working with your book.

Small publishers are seldom in the business of paying big advances, so cast aside your dreams of the big bucks up front if you're pursuing this route. The occasional small publisher might only offer authors a one-time payment for work-for-hire, but this is rare.

Before you can get your foot in the door at a small publisher, though, you need to introduce yourself in the same way you would to an agent—with a compelling query.

The Name Game

The best way to get your query read is to address it to an actual editor. How do you find out who the editors are at these small presses? Here are a few ways:

- Look on the acknowledgments page of other books from that publisher; authors often thank their editors.

- Look in *Jeff Herman's Guide to Book Publishers, Editors, and Literary Agents* or in the annual *Writer's Market* published by the same folks who do the *Writer's Digest* magazine.

- Check the publisher's website for information, or call the publishing house and ask which acquisitions editors acquire books in your genre.

- Read the free e-zine Publishers Lunch to learn the names and e-mail addresses of editors and who is buying what. Sign up at publishersmarketplace. com.

- Attend writer's conferences and meet editors face to face in pitch sessions and panels.

- Ask friends who are already published who they know.

Query an Editor

The query format you should use with a small publisher is essentially the same as outlined in Chapter 7. The only difference is that you're not trying to sell an agent; you're trying to sell an editor.

Review the advice in Chapter 7. Remember to keep your query short and to the point. But also remember that the purpose of a query is to sell yourself and your project. Talk up the market and talk up your commitment to seeing the book work. A word to the wise: if you're approaching editors directly because you've been dropped by your agent or had an unsuccessful experience with agents, keep that info to yourself. Starting off your query e-mail to an editor with a rambling explanation of why you don't have an agent will backfire.

Will you hear back from an editor at a small publisher? Yes, there's a good chance you will. How long it will take to hear back is anyone's guess. Remember the snippet from the kind folks at McSweeney's a few paragraphs back, "We apologize in advance for our very slow response." Resist the temptation to call and ask whether your e-mail got through or to follow up with endless e-mails asking about it. Even at small presses, an editor's day is hectic, often with no time to return phone calls about unsolicited queries, proposals, and manuscripts. Repeated e-mails will just tick them off.

EXPERTS SAY

Have you been dropped by your agent, who was unable to sell your project after a year or so? You're not alone. Mark Victor Hansen and Jack Canfield were dropped by their agent, too, just before the *Chicken Soup for the Soul* book sold to Health Communications. "Biggest mistake he ever made," they laugh, as the series sold more than 140 million books. Garth Stein, author of the best-selling novel *The Art of Racing in the Rain,* was "released" after his agent read the manuscript and told him he couldn't sell a book narrated by a dog. Agent Jeff Kleinman could, though.

Negotiating on Your Own

If an editor responds to your query and requests a copy of your proposal or your manuscript, you're one step closer to success. What happens then? Turn to Chapter 14 to find out. The acquisitions process for a small publisher is the same as that for a large publisher.

If the small publisher makes you an offer, then what? You can negotiate on your own, but if you decide to do so, you'll need to learn a lot in a hurry. Mark Levine's excellent book, *Negotiating a Book Contract,* can help you. Check to be sure you have the most recent edition. You can also join the Author's Guild (authorsguild.org), which offers a free contract review service to members.

Chapter 15 walks you through some of the basic points in a publishing contract. Some editors are also quite patient in explaining contract points to first-time authors. (Just don't forget they work for the house.)

> **HOT OFF THE PRESS**
>
> Lewis Buzbee, a San Francisco writer and college professor, sold his book *Alone Among Others: The Pleasures of the Bookstore,* to Jennifer at Prima Publishing on his own, without an agent. What did Jennifer find most compelling about Buzbee's proposal? The fact that he included letters of support for the book idea from publishers' sales reps. These are folks who have a terrific sense of what sells and why, so early approval from this group carried a great deal of weight in her decision. Could you pull this off, too? Maybe. Get to know booksellers, sales reps, and anyone else in the publishing world who might help you get a leg up in the process if you're doing it on your own.

An Agent, at This Point?

If you have an offer in hand, getting an agent should be no trouble now! Those same folks who weren't interested in helping you before would be happy to help you now that there's an offer on the table. But do you need an agent?

Fact is, if you don't think you can do a good job of negotiating on your own behalf, perhaps you should get an agent involved. At this point, the editor may be happy to refer you to an agent he or she has worked with before. Ask if the agent is willing to take a lower commission, though, because you got the deal on your own.

Ask yourself if it's worth it to give up 15 percent of a deal you landed on your own. It might be cheaper to hire a literary attorney (never a regular, nonliterary attorney, please) to review the contract for a flat fee or to pay the membership to the Author's Guild to use its free service.

The Hunt Is On

Small publishers and mini-majors sound great, but how do you find them? They're right there on the shelf next to the big boys! As you spend time in bookstores and online familiarizing yourself with the players in your category, you'll begin to spot the small publishers on your own. Many of them are listed in *Jeff Herman's Guide to Book Publishers, Editors, and Literary Agents* and in *Literary Market Place* (*LMP*).

If you're game, give it a try; small publishers just might be right for you.

Tight Niches

A discussion of small publishers has to include the "niche" publishers—the ones that specialize in one tight-niche market. A niche market can be anything from mountain-climbing books (The Mountaineers Press) to books on the occult (Samuel Weiser, Inc.), from Northwest travel books (Sasquatch Books in Seattle) to Southern travel books (Pelican Publishing Company). Chelsea Green is a publishing house with a slogan—"The Politics and Practice of Sustainable Living"—that tells you right up front what kinds of books it might be interested in hearing about and what it won't be interested in at all. The more familiar you become with your area of specialty, the more you'll notice niche publishers that cater directly to your market.

Don't spin your wheels trying to interest a large publisher when you can go directly to a small niche publisher that specializes in your area. These are the experts in the marketplace and will understand right away whether your book is marketable and how best to do it.

Niche publishers are very careful about the books they publish. The decision process will be slow, but if a smart niche publisher produces your book, the sales could be steady for years to come and possibly be greater than what might have been achieved by a large publisher that didn't have the same niche approach. Sure, we'd all like to be published by Knopf, but don't you think that if you wrote a book on composting, the folks at Chelsea Green might be more dedicated to keeping it around on the shelf for more than a few months?

Once Upon a Time ...

Children's books are another area in which you can sometimes deal directly with a publisher. Keep in mind that children's books include both picture books (written with an author and illustrator) and YA (young adult) novels and series. Some agents, such as Andrea Brown, specialize in representing children's books, but a large portion of children's authors does not have agents.

 DEFINITION

There are several different types of **children's books:** illustrated books, easy readers, and chapter books. Illustrated books are the lovely big picture books small children love to "read" over and over again. Easy readers are books of the "see Jane run" variety, and chapter books are longer books for more experienced readers.

How do you approach a children's book publisher about your idea? With a query, of course! Look for the names of editors in the most recent edition of *Jeff Herman's Writer's Guide to Book Publishers, Editors, and Literary Agents* or the more specialized *Writer's Guide to Children's Book Editors, Publishers, and Literary Agents.*

Another valuable resource is the Society of Children's Book Writers and Illustrators (SCBWI; scbwi.org). "I recommend so many writers to the Society of Children's Book Writers and Illustrators, it should pay me a commission!" laughs author Debra Keller. "The benefits of membership are tremendous: a list every August of all children's book publishers, the names of their editors, the submission guidelines, and what they are looking for." You don't need to have been previously published to join.

You also can call the publisher to ask for the names of its acquisitions editors and their areas of specialty. But if you do call, just get the names from the receptionist and politely hang up. Resist the urge to ask to speak to an editor directly at this point. Remember, in the early stages of getting published, all the work's done by written communication, not phone conversations. You must first prove that you can write.

You may also check the company's website to read up on its submissions guidelines. Once you discover them, pay very close attention to what they say. Do not get fancy and decide to try another approach. Guidelines have been developed over many years of publishing experience and should be heeded.

Be warned, however, that many children's publishers have ceased accepting unsolicited manuscripts altogether. These companies still will accept queries from first-time authors, though.

Many aspects of the children's book publishing industry can be quite different from regular publishing. If you plan to try to get a children's book published, pick up a copy of *The Complete Idiot's Guide to Publishing Children's Books, Third Edition.*

SLUSH PILE

Do not send an illustrated manuscript to a children's publisher. Illustrated manuscripts go first to the publisher's art department to be evaluated, not to the editor. If it doesn't meet with the art director's approval, it's rejected, and your actual words will never be seen or read. Submit only a manuscript. In children's publishing, the publisher traditionally matches authors with illustrators rather than buying a complete package from an unknown.

Poetry

Poetry is yet another category that usually doesn't require an agent—in fact, most agents don't represent poetry. If you want to have your poetry published, our best advice is to scour the poetry shelf in the library or bookstore and read more than one book on getting poetry published. Identify appropriate magazine, journal, and poetry book publishers, and query them according to their specific guidelines. Some books list appropriate publishers, but an even better technique is to read books and magazines of poetry. Ask poetry teachers as well as published poets for advice.

Don't get discouraged before you start. Poetry gets published all the time—just not very often via agents.

To Self-Publish or Not to Self-Publish?

If you've had no luck with agents and no luck submitting directly to publishers, what options do you have left? Is the only way your book will ever see its way into print if you yourself pay for it to be printed and bound?

You keep reading all these exciting stories about successful "indie" publishers. (Feel free to jump directly to Chapter 25 if you want to go in-depth about indie publishers. Otherwise, bear with us for a few more minutes ….)

Self-publishing is an old and honorable pursuit, and many of the literary world's glossiest names have published their own work at one time or another. Think we're just trying to make you feel better if this is your only option? Nope, this is the actual truth. Margaret Atwood, Virginia Woolf, Pat Conroy, Ken Kesey, … the list could go on forever. But how can you decide if self-publishing is right for you? After all, writing a book is an art. Self-publishing a book is a business.

To decide if self-publishing is the right route for you, go back to a very basic question we wanted you to consider in Chapter 1: why do you want to write a book? Now think about your answers. Which of those goals can be satisfied by self-publishing your book? Pretty much all of them could be except for fame and fortune. Sure, it has happened that a self-publisher has gone on to fame and fortune, but it is a fluke.

Do You Have What It Takes?

Not everyone is cut out to go the indie route. It requires lots of money, creativity, ingenuity, dedication, and entrepreneurial zeal. Indie e-book publishing sensation

Amanda Hocking sold a million books herself and then signed with St. Martin's because she no longer wanted the headache of doing it all herself.

Do you have what it takes? Asking yourself these questions might help you find out:

- Is publishing my book so important to me that I'm willing to pay thousands of dollars to see it happen?

- Am I willing to accept the fact that I'll probably never see that money again?

- After my book is published, am I willing to invest countless hours attempting to distribute, publicize, and market my book?

- Am I thick-skinned enough to take it if my book is criticized, ignored, or rejected by booksellers and/or the media?

- Am I persistent enough to keep going if I get that kind of treatment?

SLUSH PILE

If you're submitting an electronic query to editors or agents, check for viruses first! One hapless children's book author e-mailed a query to a long list of agents and editors (leaving the CCs showing so everyone knew it was a blanket submission) that included a vicious virus that attacked the computer of whoever opened it. Publishing folk around the country were furious. Her next submission will need to be under an assumed name ....

Speaking of Speaking ...

One of the best reasons to self-publish a book is to augment your speaking career. If you're already giving talks to rooms full of people, it might be quite easy to sell them a book you just happened to bring with you. Skip the headache of bookstore distribution, and keep all the money. Sounds great! And it can be done with a self-published book.

Wine expert Roxanne Langer decided she needed copies of her book *The 60 Minute Wine MBA* for a major talk and didn't have time or patience to wait around until the publishing world answered her, so she worked with a book designer, took her designed files to an Espresso Book Machine (learn more in Chapter 25), and 8 minutes later (yes, really) the books started to arrive. "It was amazing. I now have product to sell at my talks, and I have total control over the inventory."

Several excellent books are already available on how to self-publish a book. We really don't have enough room here to do a thorough job of covering the process, but here's a quick look at the steps you need to go through.

1. Find a copy editor and a proofreader.

2. Get the book designed and typeset.

3. Have a cover designed.

4. Find an affordable short-run printer.

5. Arrange for your book's distribution.

6. Market and publicize the book.

What if you just want to produce an indie e-book? Can you skip some of the steps? Not really. You don't need the printer, of course, but if what you want is a professional product, everything else is pretty much the same as producing a book you can hold in your hands.

Proof Positive

If your self-published book is a success, can you sell it to a larger publisher? Certainly! You have to stop selling it yourself then. If you can show a solid record of sales success with a self-published book, both agents and publishers will take you very seriously.

On the other hand, some best-selling self-publishers decide to stay indie instead of selling to a larger publisher. They might also ride it to the very top, like Amanda Hocking did, to cut a bigger deal with a large publisher.

You're on Your Own

You now know many of the circumstances in which you can try to get your work published without an agent. When submitting on your own behalf to any kind of publisher, be it a children's publisher, a niche publisher, or a small publisher, be as businesslike as possible. Review the chapters on queries and proposals before you begin to compile your materials, keeping in mind that you're directing your information to a book editor, not an agent.

Publisher Jere Calmes at Entrepreneur Press attributes one of his most successful book series to an "over-the-transom" submission (an old-fashioned term for "unsolicited," from back in the day when there was a transom opening over every office door). Here's what he likes to see in a query from an author:

> A proposal no longer than 40 pages and a very detailed table of contents. Not just the names of the chapters, but several sentences for each chapter that truly detail the information. And the more testimonials you can round up—meaningful testimonials from people who know your work and have commented upon it—the better.

An editor like Jere has the same concerns as an agent: the potential market for the book, the author's credentials, and the uniqueness of the idea. Just as an agent's career depends on finding successful authors, so, too, does the editor's career flourish when he or she finds great writers whose books sell well. Editors are always looking for new writers. Help them find you!

The Least You Need to Know

- It is possible—and quite common—to approach university presses, children's publishers, and small publishers without an agent.
- Learn the names of the editors, and approach them directly with short queries.
- Respect the system: queries first and proposals later (if requested). Don't try to call editors directly before they've had a chance to review something from you in writing.
- When you have a deal in hand, you should be able to get an agent, but ask for a reduced commission.
- Self-publishing requires both money and dedication, but it can be emotionally rewarding and can perhaps help boost your career.

Behind Closed Doors

In This Chapter

- The first hurdle: the editor
- The pub board meeting
- Competition and sales projections
- Production costs and P&Ls

So far on your mission to get published you wrote a great query and a superb book proposal. An agent answered your e-mail right away and then called you up and offered to represent you. Or no agents responded and you decided to take up the task yourself. Twelve copies of your proposal have been sent to 12 editors at the 12 publishing houses best suited for your book. Your fingers are crossed, and you're saying your prayers nightly. What happens now?

Hurry Up and Wait

Several things could happen. An editor reads her e-mail and discovers your proposal. Intrigued after reading just a few paragraphs, she prints it out and sets it aside on a stack of material she plans to take home and read more thoroughly.

Or your agent may have placed an advanced call to an editor to get him excited about the proposal before he reads it. Your proposal arrives and the editor thinks—*Ah, yes, this is the book Mr. Agent described. I must take a look at it right away; it sounded perfect for our* list. He scrolls through a few pages and decides to read it more thoroughly on his iPad during his commute home.

DEFINITION

The **list,** or plan, is a schedule of books (or types/prices) editors have committed to their bosses and their bosses have committed to their bosses for planning purposes. In any given year, an editor is responsible for bringing in a set number of titles for the list. "It's on our list," an editor might say, or "We have a few holes on our list that need filling"—these phrases are music to an agent's ears. Perhaps *your* book is just perfect for their list!

Or your agent might have gone to lunch with an editor the day before. Over a spinach salad, your agent pitched the editor a number of book projects from several clients. The editor expressed an interest in seeing one or two of them (including yours!), and the agent sent it that same afternoon. The editor decided to take it home and … you know the rest.

Editors don't read much at the office. Yes, they do read queries, but most of the real reading gets done at home. When Jennifer was an editor, she was also the mother of two small boys. Rather than read all night at home, she would go to lunch with large stacks of manuscripts and queries she'd printed out. Don't be hurt if your material comes back smudged and coffee stained; it means an editor took the time to read it thoroughly!

However it got there, and no matter in what condition it comes back to you, your proposal is now inside the doors of a publishing house.

"Sorry, Not Right for Our Needs at This Time"

Sadly, the story could easily end right here. The editor might not put your proposal on the stack she plans to take home. Perhaps she took a look at your proposal and decided to pass. Why? Well, for any one of a number of reasons. You might not make it as far as the editorial meeting for these reasons:

- It's clearly not appropriate for that publishing house—your book is about the history of fighter pilots, and this publisher publishes only vegetarian cookbooks.

- The publishing house already has a book on that topic, and it hasn't sold well.

- The publishing house already has a book on that topic, and the author of that book plans to do more in that area.

- The editor doesn't think a large market exists for your book.

Most rejections do not include any actual reason why your book was rejected. The standard line is "Thank you, but this is not right for us." Why don't editors write more? Two reasons: they don't have the time to analyze, critique, and then write to you, and they don't want to invite a response or rebuttal from you. Try to take your rejections in stride.

Who knows, you eventually might end up selling your book to that same editor at a different house. In Chapter 13, we mentioned the book series Jere Calmes of Entrepreneur Press bought after it came over the transom from a different house. It was turned down when he pitched it there, but after changing jobs and joining another house, he pitched it and was successful the second time. So be nice to editors—be very, very nice!

Publishing is a people business, and the people who work in publishing are people just like you. Sometimes they're tired, cranky, and not in the mood to buy books. If your book proposal has been rejected by one editor, don't take this as a sign that your project is doomed and will never be published by anyone. Perhaps it just was a bad day at the office when your material crossed that editor's desk. Keep trying, and go on to the next publisher.

Consider This

But if your book does make it onto the stack to be read further, then what?

Editors do quite a bit of investigating before bringing your proposal to a meeting. An editor might call your agent to ask questions or request more material. An editor might call you directly to learn more about you, the market for the book, and your plans to promote it. Editors also do more hands-on investigation: prowling around bookstores to examine the competing titles, visiting websites on the topic, asking friends in the industry how well that category is selling, and checking sales numbers of similar books on BookScan.

The phone rings, and it's an editor asking about your book. Although the questions may all relate to the book itself, the editor might have another motive. How well you present yourself on the phone is critical to your book's future success. Editors want authors who can handle themselves easily with interviews and the media. If you're tired, distracted, or otherwise unprepared to sound good on the phone, it's better to beg off and reschedule the conversation.

If the editor likes what he sees in the proposal, what he hears from you, and what his own research turns up, the next step is for him to present it to his colleagues and superiors for possible publication.

Committee Decisions

As powerful as many of them are, editors do not make the decision to publish a book on their own. That decision rests with a group of people sometimes called the *pub board* or *editorial board*. The editor who likes your book is only one voting member of this group. Other members usually include some combination of other editors; the publisher; and folks from the sales, marketing, and publicity departments. The process works something like this:

- An editor is intrigued by your proposal and decides to present it to the pub board.

- The editor brings your proposal to a meeting.

- The editor makes a short presentation about your book and attempts to drum up interest and enthusiasm.

- The editor answers questions from other members of the group. Sometimes the editor needs to do further research and presents the book in more detail at a future meeting.

DEFINITION

Unless it's a one-person publishing house, your proposal will be presented to an **editorial board,** or **pub board.** This is a group of people who collectively make the decision about what titles to publish.

"At Andrews McMeel, our first meeting is just with the other editors," explains Lane Butler. "It is more informal; with no sales or marketing staff in attendance there is less pressure. Collectively we look at the proposals and ideas not only for content, but also for ways in which it could be made stronger. We meet at least once a week, and every editor gets a chance to present one or two projects they really like. After that first meeting a proposal would go on to the acquisitions group, which does include sales and marketing."

So that's it. The fate of your book can be decided in about 10 minutes. But if you get past this point, then what happens? Does the editor call to say he wants to make an offer? No, not yet.

How's It Gonna Sell?

Even if an editor has successfully lined up support in the meeting, there's still more work to be done. Remember, publishing is a business, and in business, the bottom line is king. So the editor has to work up the numbers to see whether publishing your book will pay off. How is this done?

Editors often ask the sales department for help. Experienced sales folks can help the editor figure out what the typical orders would be for the proposed book. How many copies would Barnes & Noble buy? What about Target? Is there a chance Walmart would pick it up? Small independent bookstores across the country? They add up all these numbers and hope the result is big.

SLUSH PILE

The power and influence of the publishing sales department has grown in recent decades. Although there was a time when the typical sales department wouldn't find out what was on the list until the sales conference, it's now often included in the front-end decisions about what to publish—either just before or just after the book is approved. If the sales department doesn't think it can sell a book to its customers, the book probably doesn't get published. End of story.

The publicity department may also be polled at this point. The editor talks with the publicity folks about whether the topic of the book (or the name of the author) lends itself to publicity.

The editor might also send an e-mail to someone in the production department to check on the typical production costs for a book of this type.

All these numbers are plugged into the P&L, the profit and loss statement. If the numbers look good, the editor reports back to the pub board. And then maybe, just maybe, the title will be approved and the editor will get the go-ahead to make an offer.

The Meeting Begins

Let's take a close look at what goes on in one of these meetings. This gives you a good idea how all the information you dredged up for your proposal comes into play.

It's a Tuesday afternoon at Big Publishing Company, Inc., and all the members of the pub board are gathered in a conference room. The editors carry armloads of book proposals and other materials. In any given meeting, the fate of 10 or more books is decided. The editor printed out the materials you sent, made copies for everyone at the meeting, and has high hopes for the books he's decided to champion. Chances are most of them will fail. Harsh, but true.

Batter Up!

Editor 1 leads off with her first proposal: a book of affirmations and prayers for breast cancer survivors. She describes the focus of the book, the reason the world needs this book, the qualifications of the woman who put it together, and the impact the book could have on the women who read it.

The sales manager speaks up with a question: "How many books already exist on this topic? And just how large is the market? What are the current figures on breast cancer occurrence?"

The editor has carefully read the proposal and knows the answers to these questions because the author did her research well. It was all right there for her.

The publisher wants to know: "There is a strong title already on the subject from another publisher. How will this book be different enough to find an audience? I worry that the buyers won't see a need to order another similar title."

Once again the editor answers the questions and concerns with authority. The author of the book has researched the competing titles, talked to bookstore managers about the need, and lined up the support of a major breast cancer survivors group. A solid proposal has all the answers.

So the pub board is interested in considering this title. What happens then? Few acquisitions are made with just one meeting. The editor spends the next few days phoning and e-mailing the other departments to gather more information on how much it would cost to produce this book and how many copies they can expect to sell. She calls the agent or the author with any questions about the proposal she couldn't answer herself. She distributes copies of the proposal to those interested in reading it.

When the editor has rounded up all the answers, she makes a short follow-up presentation at the next pub board meeting (whenever that is, they get cancelled and postponed all the time, to the frustration of editors, agents, and authors who are waiting for an answer). If the numbers are right and the group is still feeling positive, the group decides to go on to the next phase: making an offer to publish the book.

Next Up!

Editor 2 gets a turn. He begins his presentation on a book about the history of base-ball cards. "This will be the first-ever book on the topic," he says proudly, reading the proposal from his laptop.

"Oh, come on!" says the publicity manager. "I am a collector myself and own at least two books on the history of baseball cards."

The editor stammers and advances through the pages of the proposal, looking for something to salvage the situation. Turns out the proposal has great graphics but not much solid information. "Ah, but this is the first time that the cards will be organized by player position rather than team! That is really unique!"

"Just like the book I have on my shelf," the publicity manager snickers.

Another book bites the dust.

HOT OFF THE PRESS

The worst thing you can do in a book proposal is lie. If you lie or fib about your qualifications, if you lie about the competing books, or if you lie about the sales history of your other books, you are headed for disaster. Editors never forget and will certainly not forget if they are made to look foolish with information you supplied. Think you can try to fool one editor at one house and then move on to the next if that fails? Don't be surprised if your first editor moves, too. A bad reputation spreads quickly and is hard to shed. Always play straight.

Show and Tell

You can see how critical the information you provide in your proposal is to your future success. When compiling a proposal, pretend you, too, are a member of a pub board. Put yourself in that person's shoes, and try to anticipate all the negative or hard-hitting questions that might be asked. Then supply the answers in your proposal. Give the editor something to work with.

Jere Calmes, a longtime acquisitions editor who is now the publisher of Entrepreneur Press, likes to think of an acquisitions meeting as a grown-up version of show and tell. "The editor has to tell people why they want to publish your book, so give them as much to show as possible!"

Second Chances?

Is there ever a second chance? If an editor flops with your proposal once, can he or she ever try it again? Seldom, but it happens. It has nothing to do with begging or pleading on your part, though.

If the editor has truly fallen in love with your book project, he might go back to square one. He might poke around some more in the marketplace, ask more questions of friends in the industry, and try to gather ammunition to convince the skeptics that this book would succeed. If the information he gathers is compelling enough, and if his own commitment to the book is strong enough, it just might work the second time around. He might suggest that you reframe or refocus your idea somewhat. Perhaps there's a way to add a celebrity or higher profile person to the project to give it the larger platform the publisher wants before it'll take a chance.

But if the answer was "no" and the editor doesn't have the heart or the interest to re-pitch the project, you have probably come to the end of the road—the end of the road with that publisher, anyway. If you've been in touch with the editor prior to his editorial presentation, chances are he'll fill you in on what kinds of problems he ran into. Use this valuable information and try to make changes to your proposal or plans before you submit it to another house.

Congratulations are in order, though. Only a tiny fraction of book projects ever make it to the pub board stage, so you have succeeded. Keep trying. If one editor was interested enough to pitch it, another one will be, too.

They Like Me! They Really Do!

What if the answer is "yes"? Go ahead and pop open the bottle of champagne. The editor succeeded with the pub board and got the go-ahead to make you an offer—way to go! Now what happens?

The editor will call you, or your agent if you have one. The conversation will sound something like this: "I've got good news! We'd like to publish your book. I'd like to make you an offer of an advance against future royalties of …."

Money, Money, Money, Money

The editor doesn't make the decision to publish on her own, nor does she decide the size of the offer on her own. In the pub board discussion or in a one-on-one with the publisher, all decision-makers determine the range of the advance. The editor then has the authority to call either the agent or the author (if there is no agent involved) to make the offer.

Understand that a smart editor will never make her highest offer first. This is particularly critical information to have if you're working without an agent. If the editor has been approved to offer $18,000, she might first offer $15,000 to give herself room to go up. It's a basic negotiating tactic. So brush up on your own negotiating skills and ask for more.

The Numbers Game

The size of the advance could vary from small to large. There's no way to predict exactly how much you'll be offered. If you have an agent, chances are he will immediately ask for a larger figure. (Remember, the more you make, the more your agent makes.) If you don't have an agent, should you ask for a bigger number, too?

It never hurts to ask, but ask for a reasonable increase over what's being offered. You might also risk looking like an egotist if you counter with what the editor thinks is an unreasonable sum. And you risk being told, "No, we won't go any higher." On the other hand, if you are just thrilled that someone wants to publish your book, take the offer.

There's much talk from agents and longtime authors about how advances are smaller now than they used to be, or that sometimes publishers are not offering an advance at all. If that's the case, you need to think hard about what your goals are and if you're willing to take a chance on your own idea.

Other Considerations in the Offer

Do you need to bone up on negotiating techniques to deal directly with an offer? Thankfully, publishing isn't a particularly cut-throat business. In Chapter 15, we walk you through each contract clause and let you know which ones are easiest to negotiate and change.

Congratulations, you are getting published!

The Least You Need to Know

- Editors present proposals to a pub board made up of representatives from several different departments.
- If the sales department is not enthusiastic about a book idea, it seldom goes any further.
- The better the information in your proposal, the easier it is for an editor to gain support for your book.
- Never lie, exaggerate, or exclude important information from your proposal; it can only hurt you.
- If you get a "yes," you'll likely be offered an advance, which you (or your agent) might be able to negotiate upward.

The Party of the First Part

In This Chapter

- Boilerplate contract clauses
- "Half-and-half" advances and beyond
- The 13 major flex points
- Rights, royalties, and remainders
- Bonuses and other contract sweeteners

An offer is in and a contract is coming. Your book project is becoming more real by the moment. Someday you really will be able to walk into a bookstore and see your book on the shelf.

But first you have to sign a contract.

We are not lawyers. After working with hundreds of contracts over the years, however, we do have a fairly good handle on what it all means. In this chapter, you learn the meaning behind many of the standard clauses found in a publishing contract. Then we give you the inside scoop on which clauses we've found to be more negotiable than others.

Whereas and *Therefore*

Regardless of the size of the publishing company, most contracts are essentially the same. Some are considerably longer than others (40 pages is the longest we've seen), but the basic points are the same. Each contract begins as a *boilerplate contract*, a kind of skeleton contract waiting to be negotiated and changed.

> **DEFINITION**
>
> The publisher's standard contract is referred to as a **boilerplate contract.** It's the standard contract that's always used, and it has not (yet) been modified with any changes you might request.

What's the purpose of a book contract? A publishing company wants to publish a work you wrote and needs to have a legal document that does the following:

- Gives the company the right to publish and sell your material in agreed-upon territories and in agreed-upon formats

- Outlines the monetary arrangements

- Establishes your right to grant the company the rights

- Spells out the responsibilities of the author and the publisher

- States a time length for the agreement

Pretty simple, isn't it? Then why does it take so many darn pages to establish those simple facts? Is that because lawyers bill by the hour? Perhaps. But the business world grows more complicated by the decade, and new legal issues crop up all the time. As you might imagine, the contract for, say, a Hemingway book would not have mentioned an e-book version. E-book rights on old contracts have become a major hot-button issue, and agents like Andrew Wylie even stepped into the fray and floated the idea that they will publish their own clients' e-books for well-known classics. That didn't go over well ….

A publishing contract has 15 major clauses. Most points are negotiable, and editors will tell you which ones are not (like the indemnity and warranty clauses). So if you want something, ask for it. You might not get it, but at least you asked—and you might get something more than you had before. Negotiating a publishing contract is all about choosing battles. Be prepared to let a few things go, and decide in advance what they will be. In the following sections, we fill you in on which points are the easiest to get changed.

> **SLUSH PILE**
>
> So you don't have an agent. Do you need a lawyer? Actually, most lawyers have little knowledge about the quirks found in publishing contracts. An editor won't be pleased to hear from your lawyer either, if he or she isn't familiar with a publishing contract. To find a lawyer who specializes in publishing, contact the Author's Guild (authorsguild.org).

The Work

One of the early paragraphs in a contract defines what is generally called the "Work." This, of course, is your book. Your book is henceforth referred to as the "Work" in the contract. You get to be the "Author," and the company is forever known as the "Publisher."

In this paragraph, the subject matter of the work is defined. If you're writing a novel, it's defined as a work of fiction, and the general focus of the book is mentioned. If you're writing a nonfiction book, the work is described as "a Work of nonfiction whose subject matter is as follows …." The expected length of your finished manuscript is also stated.

Why is this here? The publishing company needs to be sure the book you turn in is the book it had in mind when it signed you up. This clause protects the publisher from signing you up to write a novel about the Civil War, only to have you turn in a nonfiction memoir about your childhood in New Orleans.

Copyright

Standard publishing contracts state that the publisher will register the copyright to the work in the name of the author. Beware of any contract that asks you to assign all rights to the publisher or that stipulates that the publisher is the copyright holder. Unless the author gives the right away, he or she owns the copyright by virtue of having written the material. In fact, the minute you put pen to paper and write something original, it is copyrighted material without you even so much as filling out a form.

On the other hand, if you're doing "work for hire," it's standard for the publisher to own the copyright.

Tentatively Titled

This section of the contract might also contain a zinger, a phrase that refers to the book as "tentatively titled." Tentatively titled? But you thought of your title years ago, and it's all over your queries and proposals. How can the publisher refer to it as tentatively titled?

Sorry, but most publishing contracts allow the publisher the right to change the title of your book. Some state that the title can be changed only "by mutual agreement."

Your delivery date (the day your manuscript is due) also appears in this early section of the contract.

The Advance

Ah, the money part. This is where the publisher spells out exactly how much (or how little) of an advance against future royalties you will receive. The language reads something like this:

> As an advance against all monies accruing or payable to the Author under this Agreement, the Publisher will pay to the Author the sum of _____, payable as follows ….

Payable as follows? Regardless of the size of your advance, do not expect to receive it in one lump sum. Those glittering sums you read about in the paper—like the millions retired politicians or reality TV stars are offered—aren't paid out all at once either. One arrangement is for two payments: one payment upon signing the contract, and the second tied to the completion of the final manuscript. (Some of the big ones have final payment tied to publication.)

The language and terms for the final payment vary widely, with some publishers paying when you turn in the manuscript on your delivery date and other publishers not paying until the manuscript has been edited. Those are the most common advance payouts but not the only ones.

A few publishers have gone to three payments of one third each, with the final payment upon publication of the book. Others pay one third upon signing, the second third upon receipt of one half of the manuscript, and the final third upon receipt of the remainder of the manuscript. If it's your first book, they might tie a payment to completion of revisions.

Why won't they just write you a check for the whole sum? The publisher needs to know that you will follow through and turn in a manuscript on the topic and in the style you promised in your book proposal. The best way to do this is to hold back part of the money until that happens. The publisher also wants to be sure what you turn in is publishable—hence, the second payment is generally linked to receipt of an acceptable manuscript.

Grant of Rights

This is where you, as the author, grant and assign the rights to your work to the publisher. This is what gives the publisher the legal right to publish and sell your book.

In addition to the right to sell your book in bookstores and other retail outlets, this clause may also grant the publisher the right to do these things:

- License the work to book clubs
- Sell the English-language book in foreign countries
- License foreign-language editions of the work
- Produce or license electronic versions or multimedia versions
- Produce or license audio book versions
- Produce or license hardcover, trade paperback, or mass market paperback versions
- License newspaper and magazine excerpts or serializations
- License movie rights
- License commercial or merchandising rights (maybe even coffee cups and T-shirts)
- Produce other sundry items, such as Braille versions or a play based on your book

Sounds like a lot of rights, right? This is a complicated section, one agents love to tackle in detail. Publishers believe they should be granted all these rights to be given a chance to earn back the money invested in your book—and they often have whole teams of people focused on selling these rights, called subrights (see Chapter 10). On the other hand, agents like to retain as many rights as possible on behalf of the author to obtain extra income for both of you!

HOT OFF THE PRESS

As the author, you're not selling your book rights to the publisher; you're merely *licensing* the rights. When you license a right, you continue to own it for the life of your copyright, which currently is 95 years. The publisher may exercise certain rights that you grant it only for the term of the license. After that term has expired, those rights revert to you.

There is some flexibility in this clause. Although most rights categories call for a 50/50 split of monies received between the publisher and the writer, you can negotiate the percentage with the editor. The most common change has to do with first serial rights. (This is when a section of the book appears in a magazine before the book is published and available in stores. Authors can sometimes get 90/10, with the 90 in their pocket!) It's not unusual, either, for foreign rights to be split 75/25 in favor of the author.

Be aware, though, that the less money the publisher receives, the less likely it will try to market those rights. Remember that hanging on to some of your rights is only worth something if someone wants to buy them.

Royalties

In the royalty section of the contract, the publisher defines exactly what the author receives from the sale of the book. There are two different ways to calculate royalties:

- As a percentage of the retail price printed on the book

- As a percentage of the publisher's net, the actual cash the publisher receives from the sale of the book after discounts have been deducted

Royalties based on the retail price usually range from 7 to 15 percent or more. Royalties based on net may start higher, at 10 percent, and escalate from there. This kind of arrangement is going away, and we see fewer and fewer retail price contracts.

Your contract should clearly state what type of royalties you receive for each copy of your book sold. Whether a publisher pays net or retail royalties is a policy set by its financial advisers. Changing from net to retail is not typically a negotiation point.

The royalties clause might also be where you find information on what share (or "split") the author receives of any subsidiary rights income if any of the rights the publisher is granted earlier in the contract (book clubs, mass market paperback, and so on) are sold.

You also find information on how many free copies of the book the author receives after it is published and whether the author can buy more copies at an author's discount.

This is also where your royalty percentage for an e-book version should be stated. What will it be? It's anyone's guess right now. Although the early e-book contracts paid a royalty that was roughly in line with any other type of format (hardcover or paperback), writers and agents hit the roof and demanded a larger percentage. So try to get as much as you reasonably can. The e-book percentages will standardize over time.

Delivery of Manuscript and Corrections

The hard, cold truth is revealed here: the date by which you must turn in your completed manuscript. It might be a few short months, or it might be years away.

What happens if the date arrives and the publisher does not receive your finished work? The contract includes language to the effect that the publisher has the right to terminate the contract, generally upon written notification of the author by the publisher. Not right away, of course; most contracts give at least 30 days. If this happens, the contract states, the author is obligated to repay the publisher any sums advanced to the author.

The contract also includes language that allows the publisher to reject the work as unpublishable or to request specific changes to the manuscript. The contract should state a process by which the author can address the changes. If the publisher still feels that the manuscript is unacceptable, the contract can be terminated.

Once again, this language is included because the publisher needs to be protected against receiving a shoddy product. In the case of nonfiction books, the publishing house probably made its decision based on only a proposal and a sample chapter. If the book ultimately turned in does not offer the proper information or isn't written professionally, a publisher can pull the plug.

Other Deliverables

The contract outlines the publisher's expectations regarding photographs, illustrations, maps, and charts. Who pays and when it needs to be turned in is spelled out in this section.

Be advised that if your book requires photographs, you may be expected to pay for them and also any licensing fees if the photos belong to someone else. Be sure you discuss this with your agent or editor.

Options

The publisher is taking a chance on your book. If it becomes a success, the house might want to publish more of your work. In the *option clause*, the contract states that the publisher gets the first crack at your next work, the book you write after the book under contract. The language gives your publisher the exclusive right to consider your next work and describes how long the publisher has to make an offer. It may also say that if your publisher bids on the next work, you cannot sell the next work to another publisher for a lesser sum. It also specifies the earliest date the next work can be submitted for consideration.

> **DEFINITION**
>
> Most contracts contain an **option clause** for the author's next work. This means that the publisher gets first crack at the next book you write, or the next book of the same type.

The clause might also cover competing works. The publisher doesn't want you to publish a similar book with a different publisher that would compete with this one.

The option clause and the noncompete clause can sometimes cause trouble for working writers. Later in this chapter, you find some ways to deal with this issue.

Author's Representations, Warranties, and Indemnity

In this clause, you, as the author, are assuring the publisher that the work is original and that you have the "sole and exclusive right to make the grant of rights set forth herein …." You also are assuring the publisher that you are not slandering, libeling, or invading anyone's privacy with your work.

If legal action arises from the publication of your book, this clause allows the publisher to stand aside and point directly to you: "He's the one you want; he wrote the words. We just printed the darn thing." This clause might also outline the legal procedure if a lawsuit arises. Some publishers carry libel insurance; some do not. This clause is also going to point out that in the case of a lawsuit, the publisher will manage the defense and provide the legal team. This is because most large publishers have legal teams who know publishing law inside and out and are going to have the best idea of how to handle a situation.

Although you might or might not agree with the wording in these clauses, this section of the contract is often not up for negotiation.

There have been some interesting developments in this area, mainly having to do with Twitter posts. Just after the Egyptian uprising, a publisher announced an instant e-book based on tweets from protestors. Hmmm, who owns a tweet? How can you track down and get permission for every tweet? If you're putting together a book based on something like this, start talking to your editor now about what kinds of legal releases the publisher will expect you to chase down.

Obligations of the Publisher

You have promised to deliver a manuscript by a certain date, and in this clause the publisher promises to publish the manuscript by a certain date. Other than exceptions mentioned in the contract (such as labor strikes, acts of God, or other circumstances beyond the publisher's control), if the publisher does not publish it, what then? There should be language that allows the author to terminate the agreement and keep the advance.

Many standard publishing contracts give the publisher a full 18 months to publish—an eternity in today's world.

Accounting

You've already been informed about the amount of royalties you'll receive, but when exactly will this be paid to you? The contract has a paragraph that outlines the schedule. Some publishers pay twice a year; some pay only once a year.

This section should also include language describing what happens in the case of overpayment (if the publisher's accounting department accidentally sends you too much money!) or if audits are requested by the author. It is within any author's right to request an audit if inadvertent irregularities in payments arise.

Overstock, Out of Print, or Reversion of Rights

If your book goes out of print, or if the sales dwindle down to nothing, what then? The answers are found in this section of the contract. Most contracts state that if the book goes out of print for a particular length of time, the rights revert to the author.

Currently, this clause is a huge flashpoint, thanks to the existence of print on demand (POD). It used to be that if your book stopped selling, you could eventually get the rights back to your material. But if a publisher can keep it "in print" forever simply by printing a copy whenever one is ordered, then what? Again, something to talk about seriously with your agent or editor to be sure you understand the implication.

This clause also gives the publisher the right to sell your book at *remainder* prices, if need be.

DEFINITION

When a book ends up being sold at a steeply discounted price, it is called **remaindering.** Books are sold for pennies on the dollar to remainder companies (who then sell them back to bookstores for the bargain tables). Before a book is remaindered, most publishers offer the author the chance to buy copies at bargain prices.

Assignment

After you sign the contract, your heirs are legally bound by it as well. This means that if you die, the publisher still has the rights to the book. This clause also allows the publisher to assign the rights to your book to a new company if your publisher sells the business.

Bankruptcy

This clause covers the possibility of the publisher's bankruptcy, not yours. Your book rights are an asset now, and according to most contracts, if the publisher goes bankrupt, the author may buy back the rights to the book or the publisher's assets will be sold. But it may leave the publisher the right to sell any remaining copies of the book in inventory without paying any royalties.

Agency Clause

If you're represented by an agent, an agency clause will appear in your contract. If you're not using an agent, this clause won't appear.

The agency clause names the agent as the person to whom the publisher should send all monies accruing to this book. The agent will then subtract his or her percentage and pass on the balance to you. As long as the book remains under contract to this publisher, the agent receives the royalty check.

What happens if you and your agent someday have a falling out and part ways, or if you decide to change agents? You are committed to the agent stated in your contract. You won't be able to call the publisher and ask them to start sending checks directly to you or your new agent. The checks for this title will still go to the agent listed in the contract unless both you and the agent send a letter to the publisher.

HOT OFF THE PRESS

"Verification of facts" is also a hot-button issue in publishing due to the bad taste (bad publicity for the publishing industry) left by a few flagrant examples like James Frey's *A Million Little Pieces* or the elderly gentleman who claimed that he was kept alive in a concentration camp by a little girl who would bring him apples. Except it wasn't true, as the publisher discovered just before the book was headed to the printer. Some publishers have begun to spot check nonfiction works in a way they never did before, just to protect themselves from embarrassment.

Electronic Rights

The term *electronic rights* is very broad and can mean different things, so it's important to look at each right individually.

Verbatim electronic rights. This is the right to make a book available online, noninteractively, or on a handheld device such as a Kindle, a Nook, an iPad, or whatever new thing is invented next. This is also known as "electronic display rights."

Database. This refers to an electronic collection of writings such as an anthology or a cookbook.

Interactive. This is an electronic version of the book enhanced by a third party (the publisher, for example) with material, such as audio or video elements or illustrations, that allows the reader to manipulate the text. You might have heard this referred to as a "vook," or video-enhanced book. Publishers increasingly either are insisting on keeping this right or are retaining the first option of exploiting it. Even when an author does keep this right, it's important not to compete with the published version of the book. The publisher might get angry and might have cause to litigate, and it's not necessarily beneficial to the author.

Print on demand. This refers to short-run printing, using an electronic file to print a small number of copies of the book, as and when they are needed, relatively inexpensively. In the past, it was very expensive to print a small number of books; even 1,000 was considered small. Now books can be printed one or a few at a time. When publishers control print on demand, they either use it to authorize wholesalers or retailers to print copies as needed or they do so themselves. When authors control print on demand, they can publish books themselves through services such as those offered by Xlibris or with the Espresso Book Machine.

Print on demand seems to be most valuable to published authors whose books no longer generate enough sales to warrant standard print runs but who have found an audience. Another value to print on demand applies to promotional speakers or people who make a living giving seminars. These authors can sell books from a table in the back of the room. This is a cheap way to make professional-looking books available.

So Is Anything Negotiable?

Most things in life are negotiable, particularly contracts. As we mentioned before, we've each spent hundreds of hours working with publishing contracts, so we know a thing or two about where publishers might be willing to make changes. Don't take this as legal advice, but rather as guidance from two learned colleagues.

Here are the 13 major flex points:

- Who pays for the index
- Who pays for illustrations, photos, and similar parts
- What sales territories the publisher has the rights to
- Splits and serial rights issues
- Commercial and dramatic rights/merchandising rights
- How many free copies the author receives
- The delivery date
- An author expense budget
- High-discount/reduced royalties clauses
- Joint accounting
- Next work and option clauses
- Electronic rights
- Reversion of rights

We've seen publishers make concessions in these clauses many times. Let's examine them closely.

Who Pays for the Index?

Most contracts call for the author either to provide the index or to pay for a professional index. Ever tried to do an index? Forget it. We recommend asking that the publisher pay for the index or at least split the cost with the author. Indexing can cost several dollars a page, so the bill can be steep. If the publisher won't pay the entire amount or won't split the cost, ask for a cap on the cost.

If you end up having to pay for the cost of the index, be sure it comes out of your future royalties so you don't have to pay for it out of your advance or out of your pocket.

Who Pays for Illustrations, Photographs, and Other Such Things?

For books in which photographs play a central part, the cost is usually borne by the author. When designing the book, if the publisher thinks photographs add to the book (food photography, for instance), the publisher should pay. The publisher usually pays for illustrations that decorate the book, but the author pays for illustrations for necessary charts.

Be sure you understand who pays for what, and feel free to ask the publisher to pay a larger share. Sometimes the author needs to deliver only what is known as scrap art: rough sketches of suggested art for the publisher to have drawn professionally.

The Sales Territory

The publisher will, quite literally, ask to publish the book in every language in every format throughout the whole world—not just the United States and Canada but tiny territories you've never even heard of. It wants the right to publish the book in the English language throughout the whole world, and it also requests the right to license foreign publishers to translate the book into other languages.

Some publishers do exploit these foreign rights well; others routinely distribute in the United States and Canada and let all the other territories languish. If you have an agent, your agent might want to keep foreign rights on your behalf and try to sell them directly to foreign publishers, so he or she will try to retain this right for you.

When publishers license translation rights, they split the monies received from foreign publishers with the author. If you don't have an agent, at least ask if there's any flexibility regarding the split. Some contracts call for a 50/50 split between the publisher and the author on the money from the sale of these rights, but you can always ask for a better cut. How about 75/25, with 75 percent going to the author?

Splits and Serials

As with the size of the territory, there are two questions with regard to serial rights. One, who controls the rights? And two, what's the split? If you have an agent, he or she might want to try to keep control of the *serialization* rights. But if you (or your agent) don't have the contacts to try to sell *first serial* rights to a magazine or newspaper, you might as well let the publisher's rights department try. But again, ask about the split. It's not unusual for the author to receive 90 percent of the money from a first serial rights sale.

DEFINITION

When an excerpt from the book appears just before the book is published, this is a **first serial.** Any excerpts that appear after the book has been published are known as *second serials.* These strange-sounding terms come from the word **serialization.**

Commercial and Dramatic Rights

These are the movie and play rights. Do you see your book as a perfect movie of the week or as the basis for a Broadway musical? Then either fight to control these rights all yourself or reduce the publisher's split.

Once again, if you keep these on your side of the table, the dramatic rights are useless unless you know how to sell them or believe the movie world will beat a path to your door. And as for audio rights, agent Andrea Hurst suggests not granting them unless the publisher itself has an audio division.

Free Author's Copies

Most publishing contracts give the author a scant 5 or 10 free copies. Hey, you've got a big family! Your mom wants one, your great-aunt, your old next-door neighbor …. You need more free books, and you can probably get them. This is an easy place for an editor to give up a little something. Ask for 25, anyway, and see what you get.

Publishers usually are generous with free copies used for publicity or review purposes, so if you have good opportunities for promoting the book yourself, ask for some free publicity copies.

Try to get at least a 50 percent discount on the cover price for any additional books you want to buy. If you plan to give lots of speeches and sell books, try to get an even better quantity discount. Bear in mind that you'll have to pay the shipping charges on these purchases and that books are heavy objects. You need to factor in the shipping costs when deciding what makes up an attractive per-book purchase price.

The Delivery Date

By the time you get to the contract stage, the publishing company might already have a pub date in mind. But you can always try to get a little extra time here—a few weeks or an extra month or so. Be kind to your editor, though. If you don't need the extra time, don't ask for it.

Expense Budgets

These are fairly rare. Expenses are assumed to be the author's responsibility—that's what an advance is for. Sometimes cookbook authors get baking allowances to help with the cost of buying ingredients. Sometimes the authors of anthologies or compilations can get a *permissions* budget. It never hurts to try, though.

DEFINITION

If you're using material to which you do not own the copyright, you need to secure the proper **permissions.** To quote or reprint from newspapers, magazines, or other books, you must contact that company's permissions department. Sometimes a fee is involved, which generally falls on the author.

High-Discount/Reduced Royalty Clauses

These are tough. Publishers claim the deep discounts so prevalent today have cut into their margins and they need to reduce royalties to stay in business. Agents (and authors) claim publishers reduce royalties to practically nothing. Always try to get some concessions in this area. Publishers will also ask for reduced royalty rates on small print runs. You can try to negotiate the size of the print run that triggers this.

If your royalties are based on net and not list price of the book (see the section on royalties earlier in this chapter), you or your agent might want to ask for a higher starting royalty rate. Or perhaps ask that the royalty rate escalate as the book sells more copies—for example, a starting percentage on the first 10,000 copies sold, a higher percent on the next 5,000 copies, and the highest percentage on all copies sold in excess of 15,000.

Joint Accounting

Joint accounting? What's that mean? It means nothing on your first book. It means a great deal if you publish a second book with the same publisher, however. With joint accounting, all monies from both of your books go into the same big pot. So if you haven't earned out the advance on your first book and your second book does really well, the publisher will ding your account for the negative royalty balance on the first one.

We think each book should stand on its own, and we recommend asking to get this clause eliminated.

Options Clauses

If you and your publisher get along well, you'll want to work together again. If you don't get along, you don't want to be legally bound to offer it your next book.

If you're a working writer with lots of books in the works and in various stages of publication, this needs to be stated in the contract. Some contracts actually seek to prevent you from signing another contract with another publisher until this book is published—and publication can be months (even years) after you've completed the manuscript. If this is a problem, speak up.

Electronic Rights

Unfortunately, as the field of electronic publishing is changing so rapidly and rights appear to be more lucrative, publishers are becoming less willing to budge from their very stringent boilerplates on the matter. They want to keep a great big bag full of rights.

This issue continues to evolve daily. A recent blog discussion between best-seller Barry Eisler and fellow author Joe Konrath on Eisler's blog came down firmly on the side of writers doing their own e-book publishing rather than let "legacy publishers" do it. Follow the conversation at barryeisler.blogspot.com.

HOT OFF THE PRESS

Just what should writers make on the e-book version of their work? Publishers tried hard to keep the rates in line with paper versions but have had pushback because of the assumption that an e-book version is cheaper to produce (no printing, no paper, no messy returns process) and so the publisher should pass along a greater share of the profits.

Here's an electronic clause that we feel is fair to the author:

> "Electronic book" rights, which for the purposes of this agreement shall be limited to the right to digitize, reproduce, transmit, display, download, or otherwise transfer, manufacture, publish, distribute, and/or sell the verbatim text of the Work, or a portion thereof, in an electronic format in any media and by any means, on any platform now known or hereafter developed, but without enhancement (such as video, extrinsic illustrations, audio, or any other contributions not present in the printed edition of the Work). Any such display, transmission, or transfer of more than a single chapter of the Work must be encrypted to prevent unauthorized reproduction. Publisher acknowledges and agrees that such grant of electronic display rights does not include any grant of electronic version or interactive multimedia rights, and that such rights are expressly reserved to Author.

Reversion of Rights

Some contracts state that as long as the publisher keeps the book in print somewhere (even if it's available only in New Zealand), the rights won't revert to the author. It's generally in the best interest of the author that the rights to the book revert when the book is out of print in book form in the United States. Ask and see.

It's becoming more important to note that the availability of print on demand copies or electronic copies has the potential to keep a contract in effect forever if it's not expressly excluded from the definition of "in print."

Publishers might say this is beneficial to the author, but it prevents the author from having the book reissued by another publisher who might promote it, which actually might happen if a new book by the author becomes successful. It also hinders the author's ability to reuse the material in other, newer works on the same subject. In any case, it's just as easy for an author to make her book available through print on demand as it is for the publisher, and the author can keep 100 percent of the profits without having to earn out an advance.

If you can neither keep the print on demand rights nor get the publisher to exclude print on demand from the out-of-print clause, then at least request vociferously that a clause be added stating that unless the book sells a certain number of copies (for example, 250) in a royalty period, the work shall be considered out of print. Many publishers will find this a fair compromise.

> **SLUSH PILE**
>
> This chapter is not all you need to negotiate a contract. If you don't have an agent, consult a literary lawyer or at least a good book, such as *Negotiating a Book Contract* by Mark Levine. The Author's Guild in New York can also be a good resource, if you want to join.

The Least You Need to Know

- A publishing contract grants the publisher the right to publish and sell your book.
- You should receive a small payment, called a royalty, on every copy of your book sold.
- Exactly what rights are granted to the publisher is open to negotiation.
- Under most contracts, the publisher has the final decision regarding the book's actual title and the cover artwork.
- Some contract terms are more negotiable than others, such as free copies to the author, first serial rights, and merchandising rights.
- If you plan to negotiate on your own, get help from a literary lawyer, or get a good book on publishing contracts. The family lawyer probably won't be much help here.

Working with a Publisher

Congratulations! You've got a publisher! But now what happens? In Part 4, you get a complete overview of the actual book publishing process and learn how to work effectively with all the players. From meeting deadlines, to sending files or uploading graphics, to keeping an editor happy, to understanding the retail book process, it's all here.

You also learn the basics of book publicity, a critical element in the future success of your book. Understand what the publisher can (and can't) do for you and what you can do for yourself.

In addition, you learn a thing or two about what works with social networking, and what parts of the online world are worth your while. You can't do everything—no one can—but we help you decide just where to put maximum effort to help your book soar.

I Signed a Contract— Now What?

Chapter

16

In This Chapter

- Deadlines, deadlines …
- That first advance check
- Assembling attention-grabbing sales materials
- What your book is going through
- The loud ticking of the clock

You've done it! You've signed a book publishing contract! That means now you have to produce a manuscript. No more talking about how "someday" you plan to write a book—you have to *now*. In fact, you are legally obligated to write one. This was the very thing you sought so hard, but now that it's happened, it can be intimidating.

Allow us to repeat what we believe is the central message of this book: the book publishing business is a business, and to succeed in book publishing as an author, you must be businesslike.

You wrote a businesslike query. You put together a businesslike proposal. You conducted contract negotiations in a businesslike manner. Now you must continue to behave in a professional manner during the next phases of the process. No artistic suffering, no writer's block—and the dog can't eat your manuscript. Remember to use professional behavior at all times and in all interactions with your publisher.

Deadlines Loom

Deadlines can sound so final—and they are. When a contract specifies a deadline for a completed manuscript, it's not just an arbitrary date. It's a date that needs to be met because of these reasons:

* You need to maintain a good working relationship with your editor and publisher.

* Your publisher has to plan for the publication of your book in advance so it can be sold and marketed.

* If you do not meet the deadline, your chances to be published might disappear.

Think back to those idyllic days when you first decided to write a book. You were completely in charge of the schedule for the project. You decided when you would sit down and write, when you would wander down to the bookstore for a low-fat cappuccino and a little bit of research, and when you'd finish the query.

But those leisurely days are behind you. After you sign a contract with a publishing house, you may no longer do things at your own pace. You must meet the deadlines specified in the contract. You also have to think about something else—meeting the exact *word count* or *page count* specified in your contract.

DEFINITION

Some contracts specify a **word count** for the completed manuscript. This is the minimum number of words your manuscript must contain to live up to the contract. Some contracts might specify a **page count,** the minimum number of pages that must be in the manuscript. Sometimes there is a maximum word count or page count, which ensures you don't promise a novella and deliver *War and Peace.*

Ready, Set ...

Why is meeting deadlines so important? The minute a book is scheduled for an upcoming season, the following wheels are set into motion:

* The book is scheduled for publication.

* The catalog copywriters begin to write.

- The cover designer begins to design.

- The accountants begin to forecast costs and expenses.

- The sales department starts planning the best way to sell your book.

- The publicity department begins to think about publicizing your book.

- The subrights department begins to think about to whom they can sell foreign rights or which magazines might pay to excerpt.

- Your editor makes plans for editing your book.

So as you can see, this is no longer just a solitary endeavor for you, your imagination, and your computer. A large structure has just been put into place that depends on the timely arrival of your fully completed manuscript.

We'll examine some of these things more closely in later chapters so you have a better understanding of the sales process, the publicity process, and the editorial process. But for right now, keep that image in your mind—the image of a cast and crew of several people all waiting anxiously to begin working on your book.

This image isn't meant to scare you. But on those days when you just don't feel like working (even if you know it will set the project back a week or two), remember what's happening inside the publishing house. The entire house is counting on you to meet a deadline.

More Time, Please?

You tried hard to meet the deadline, but the book just won't be done on time. What can you do? You can ask your editor for an extension on the deadline—that is, an officially sanctioned excuse note.

"Don't wait until the last minute to ask for an extension," warns Steve Martin of Sage Publishing. "Better to recognize your need for extra time as early as possible and ask accordingly." If you don't warn your editor that you won't make the deadline and then call the day your book is due … well, this is not a good thing. No editor wants to hear bad news at the very last minute.

Plan ahead, but don't count on an extension, and never ask for an extension of an extension. Do try to get your editor to put the extension in writing. Read your contract and be sure you're aware of what will happen if you ask for more time. At many houses, the failure to meet a new deadline can be grounds for cancellation.

Bear in mind that if you need to ask for an extension on your deadline, the reason is immaterial. The editor doesn't really care if your computer crashed, your house was destroyed in a mudslide, or there has been a death in the family. This sounds cruel, but it's true. One excuse is no better than another. If the book is late, the editor is in trouble. It doesn't matter why.

Where's My Advance?

You signed a contract promising to deliver a completed manuscript by a certain date. The publishing company also signed that contract and promised to send you an advance. But it's been weeks, and the money isn't here. You have to meet a deadline; shouldn't there be some deadline they have to meet, too?

The simple answer is "no." The company should be timely, but sometimes it can take many months to see the first of your payments. Welcome to the world of business.

HOT OFF THE PRESS

When does a contract become a signed contract? Most publishers send a contract to you to sign and then you send it back for them to "countersign." It might have to be countersigned by more than one person in-house. After the publisher countersigns the contract, a check request for your "on signing" advance is processed. The publisher will also send you a copy of your contract. Your contract then will go to the royalty department, which will set up an account for your new book and process the check. Depending on the department and size of publisher, this entire process can take up to 4 to 6 weeks.

It seems awfully unfair, doesn't it? Yes, but try to be businesslike about it. If you have an agent, let your agent nudge the editor about when the first payment will arrive. If you don't have an agent, tread as gently on the topic as you can. You're just starting out in your relationship with your editor, so don't jeopardize it now.

Should you threaten to stop working on the book until you get your first check? Once again, the simple answer is "no." Yes, it stinks that you're working hard to meet a deadline and the money hasn't yet shown up. But it's better for your book—and your career—to keep working. If you threaten to stop working, you only hurt yourself.

Remember, editors don't cut checks; the royalty department generally does. No matter how sympathetic your editor is that you haven't yet received a check, she cannot write one for you. She might be able to walk down the hall and ask, nudge, or lobby, but she cannot write the check. So don't hold your editor responsible because the check hasn't arrived yet.

The Sizzle for Your Steak

You and your editor have had a conversation or two about your book, and she has asked you for quite a bit of backup material. This might seem like unimportant stuff to you. Shouldn't you concentrate on writing and not have to worry about sending off the bunch of newspaper clippings, online mentions, and magazine articles she's asked for?

As you learned a few paragraphs ago, much is happening at the publishing house while you work away on your book. One of those things is hype. The fate of your book may depend on several things, including how excited the salespeople are, how sexy the catalog copy is, and how jazzed up your editor is.

Bend Over Backward

While you're working hard to meet your manuscript deadlines, you also need to work hard to supply the things the folks at the publishing house need—particularly *when* they need it.

If someone from the publicity department e-mails asking about the recent big media profile you included in your proposal, just answer back with a link. Don't tell them to get it from your editor. If someone from the editorial department calls and asks about where you went to school, answer the question. Don't tell the caller the answer can be found in your proposal.

Will You Say "I Love It"?

Your editor (or the copywriter, or the publicist) might also ask you about endorsements. Your proposal bragged about an endorsement or two, and now you need to produce them! Why do they need endorsements so long before the book is published?

Endorsements aren't just used on the back of the book or in advertisements—they're sometimes used in catalog copy as well. Both fiction and nonfiction books routinely have glowing blurbs in sales material or printed on the book itself. (The catalog and book covers are usually produced 6 to 8 months before your book is published. If your book will be publicized with bound galleys 4 months before publication, your publisher will need cover quotes and other materials even months earlier.)

You need to spend time and energy rounding up endorsements for your book, often both professional and celebrity ones. But you will be amazed at how the words, "I'm under contract to Publisher X to write a book ..." helps you open doors and get responses to requests for endorsements. You'll find that this is a great time to expand your personal and professional network. And never forget that most folks love to see their name in print!

Don't be hurt or insulted if the high-profile person you approach says, "Sure, but can you write it for me and send it to me to approve?" This is actually very routine and happens more often than not.

You're Excited; They're Excited

Understand that publishing people will ask you all kinds of silly questions and for all kinds of silly stuff. Just smile and provide the answers and materials they need. The easier you make it for them, the more excited they will be about you and your book. Conversely, the less cooperative you are with them, the more their excitement will dim.

The more enthusiasm that builds around you and your book, the better your chances for strong sales. You can help create the excitement and enthusiasm by supplying your publisher with as much information as possible to create a *buzz*, the impression that you and your book are destined for greatness. Companies like Random House now routinely tweet about books months before they arrive to stir up interest and build buzz among both booksellers and readers.

DEFINITION

The word-of-mouth publicity created before a book is actually published is the **buzz.** You want a lot of buzz for your book, from the publicity department to the sales department. The more buzz, the better.

I Haven't Heard from My Editor in Months!

You're working diligently to meet your deadline. You've created a writing schedule, and you sit down to write every day, regardless of whether you feel creative. You take your contract deadline seriously. So why haven't you heard from your editor in a while? Has she forgotten about you?

No. No one will forget about you. But yes, there may be long stretches when you won't hear from anyone.

Here's another reality check from the world of publishing: your editor is responsible for many books at once, perhaps as few as a dozen or as many as 30. It depends on the size of the publishing house and how many editors are on staff. What's more, all the books the editor oversees are in different stages—acquisitions, contract negotiation, manuscript review, typesetting, publicity—so her attention is sometimes fragmented.

Speaking as longtime editors, we can assure you not to worry about the long absences. If an editor leaves you alone for a while, take it as a sign of trust. The editor is probably delighted you are a professional who is working away on your own, not needing constant encouragement and reinforcement from her. Editors adore writers who don't need constant attention.

What's Going on with My Book?

You are writing easily and are pleased with the progress you've made so far. Your check for the first half of the advance has arrived, and your editor has expressed his or her confidence in your ability to do the job. Let's leave you alone for a moment and check in to see what's happening at the publishing house.

You aren't alone. It may seem that way as you write deep into the night, with your computer screen glowing in the darkness. But you are not alone. Much is happening with your book. Editorial and marketing are finalizing the title of your book with any subtitles or taglines. Copywriters are producing copy for the catalog, which the sales reps will take with them to sell your book. Cover designers, art directors, and marketing folks are designing a cover for your book.

EXPERTS SAY

If you thought writing a book was a lonely pursuit, just wait until you sit through those long silent months of anticipation until your book arrives in finished form! "You need to involve yourself in lots of non-book-related things during this phase," one much-published author recommends. "Go hiking, build a house with Habitat for Humanity, anything to keep yourself from obsessing about what is going on with your book!"

What's in a Name?

You learned in Chapter 15 that the publisher has the final say over your book title. If the publisher does change your book's title, it won't be a casual decision. The title of your book will be discussed again and again. In every meeting on any marketing issue—from catalog copy to cover design and everything in between—the title will be reexamined.

When a group of people clusters around a table to see the sketches for your book's cover, the title will be questioned.

When a group of people sits together to examine the sales department issues for your book, the title will be questioned.

When your book is presented to the sales department (more about that in Chapter 20), the title will be questioned.

Why does everyone care so much about what your book is eventually named? Because a good name can make a book, and a lousy name can kill it. When these same folks aren't obsessing over the title of your book, they're probably obsessing over the subtitle, if your book has one, which is equally critical to the success of your book.

Catalog Copy

Using your own book proposal as a basis, a copywriter is struggling away to describe your book in 100 words or less for the catalog the sales representatives use. On rare occasions, a copywriter may call you to learn more about the book. The more he or she knows, the easier it is to choose the most important points that must be included in the 100-word description.

HOT OFF THE PRESS

Books are cataloged and sold by seasons. Winter season is typically for books that publish January through April, spring/summer season is for books that publish May through August, and fall season is for books published in September through December. When a publisher schedules a publication month for your book, it will take into account any "seasonality" or if there's a time during the year books on your topic are more popular. For example, January is the big month for weight loss and fitness books, September is the big month for cookbooks and gift books, and July is usually the big month for back-to-school topics. With fiction, serious lit titles are usually scheduled for fall.

We previously mentioned that the day of the printed sales catalog for forthcoming titles has dwindled to almost nothing, but some still use them, and if they don't, the company has an electronic catalog on its website for bookseller customers.

Judging a Book by Its Cover

Another busy person at the publishing company is the cover designer. This person's title might vary somewhat, from art director to cover coordinator. But somewhere, someone is working on designing a cover for your book.

The same group of people who met to decide whether to publish your book might also be getting together to discuss the cover ideas. Or it might be a group that includes more folks from sales and marketing and fewer from editorial. Regardless of the group's makeup, its task is a critical one: to decide how to best convey your book's message in such a way that it accomplishes these points:

- The cover is eye-catching and unique.
- The title can be read from a distance.
- The purpose of the book is immediately clear.

This is easier said than done. The proper solution for each book is different.

Will these cover folks include you in their discussion? Possibly. Another harsh fact (are there more?) is that, as with the title, the publisher has the contractual right to determine what the cover says and what it looks like. As the author, you might be included as a courtesy (this is called "consultation"), but it isn't guaranteed.

The Good, the Bad, and the Ugly

What if you don't like the title? If your editor sends you a copy of the cover in the works (not all do) or you read the catalog copy and you think it stinks, do not react immediately. Count to 10. Count to 20 if you still aren't cooled down. Never make a phone call to your publishing house in the heat of the moment.

SLUSH PILE

You might find yourself talking to someone from the publishing company who knows very little about your book. Perhaps it's the copywriter, a publicity person, or an editorial assistant. If this happens (and it probably will), don't be snippy. Understand that yours is just one of many books that person is handling. Be polite, and use this as an opportunity to educate, not attack.

The best way to convey your thoughts about the cover is in writing rather than in a phone call. Write a measured, professional message in which you offer alternative suggestions. Don't just offer criticism in your letter. Make useful suggestions, too. Jennifer received a thoughtful e-mail from two of her authors once with their thoughts on the cover. They made professional suggestions regarding the type size and colors on the cover and also pointed out that as a married couple they preferred their names read somewhat differently than shown—critical information they needed to pass along, and it was appreciated.

If you have an agent, let the agent know how you feel about the cover. With your agent to back you up, the publisher just might make some changes. But once again, we need to remind you, the publisher has final say and you (like almost every author in the history of the world) might have to live with a cover you dislike.

The Clock's Ticking

But enough about these other people—let's get back to you and your computer again. The time is ticking away, and the deadline looms closer ....

Although this is a book about getting published, not about actually writing a book, we can't resist offering you a few suggestions. Here are some helpful hints to meet a deadline:

- Write every day, even if it's for just 15 minutes.

- Set small goals, and reward yourself when you meet them.

- Turn off your phone; quit checking e-mail and Facebook; and pull the plug on electronic gaming, television, and even your iPod if it distracts you.

- Take yourself away for a weekend to write in solitude.

- If you find yourself stuck on writing, go do research for a little while instead; then come back to your writing.

- If you're stuck on Chapter 3, work on Chapter 5 instead.

- Write your ending first and then go back and fill in everything that comes before it.

- Call your mom and ask her to scold you into writing.

- Find a buddy writer, join a group, tweet your progress to friends and fans—anything to report regularly on your progress.

Remember the old writing adage: if you write just 1 page a day, in 1 year you will have a 365-page book. We hope your deadline leaves you that much time!

The Least You Need to Know

- Maintain your businesslike attitude, particularly about meeting manuscript deadlines.
- If you're going to miss a deadline, give your editor as much warning as possible. Don't wait until the last minute to ask for an extension.
- Long before your book is published, you need to provide material for the sales, marketing, and publicity departments.
- There'll be long periods of time when you don't hear from anyone at your publisher. Don't worry, they haven't forgotten about you.
- While you're writing the book, other people are also working on your book, including the cover designer and the catalog copywriter.
- Keep seeking endorsements for your book while you're writing.

Saying Good-Bye to Your Baby

In This Chapter

- Tips on typing and formatting your manuscript
- Polishing your prose
- What to do about the art
- Acknowledging the proper people

You've met your deadline, posted that milestone on Facebook for all your friends to cheer, and with a pounding heart you are now preparing to hit "Send" on your manuscript. Is there a right way or a wrong way to submit it?

To keep your editor happy (and don't you just love the phrase "your editor"?), you need to submit a clean and polished manuscript prepared according to the publishing house's rules.

Go with the Guidelines

Each publisher has its own rules, or *manuscript guidelines*, you'll need to follow. Typical manuscript guidelines stipulate things such as the following:

- What type of word-processing software is acceptable, such as the most current version of Microsoft Word.

- What type of file to send (zipped or not?) and whether to submit by e-mail or upload to an ftp server. (Some large publishers have a dedicated site on which to transfer large files.)

- Do they want a printed hard copy of the manuscript. (Yes, some publishers still want paper!)

DEFINITION

Manuscript guidelines (or author guidelines) pertain to the actual formatting, disc preparation, and hard copy requirements of the final manuscript. These guidelines vary among publishing houses and sometimes among editors within a house. Be sure you have a copy of the manuscript guidelines in hand before you start to prepare your manuscript.

Submitting your manuscript on a disc was the old-fashioned method, and before that, authors proudly walked to the post office to mail off a precious manuscript to their publisher. You can thank heavens we all save on postage nowadays. Today, you will be asked to submit electronically via e-mail or ftp. Moreover, when e-mailing your chapters, you might be asked to follow guidelines similar to these:

- Create an individual file for each chapter of the book. Do not write your entire book in one file.

- Save the files as attachments to an e-mail. *Do not* cut and paste text into the e-mail message area.

- Save all files as Microsoft Word docs or compatible (per your publisher's instructions). To ensure that your editor can read your files, send a test file first using only one chapter.

- If at all possible, avoid submitting incomplete files. If you must update a file after it's been submitted, talk to your editor and get instructions on the best way to do this.

- Be sure you're using an Internet provider that lets you send and receive multiple files.

- To reduce the number of e-mail submissions and maximize the number of files submitted per e-mail, you might want to utilize compression software such as WinZip (or StuffIt if you're on a Macintosh). Be sure your Internet provider allows zipped files, and also ask if your editor wants it that way. Some publishing houses quarantine e-mails with zipped files.

Sure, you can be creative in *what* you write, but most publishing houses are firm on *how* you write what you submit to them. Follow their guidelines ... or else.

HOT OFF THE PRESS

Submitting your manuscript by e-mail? Don't submit and just assume your editor received the files. A project editor at Prima Publishing told us about the stressful time an author e-mailed his entire manuscript at the very last minute on the day it was due in a text format that was unreadable. Then the author left on a month-long trip traveling to an inaccessible part of the Middle East and was unreachable. "It caused quite a panic for a day or two," remembers the editor, "but luckily his assistant also had a copy in a better format."

The Best Software

By definition, the best software for you to use is the software stipulated in the manuscript guidelines. But when you first started writing so many months (or years) ago, who knew what publisher you would end up with and what kind of software that publisher would require or recommend?

Your best bet, then, is to stick with the largest and most popular program—Microsoft Word in a newish version. As a general rule, the more current the version of your program, the better. Another consideration: most editors work on PCs, not on Macs.

If you're submitting electronically, chances are your publishing house editors will edit the files electronically. Programs such as Microsoft Word have features that allow editors to track their changes, make comments, and edit your manuscript so you can see very clearly any additions or deletions. It's worth it for you to become familiar with the revision features in your software. You will most likely need to use them.

If your personal equipment isn't up to current standards, spend time and money at your local library, a FedEx Kinko's, or another business where you can rent computer time.

Proper Formatting

Back in the days before computers, *formatting* was pretty straightforward. Your editor would ask you to submit your manuscript neatly typewritten (with a new ribbon!) on standard, white, 8½×11-inch, high-quality bond paper. Doesn't that sound quaint? Margins were to measure 1 inch all around, and text was to be double-spaced with ½-inch indentations.

It was quite simple, actually. The tricky stuff such as italics, bold, *headings*, and the like were left to the typesetter.

DEFINITION

Formatting refers to the set of instructions that determines the way the printed words appear on the page, including things such as margins, indents, type size, and fonts. A **heading** (often called a head) is the title introducing a chapter or subdivision of the text. Typically, a manuscript has a hierarchy of different-size headings throughout, which you need to designate as Head 1, 2, 3, or Head A, B, and C. Your author guidelines will specify how your publisher wants heads handled.

Those days (and the typesetters) are gone at most publishing houses. In the age of computerized publishing, the rules have changed considerably, for both the publisher and the writer. Now formatting requirements are designed to facilitate the production process. More than one author has grumbled about the extra work, but it's a fact of life these days.

How you're asked to format your electronic manuscript files varies somewhat from publisher to publisher. It depends entirely on the publisher's computer sophistication and editorial conventions. However, some fairly standard formatting requirements exist:

- One-inch margins around the page
- Standard 12-point type in a typewriter font, such as Courier or Times New Roman
- Single line spaces between paragraphs rather than indents
- Double-spaced text
- Unjustified text—that is, left aligned
- No double hard returns
- One computer file per chapter, named according to the house's naming convention
- Hard copy printed on a desk jet or laser-quality printer, on good, $8^{1}/_{2}{\times}11$-inch white paper
- No double spaces after periods

Most publishing houses have prepared very detailed formatting guidelines for writers under contract. These guidelines often specify particular coding for various design elements such as headings. Many publishers send these guidelines out when they return the signed contract. Don't wait for that—as you know from Chapter 15, you might have finished the book before the signed contract comes! If you have any questions at all, just ask your editor to send the guidelines early.

Don't assume these guidelines are just suggestions and you really don't have to follow the page setup guidelines or formatting instructions. Also, don't assume your publisher will just fix the problems itself and not bother you with it. You might get lucky, and you might not. It's terrible to have worked so hard to meet a deadline only to have your editor send your entire manuscript back to you to be put into the proper format. It could also jeopardize the schedule for your entire project. The work has to be done—and if it's your responsibility, it's going to fall to you.

You should also understand that not following the publisher's guidelines could affect the page count (if they ask for 1-inch margins, for instance, and you use 1.25 inches instead), which could make your book run too long or too short.

If you don't understand something in the publisher's guidelines, do speak up. And do it sooner rather than later. Editors and production people are happy to explain and can easily clear up any confusion. Remember, there are no stupid questions in life.

File Management Matters

You'll turn in your chapters, each tucked neatly into an individual file, cleverly named. Sometimes too cleverly named …. Choose clear file names like "Chap. 1" and so forth. Stay away from using the actual name of the chapter—"Chapter One, How It All Began." Clearly named files are critical because when the developmental editing or copy editing phase begins, many versions of your files will be flying back and forth through cyberspace, and it is easy to become confused. We like to do it this way:

> Chap1
>
> Chap1-revise
>
> Chap1-revise2
>
> Chap1-final

You'll develop a system that works for you, or your publisher might have a system it wants you to use. Just remember to keep it as simple and clear as possible so you (or your editor) can tell at a glance which version of the chapter this is. Needless to say, do not turn in multiple versions of a chapter, only the final one.

SLUSH PILE

Come on, does any of this advice about files really still matter? Sure it does. Just ask Jonathan Franzen, whose novel *Freedom* was published in England by HarperCollins, only to have those copies quickly pulled and pulped. Seems British typesetters accidently opened and copied the wrong computer file during production—a very costly mistake.

What About the Pictures?

Many book projects include *interior art*, a term that in book publishing refers to the photographs, illustrations, maps, and cartoons that might appear on the pages of the book. If your book does have interior art, you need to find out exactly what your responsibilities are concerning it. It is best to be sure you understand your responsibilities before signing the contract, not after.

Some publishers—particularly the larger ones—provide all the art, and they like it that way. If this is the case, you, as the author, might be encouraged to contribute ideas for possible art. Or you might well be discouraged from contributing art ideas. Check your book contract to see what your publisher expects from you.

What if you're responsible for providing art? You'll have to provide it in the proper way. Here again, this varies from publisher to publisher. Most often, it depends on the production department's technical sophistication, but let's look at some possible scenarios.

If you're providing black-and-white photographs, you might be asked to provide simple 8×10-inch black-and-white glossies. Or you might be asked to provide color slides or electronic versions that you've scanned and delivered electronically in GIF or JPEG files at the publisher's required resolution.

If you're providing maps, you might be asked to provide simple sketches that the publisher's art department can use to render final art. Or you might be asked to deliver *camera-ready*, professional-quality maps.

DEFINITION

Camera-ready art refers to the finished artwork that is ready to be photographed or scanned, without alteration, for reproduction. Sometimes it's called *mechanicals*.

If you're providing actual illustrations (this is unlikely), you might be asked to deliver the originals or the camera-ready versions of those originals.

Including art or photographs in a book can increase its production cost—and, thus, its price—considerably. So despite your opinion, if the publisher decides not to include art in the book, try to understand and be gracious. This is a business decision, not an emotional one.

Permissions

Regardless of the form, remember that you must also obtain written permission to reprint any art that's not your own or that's not in the *public domain*.

> **DEFINITION**
>
> Written work or artwork no longer protected by copyright law is in the **public domain** and can be used by anyone without permission or cost. Artwork that's free to be used by anyone without obtaining permission is called *clip art*. One caution though: just because something is online doesn't mean it's in the public domain.

Art is not the only thing that requires permission or a signed release form from the copyright holder. Many new writers make the mistake of not paying enough attention to the fact that they probably need permissions or releases when dealing with the following:

- Artwork, photographs, or screen shots from websites

- Interview subjects whose comments and names you plan to include in the book

- Quotes taken from other published works such as books, magazines, or websites (Just because you found it online doesn't mean it's public domain.)

- Song lyrics (Expect to pay dearly—ASCAP is fierce.)

- Contributions from other writers, such as in a story collection or when you've asked a writer to make a substantial written contribution to your book

Ask your editor early in the game if the publishing house has a standard release form you can use. If you aren't clear on how or when to seek permission, your editor might be able to hook you up for a conversation with someone in the legal department so you have a better understanding.

Identify early in your project what material you will need, including releases, permissions, and who you'll need to contact. Keep good records, and organize your paperwork. Your editor will be expecting all this documentation with your final submission.

Plagiarism

Plagiarism is a very real issue for publishing houses today. There are many misconceptions about what kind of material is *fair use*, how much you can use before permission must be obtained, and how it must be cited.

DEFINITION

Fair use could be the most misunderstood concept in writing today. Many authors think using two sentences is fine, while others think there's a 500-word rule. The truth is, fair use can vary greatly depending on the size, type, and content of the original work. The legal definition has more to do with *how* the content is used, not so much *how much* of it is used. If you're excerpting material from other sources, be sure to check with your editor and get the publisher's guidelines for use.

If you plagiarize, you will be caught. Several romance writers and novelists have been caught in recent years, and more than one big name historian has been red-faced over this issue. We've known several editors who have had projects fall through because authors submitted a manuscript full of uncited or improperly used material.

"We don't think most of them deliberately set out to plagiarize work. We just think most of them don't truly understand what they are doing is wrong," one editor told us. "We had a fully written manuscript almost published when an editor did a routine check of material. The authors had done their research using websites and cut and pasted material from various sites into their book with no rewrites and no cites!" The authors' response about the plagiarized material? They said, "It was on the Internet. You can't copyright material on the Internet. It's free." Needless to say, their book wasn't published.

Publishers do spot checks on manuscripts, and some even go through legal vetting. But contrary to popular belief, rewriting isn't enough. Be sure you talk with your editor in advance of using material from other sources. Publishers are often the most up-to-date sources of information on what's happening in copyright law, as their cases are often defining the standard.

Show Them the Money

Few new writers understand that if a fee is required to include material (such as a poem or song lyric), it is your responsibility as the author to pay it. Check your contract, and you will find that in almost all cases the author is responsible.

Keep this in mind when you're writing your manuscript so you don't have to go back and cut things you literally can't afford, like that great Rolling Stones lyric you think sets the tone for your whole book. When you find out how many hundreds of dollars just a few lines can cost, you might quickly change your mind.

"I'd Like to Thank My First-Grade Teacher …"

Ah, the acknowledgments section. Here is your chance to tell the world where you learned to write, who has influenced you in your life, and to whom you will feel eternally grateful.

Many writers turn in the acknowledgments section of their manuscript last. And because it's sometimes quite lengthy, it might seem to the editor that the author spent the most time writing this section of the book.

As a reader, aren't you annoyed by the endless log-rolling and name-dropping that goes on in the books you've bought? Don't put your own readers through the very experience that annoys you!

Again, we would like to impress upon you that the most businesslike and professional approach to the acknowledgments section is to keep it short, perhaps just a few paragraphs. Understand that if you turn in a long one, you just might be asked to cut it.

Garbage In, Garbage Out

GIGO is old school tech-talk for the phrase "garbage in, garbage out," an expression as applicable to publishing as it is to computers. The cleaner the manuscript you send to your publisher, the cleaner the book that comes out from your publisher.

Writers often complain about the finished product, as if that product were completely out of their hands. Particularly loathsome to writers are unnecessary tinkering by copy editors, typos, and formatting bloopers.

Yet as the writer, you have more control over this process than you might think. If you turn in a manuscript riddled with grammatical errors, typos, and formatting inconsistencies, you're asking for trouble.

EXPERTS SAY

The Chicago Manual of Style is the book publishing bible and every writer's best friend. It's a veritable treasure trove of information that addresses all the spelling, grammar, and language usage issues you're likely to encounter in a lifetime of writing. "Using *The Chicago Manual of Style* as your guide marks you as a professional and impresses your editor," says book doctor John Waters. Find it in the reference section of the bookstore or search it online at chicagomanualofstyle.org.

So polish your prose. Check your grammar and your spelling. Follow your publisher's formatting guidelines to the letter. You'll be glad you did (and you'll impress your editor to boot!). If you've forgotten everything you learned in English class, take a look at *The Complete Idiot's Guide to Grammar and Style*, now in its second edition, for a refresher course.

Bye-Bye, Book!

Good job! You've prepared your manuscript in strict accordance with the publisher's guidelines. Your manuscript is now ready to begin the labyrinthine journey known as the editorial and production process. It's ready to become a book. Read on to learn exactly how this happens.

The Least You Need to Know

- Computer illiteracy is not acceptable in today's publishing world. You must know how to do everything the publisher expects from you.
- Few publishers accept old-school manuscripts on paper anymore; editing and production is all electronic these days.
- Save each chapter in an individual file, never write a book as one long file, and be sure to manage your files during the editing phase.
- Ask your publisher early on for manuscript guidelines—and follow them!
- Remember that getting signed permissions and paying any required fees are your responsibility as the author.
- Clean up your text, give it any final touch-ups, hold your breath, and send your manuscript on its way!

Welcome to the Home Team!

Chapter 18

In This Chapter

- Book production, step by step
- Who's who in the publishing business
- Tips for responding to editorial queries and changes
- Production deadlines to be aware of

Much is often made of the solitary nature of the writer's life. Some writers—loners and dreamers at heart—like it that way.

Well, writing a book may be a solo act, but making a book is a collaborative one. Making a book requires that the author put aside his or her artistic, sensitive, prideful self and join forces with the cast of folks needed to produce a bound book. Maybe for the first time since you started writing your book, you've joined a team.

The process of producing a book is by no means simple. You, the writer, have provided the text of the book. But a book is much more than simply text. It's a product that must be polished, designed, manufactured, marketed, promoted, sold, and shipped into retail outlets all over the country, warehouses for online retailers, and, finally, sold to readers.

Production in a Nutshell

Here are the steps to producing a book:

- Developmental edit
- Copy edit

- Interior design
- Front, spine, and back cover copy and design
- Indexing
- Final page proofs and proofreading
- *Bluelines*
- *F&Gs*
- E-book formatting

DEFINITION

The term **bluelines,** sometimes called *blues,* refers to the cheap proof—the test run off the press that's usually blue (hence the name)—the printer sends to the publisher to check before proceeding with the actual printing. The **F&Gs** are the sheets of a book that have been "folded and gathered" in preparation for printing. In the rush to market, many publishers do not bother to review F&Gs, having already reviewed the bluelines. A notable exception to this is heavily illustrated books. *BLAD* is another old school design term for "basic layout and design."

Join the Team!

You are now part of a team of talented and resourceful publishing professionals whose contribution—whether it's the copy edit or the cover illustration—is as important to them as your words are to you. Let's meet this team and learn how you can make yourself a welcome addition to it.

We'll introduce you to these publishing professionals in the order you're most likely to meet them—or hear of them, as the case may be.

The Acquisitions Editor

The first person to read the manuscript you've turned in is usually your old friend, the acquisitions editor. By definition, this person is already a big fan of yours, having had the wisdom and foresight to offer you a book contract in the first place.

The acquisitions editor works for a publisher, an editor in chief, or a publishing director who may oversee an entire imprint or topic of publishing for a house. The publisher also approves any final financial decisions the acquisitions editor makes. While you won't work directly with a publisher, he or she is aware of the decisions being made on your book.

But I Thought You Liked It!

At this point in the process, however, your biggest fan may become your worst critic, all in the name of making the best book possible. She'll take a big-picture look at your manuscript, performing what's called a *content edit*. She'll review your manuscript for the following:

- Content
- Style
- Voice
- Structure
- Pacing
- And more

SLUSH PILE

Even if you think you're done, you might not be. Jennifer went through a blue period in her career as an author when every one of her completed projects came back with a request for more material. Be cheerful, and supply the publisher what it needs.

Especially for Fiction

If the book is fiction or creative nonfiction, the acquisitions editor will also be looking to see how you've handled these elements:

- Setting
- Plot
- Characterization

- Dialogue

- Point(s) of view

- Narrative

- Themes

- And more

When your editor has completed her review, typically she'll write up her comments, proposed changes, and questions and forward them on to you. As we'll discuss later in this chapter, it's your job to incorporate all her changes with grace, professionalism, and speed—especially if you want to get your hands on that acceptance check. (The acceptance check doesn't come until these changes are made to your acquisitions editor's satisfaction.)

The Developmental Editor

If your acquisitions editor believes substantial changes must be made to your manuscript before approving it for publication, she may assign it to a developmental editor. In some houses, the acquisitions editor and the developmental editor are the same person. Developmental editors work on actual content, helping you rework and reorganize your manuscript to the publishing house's expectations. And don't be hurt if your book does get a developmental edit. It's standard practice in many places and shouldn't be taken as a sign that your book was thought to be in bad shape.

If you are for any reason unable or unwilling to make the changes requested, the developmental editor may serve as a book doctor, rewriting your book as she and the acquisitions editor see fit. If they use an outside person, the fee for this developmental editing either is paid by the publisher outright at no cost to you or is paid by the publisher and then charged back to you against your royalties.

The Production or Project Editor

When you and your acquisitions editor have ironed out all the big-picture issues, you and your manuscript are handed off to the production editor, who runs your manuscript through the next lap in this publishing relay.

Just as your acquisitions editor has seen you safely through the acquisitions process (from query to signed contract to acceptance of the final manuscript), your production editor sees you safely through the production process (from copy edit to final proofs to bluelines to printed book).

In some publishing houses, the production editor also assumes responsibility for the content editing, either doing the edit herself or sending it out to a freelance developmental editor.

The Copy Editor

The way some writers rant and rave about copy editors, you'd think they were insensitive, intolerant, inflexible … well, you get the picture.

Wrong! Copy editors can be a writer's best friend. Sure, they're a little picky, but then they're paid to be picky. Who else catches all your inadvertent misspellings, grammatical errors, questionable punctuation, and inconsistent capitalization? Not to mention all those other things you didn't even know those meticulous copy editors check, including these elements:

- Pagination
- Illustrations
- Front and back matter
- Contradictions and ambiguities
- Parochialisms and anachronisms
- Abbreviations and contractions
- Accuracy of names, dates, and places
- Cross-references
- Coding for headings, illustrations, and the like

Who (and where) your copy editor is varies according to the publishing house. At some houses, the production editor does the copy editing herself. At other houses, the production editor sends the manuscript to the copy editing department, where an in-house copy editor does the job. At still others, the production editor sends your manuscript out to a freelance copy editor.

No matter where she comes from, the copy editor deserves your respect and maybe even your undying love.

The Art Director

The art director is the person responsible for the way your book looks, both inside and out. In large houses, the art director heads up a design department that creates the interior and cover designs for each title. In smaller houses, the art director may create the designs herself or send them out to freelance designers.

Interior Design

Interior design varies greatly in its complexity, depending on the type of book you've written. Novels, made up primarily of *text*, typically require very simple interior designs. Nonfiction books can run the gamut from simple text to highly illustrated to books like the one you hold in your hands. This nonfiction book, *The Complete Idiot's Guide to Getting Published*, *Fifth Edition*, incorporates a number of design elements such as *sidebars*, bullets, and numbered lists.

DEFINITION

Words on a page are called **text.** Text set aside in a box or that runs down the side in a smaller size type is a sidebar. **Sidebars** are like little asides in a conversation.

If the design of your book dictates that text be arranged in a certain way (like this one does), you may be asked to write the text accordingly (like we were).

Cover Design

You may not be able to judge a book by its cover, but you can sell a book by one! The cover is a book's major sales tool. Now maybe you can see why it's important for the publisher to state flatly in the contract that the cover text and design is its decision, not yours.

Moreover, the cover is usually the most expensive piece of the production process—it typically costs thousands of dollars for even the most basic cover and can cost thousands more if the cover includes an illustration or photograph.

For a how-to book, the art director may choose a straightforward type of solution with no illustration. For books such as novels, the illustration is paramount.

The art director presents his designs for your book's interior and front and back covers to a panel that includes your editor, the marketing director, and the publisher, as well as sales, publicity, and pretty much anyone who was there in the meeting when they decided to buy your book so long ago.

The Copywriter

The copywriter writes the copy, or text, that appears on the cover of your book (front and back) as well as the inside flaps on a hardcover book. The cover copy must work with the cover design to entice the bookstore browser to pick up your book and buy it, right then and there. In effect, this is sales copy.

At some houses, the acquisitions editors write the copy for the books they acquire; at other houses, in-house copywriters in the marketing department write the copy. No matter who writes it, this sort of copy is an art form.

Will this be the same copywriter who wrote the description of your book for the catalog? It might be. But it might also be someone who is new to the project, so be kind and patient if that person calls you for information.

The Proofreader

The proofreader is the last person to read the formatted book pages before they're shipped off to the printer for manufacturing. The proofreader's job is to catch glaring mistakes such as typos, pagination problems, and so forth. Think of proofreading as a last-ditch quality-control effort.

Here again, who does the proofreading depends on the house. At larger houses, in-house proofreaders in the proofreading department perform this function; in smaller houses, the proofreading may be done by editorial assistants or may be sent out to freelancers.

The Indexer

Not every book needs an index, so not every book has an indexer. Also, not every house has in-house indexers, but these folks do work here toward the end. Many indexers today work electronically, while others work on index cards. Indexing is a fine and traditional art in itself, and the finished index adds greatly to the usefulness of a book.

Indexes are critical to libraries. Many a book has lost library sales because it doesn't have an index.

The Manufacturing Manager

The manufacturing manager is your publishing house's liaison with the printers. He's typically in charge of buying the paper on which to print the books and decides which printing company to use.

In this age of escalating paper prices, many manufacturing managers are buying cheaper paper to keep costs down. As an author, you should know that paper is another very expensive component of the book—something like 70 percent. Complain to your editor if you like, but there may be nothing your editor can do about it, to his frustration as much as to yours!

Over to You Now

Okay, now you've met the major players in the editorial and production processes at most publishing houses. Now let's go step by step through the interactions you'll have with some of these people as your book is produced.

As we've tried to make clear in the last several pages, much of what goes on at your publishing house is out of your control and is in the hands of your team members. Also, the order as we've described it might vary slightly from house to house. But when the ball does bounce back into your court, you want to be sure you do your part to keep the process going smoothly.

Responding to Your Editor's Comments

Your part first comes into play when your acquisitions editor reads your final manuscript and delivers her content editing comments. No matter how pristine your manuscript, you can expect revision suggestions that include the following:

- Cuts (where you run too long)
- Additions (where you leave too much unsaid)
- Clarifications (where you might confuse the reader)
- Rearrangements (where your structure falters)
- Rethinking of sections (where you veer off track)

"But I gave them a perfect book," co-author Jennifer once heard an unhappy author lament. Wrong. There is no such thing as a perfect book, and that attitude won't make you any friends at your publisher. There's always room for improvement, even if it's only a buff and polish.

Especially for Fiction

If you're writing fiction, you can also expect comments concerning these factors:

- Characters who work and characters who don't
- Holes in the plot or plot contradictions
- Milking certain scenes and eliminating others
- Building suspense or stepping up the pace
- Dramatizing your beginning
- Sustaining interest in your middle
- Nailing your ending

What's Best for the Book

Take these comments in the spirit in which they are given. Your editor's only interest is in making your good book even better. No one is trying to hurt your feelings. The book's success (for both you and your editor) depends on it being the best book it can possibly be.

Sometimes editors are better at seeing what's wrong than they are at seeing how to fix it. Take a hard look at the problems your editor has identified, and if you don't like her solutions, come up with your own. Feel free to discuss these issues with your editor, but don't drive her crazy over every detail. (You learn more on maintaining this all-important relationship with your editor in Chapter 19.)

HOT OFF THE PRESS

The publishing industry is replete with writers who have sabotaged their own book projects—and ultimately their careers—by objecting too strenuously to editorial comments. A case in point: a writer sold a book proposal to a major publisher about marriage and the devastating effects of adultery on the bonds of matrimony. When the manuscript came in, however, the editor objected to large sections in which the writer examined the feelings of the third party (the other man or woman). The editor insisted that the section be cut; it was inappropriate in a book about marriage. The writer insisted that it remain. The impasse was never resolved, and the manuscript was declared unacceptable. Deal over.

Get the job done, make the changes your editor needs, and get the manuscript back to her within the deadline she's given you. If you are slow in this step, you jeopardize the production schedule, and your book may not be published on time. This is not a good thing. Not a good thing at all.

Copy Editing Changes and Queries

When you've made the content changes as requested by your acquisitions editor, your manuscript is handed off to the production editor. He reviews the manuscript and chooses a copy editor based on that review. The copy editor makes her edits, which most likely include *author queries*.

DEFINITION

Author queries are questions the copy editor needs you, the writer, to answer before the text proceeds to the layout stage. These questions can relate to meaning, accuracy, and research, among other things.

It's your job to answer these queries as completely and swiftly as possible. If the copy editor seems a little overzealous, keep in mind that, by definition, copy editors are suspicious of everybody's copy. Don't take it personally—they are merely doing their job.

Of course, there are times when copy editors really do go overboard. If you feel this is the case, first get the opinions of other publishing pros as a double-check. If they, too, agree that the edit is excessive, talk to your acquisitions editor first. He may want to handle it himself. Be polite—no ranting and raving. If your editor agrees with you, he might tell the copy editor to tone it down, or he may reassign the job to someone else.

More Deadlines to Meet

After the copy editing process is completed, your manuscript is ready to go to layout. In the typesetting days of old (before computers), authors received galleys to review. Galleys were long proofs pulled off the machine before the copy was divided into pages.

Ask your editor if you can see a sample design for the interior layout for your book. Many houses use standard designs, but some books have custom designs. They can just e-mail you a sample layout page in a PDF file so you can have an idea of what your finished book will look like.

Galleys are mostly history now. What you are more likely to receive are page proofs, straight from the layout person's (also called the *compositor*) laser printer. These page proofs are reviewed by a number of people, including the proofreader, the acquisitions editor, the production editor, the developmental editor, the art director, the manufacturing manager, sometimes the publisher, and then last but not least, you, the writer.

DEFINITION

Manuscripts are no longer sent off to typesetters but rather to **compositors.** The compositor then formats the book on a computer and gets it ready to go to the printer.

Page Proofs

As the author, you'll usually review what's known as the first pass, the first set of page proofs from the layout person. Chances are you will be asked to view them electronically rather than get an actual set in the mail.

Do not go overboard on corrections or additions here; your opportunity to make big changes was during the copy editing phase. This stage is really just to catch layout errors and typos. Don't panic if you do see a few typos. Chances are a proofreader is looking at pages at the same time you are. Changes at this stage are very expensive. And if you make too many, you have to pay for them. Check your contract for details; each publisher draws the line at a different place. Even if you don't get charged, you'll possibly delay publication.

Usually there are two more passes of page proofs, but the author seldom sees these. One ensures that the first-pass changes have been made without introducing new errors and then there's one more: the final pass just before the book is shipped to the printer.

HOT OFF THE PRESS

Is the e-book version of your book just plain type on the page? No. It's a fully produced version that's designed and scaled to be viewed on an e-reader. In most cases, the publisher sends the finished and edited files to an outside firm that specializes in converting files into e-book versions.

Stop the Presses!

As the printer prepares to print your book (a process known as "make ready"), he first makes a proof. This proof, as we learned earlier, is called the bluelines. Publishing pros just call them "the blues."

Will you get to see the bluelines? Probably not. Blues are meant to be reviewed posthaste by the production editor only hours before the presses actually start to roll. Although some writers may insist on reviewing the bluelines, very few are allowed to do so. Without the clout of a best-selling track record behind you, you won't see the bluelines.

Even if you could, who'd want to? Leave the last-minute quality control to the pros, and get started on your next book. There's no better feeling in the world for a writer than to have one book at the printer and another one in the computer.

The Least You Need to Know

- The editorial and production processes require teamwork; this means cooperation between the publishing staff and you, the author.
- Try not to take editorial criticism personally; the editor's goal is to help you write the best book possible.
- Make all requested changes, and answer all editorial queries promptly so you don't delay production.
- The later it is in the production process, the less likely you will be allowed to make changes to your book.

Proper Care and Feeding of Your Editor

Chapter 19

In This Chapter

- Be good to your editor!
- A day in the editing life
- Getting through to your editor when you need to
- 'Fessing up when things aren't going well
- Keeping everybody on your side

Your manuscript has now left the safety of your nurturing arms and has headed off to the big city. Its fate is now in the hands of strangers, many of whom will remain strangers.

The notable exception to this is your editor. He or she is your link to this strange new world, so it's in your best interest to make this person your new friend.

Make a Friend for Life

Writers and editors as friends? It works for many famous pairings. Recent biographies of Jackie Onassis's time as a New York acquisitions editor gave example after example of how the famously reticent former First Lady dropped her guard with her own writers. Handwritten notes and thoughtful gifts—what writer wouldn't flourish if sent those kinds of things?

Well, not every editor/author pairing will turn out like that, but yes, you can be friendly with your editor.

Your Book's Best Advocate—and Yours, Too!

David Gernert, former editor for a guy named John Grisham, is literally John Grisham's advocate (because he quit his job at Doubleday and became Grisham's agent). Your editor, having acquired your project for the publishing house, is your book's advocate. And you want your editor to become *your* advocate, too.

The trick is to fuel your editor's enthusiasm for you and your book as your manuscript makes its way through the editorial and production processes. Be sure to maintain your editor's enthusiasm after the book is published, too, all the way through the marketing and promotion. At every point, your editor is crucial to the success of your book.

HOT OFF THE PRESS

The most celebrated editor of all time was the legendary Maxwell E. Perkins of Scribner's. Editor and friend to such luminaries as Thomas Wolfe, Perkins was renowned for his ability to draw the best work out of his authors. "Do not ever defer to my judgment," he admonished F. Scott Fitzgerald in one of his remarkable letters. It's worth noting that, despite Perkins's warning, Fitzgerald took his editor's comments and criticism seriously—to his and his work's great credit.

However, while your editor's excitement was initially high when the book was signed, this may fade over time. This apparent loss of enthusiasm and/or interest in your project is more a function of workload than anything else.

Remember, at any given time, your editor is juggling three lists:

- The list of books currently being acquired

- The list of books currently being produced

- The list of books currently being promoted

Depending on the house, this can add up to anywhere between 20 and 100 books per editor. That's a lot of books to track. When it comes to your editor's interest, there's quite a bit of competition for you and your book.

It's your job to sustain this interest and to accomplish this with grace and professionalism. This means you'll need to learn as much as you can about editors and how they operate. Let's observe an editor in the field, so to speak, and find out how she spends her time.

Editor for a Day

Your editor's day typically begins early. Although the workday may officially begin at 9 A.M., many early-bird editors are already at their desks by 8 A.M.—and many can be found at their desks long after 5 P.M.

As you've learned before, there's little time in the editor's day to do the "real" work of reading and evaluating manuscripts and proposals. You'll recall that most of this work is done on the editor's own time, either at home or on the train, subway, or carpool. Many an editor has fallen asleep at night next to a stack of manuscripts or the eerie blue glow of a computer screen.

8 A.M.

At your editor's office, the early birds are getting as much done as they can before the daily meetings start up:

Reading and responding to e-mail. One editor we know gets 200-plus e-mails a day from authors as well as agents, other editors, and all manner of in-house staffers. Editors feel as overwhelmed by e-mail as do folks in other parts of the business world.

Going through snail mail. Yes, it still arrives. Mostly contracts and other assorted things that still crawl across the country in paper form. With any luck, your editor has an editorial assistant who sorts through the mail first. Still, many editors prefer to perform this formidable task themselves, handling contracts from agents, catalogs from other publishers, trade publications and newsletters, interoffice correspondence, faxes, and wow, maybe even the occasional exotic postcard from a long-time author.

Making overseas and transcontinental phone calls. Many editors conduct a great deal of business with foreign publishers. They evaluate projects, make deals for translations, and work together on other projects. The best time to call Europe is early in the day. Likewise, West Coast editors are calling the East Coast as early as they can, and editors on the East Coast are waiting until later in the day to do business with the Westies.

Writing rejections. Yes, some editors do write their own rejection letters. This is a time-consuming job, but many editors consider it a professional courtesy crucial to maintaining good writer-editor or agent-editor relations. Let it never be said that editors don't care about writer's feelings! Let it also never be said that they want to ruin a good relationship with a big-deal agent, so it's always important to tread lightly on those rejections.

9 A.M.

By 9 A.M., the meetings start. Ask any editor how she spends her day, and she will likely say (with some irritation), "In meetings!"

The first meeting on the schedule is the production meeting. Here, your editor meets with the production editors to discuss the problems and issues regarding books currently in production. At today's meeting, your editor learns that a conflict concerning the copy edit of one title has arisen. The writer is unhappy with the copy edit and is dragging his heels on responding to the author queries. The production editor asks for your editor's help in resolving the issue. They will try to meet later in the day to call the writer together and work things out.

> **HOT OFF THE PRESS**
>
> Most acquisitions editors toil in relative obscurity. But a handful have become industry superstars and have earned the biggest reward of all: their own imprint. When this happens, an editor's name is right up there on the book's spine with the publisher. And so you have Nan A. Talese Books/Doubleday and Reagan Arthur Books. That means these editors run their own mini-publishing companies inside a larger house. Both editors have had multiple best-sellers from high-profile names. So there you have another reason to be nice to your editor: she might have her own imprint someday.

10 A.M.

By this time, the production meeting has ended and the cover meeting has begun. At a cover meeting, the art director, editors, marketing execs, and often the publisher get together to brainstorm ideas for new covers and to review covers already in the design process. At today's meeting, they discuss ideas for four new covers and review the art for front covers on four books in production.

One cover for a new cookbook gives them particular trouble. Cookbooks are expensive books to produce, especially when the front cover boasts a beautiful photograph of a savory dish. Cover photos featuring recipes from the cookbook require a photo shoot, a top photographer, a food stylist, the cooperation of the cookbook author, and, of course, the food. It's an expensive production from start to finish.

Even then, the results aren't guaranteed. Maybe the final photos are not what anyone—including your editor—had hoped they would be. The art director is defensive, the marketing executive is fighting for another photo shoot, and the publisher is unhappy at the prospect of doubling the cover costs with another shoot.

Your editor knows the cookbook author (a best-selling author currently being wooed by other publishers) won't like the photo either. "If we run with this cover, we could be giving the agent the ammunition she needs to convince the author to switch houses," your editor argues. The publisher reluctantly agrees and approves a new photo shoot.

Noon

By the time these and other issues have been resolved, it's after 12 P.M. Your editor, late for a luncheon with a top agent, runs down the street to the appointed restaurant, cell phone in hand. Once there, she sits down for a quick bite (no three-martini lunch, this) with the agent. In between bites, the agent pitches a few of his clients' top projects.

As the editor pays for lunch, the agent tells her he will be in touch with her on the projects that most piqued her interest.

1:30 P.M.

Your editor rushes into her office to check her messages before the next meeting begins. As quickly as possible, she returns the most urgent phone calls. One is to an agent about a final contract point, one is to an author about a rewrite in progress, and one is to a rights manager trying to close a deal with a book club.

By the time she hangs up the phone, 45 minutes have gone by. She has only 15 minutes to collect her thoughts (and her information) for the most trying meeting of the day: the acquisitions meeting with the pub board. This is the meeting in which editors try to sell their colleagues and bosses on projects they'd like to sign for publication.

The degree of formality at these meetings may vary from house to house, but the pressure does not. Your editor, and the projects she pitches, falls under close scrutiny during these meetings. As you read in Chapter 14, each editor at the meeting presents one or more titles. This round-robin approach continues until all the books have been discussed or the time is up. Not surprisingly, acquisitions meetings often run late.

At today's meeting, your editor is able to present two projects. The first, a follow-up book by an author whose first book did very well, is an easy sell. The other, an off-beat project by a first-time author the editor loves, is not. Despite her passion for the project, she fails to convince her peers and will have to turn down the writer.

5 P.M.

Your editor finally returns to her office. Again, she listens to her voicemail messages and returns the most urgent calls. She checks her e-mail and her snail mail for after-noon FedEx packages. She sorts through her inbox, pulling out the catalog copy for a couple new books left there by the copywriter, which must be reviewed and returned before she goes home. Ditto for the proofs of two covers for books due to ship to the printer the next day.

Depending on how late she works, she may also make the less urgent calls on her list and write more rejection letters. She writes a very encouraging and complimentary rejection note to the writer whose project she was unable to sell at her acquisitions meeting earlier in the day. She recommends another editor at another house to the writer.

6 P.M.

She packs up the manuscripts she hopes to review at home that evening and leaves the office.

11:30 P.M.

Your tired editor falls asleep, a damp and crumpled stack of proposals in her lap, her computer still on and open to the e-mail she didn't get to earlier.

Tomorrow brings more of the same. It's a tough job, but your editor loves doing it. It's her love for her work that keeps her coming back, despite the relatively low pay and heavy workload.

Why Doesn't My Editor Ever Call Me?

Unless you slept through the last couple pages, you now know why. She's busy—busier than you imagined. But don't panic that she hasn't called lately. Generally, no news is good news.

Still, you want to believe your editor has not forgotten you and your book. If you need to discuss an issue, call and talk to her about it. Given the time she spends in meetings, you may often be reduced to leaving messages on her voicemail. Voicemail can be frustrating, but don't allow your frustrations to influence the message you leave. Be brief and succinct. Be sure to let her know the best time to return your call so you two don't wind up playing phone tag. An even better way to get together on the phone is to schedule a time via an e-mail exchange or just use e-mail to send regular updates.

EXPERTS SAY

"There's a fine line between too much contact and too little," one weary editor admits. "The first note to strike is one of professionalism. If you treat your editor like a pro, odds are she'll return the favor."

If you don't hear back from your editor in a reasonable amount of time, you can do a number of things.

If your editor has an assistant, try getting through to him. Often he may be able to resolve the situation himself. Befriend the assistant. Not only can he help you now, but he may be able to help you later—when he's an acquisitions editor himself!

If an issue has come up during the editorial or production process, try to resolve it with the production editor first. Only as a last resort should you antagonize your production editor by running around him to your acquisitions editor.

The same thing goes for going over your editor's head to her boss. Before you do anything like this, talk to your agent. Let your agent talk to your editor or her boss. This is one of the biggest advantages of having an agent: you get to stay pals with the editor while your agent looks like a meanie. If you don't have an agent, do the best you can to work it out with your editor. If you do go over her head (and we advise against it), proceed at your own peril.

If you feel you need to go over your editor's head, find out who her boss is and politely raise the issue at that level. One busy editor we know at a large house was surprised when an unhappy author sent an e-mail to the CEO of the publishing company's parent corporation complaining that his book hadn't received enough marketing attention. "I got a call from the CEO's assistant in London asking about the e-mail she'd received and if I could shed some light on the situation," she said. "Of course, the CEO understood the situation from our perspective, and the author didn't get what he'd hoped. If he'd actually gone to my real boss—my publisher—he might have had his concern heard with a more sympathetic ear."

SLUSH PILE

Have an attitude? Don't. One writer we know turned in a manuscript twice as long as the contract specified and then refused to speak to her editor about it by phone. The writer demanded that, from now on, the staff communicate with her only by e-mail. The book was eventually published, but by then she'd made enemies all over the building. Did she sell them another book? No.

When to Confess You're in Trouble

We've said this before—if you're running behind, tell your editor sooner as opposed to later. If for any reason you find yourself unable to meet your deadline, complete your rewrites, or turn around your author queries, speak up. Let your editor know as soon as possible.

The sooner she knows, the sooner she'll be able to do damage control. Damage control? Yes, your lateness will cause damage. Your editor will need to rework production schedules and perhaps postpone the publication of your book.

Writers hate to deliver bad news to editors. But the longer you wait, the fewer your editor's damage control options. You have to tell her straight away, while she can still do something to save your book! As long as you speak up soon, odds are that your editor will understand.

Remember that books are published in seasons, and if your book misses the manuscript deadline, it might need to be pushed out to another season. This is important info to have as early as possible because it might mean your book will have to be presented again by the sales force. If there's a chance your book will slip, your publisher needs to know sooner rather than later.

Play Nice

As you've seen, editors are hardworking, underpaid people who love books and writers. They are also often job-hoppers, jumping from one publishing house to another. In New York, where much of the book publishing industry operates, switching houses is as easy as crossing the street.

This revolving-door pattern is one many writers come to hate. It's what's known as the "orphan syndrome": you develop a good relationship with one editor, only to lose that editor to another house. Your new editor—often a hastily promoted assistant—may lack the experience your departed editor had. Worse, she may lack enthusiasm for your project. Then you find that you and your book are orphans with no strong sponsor.

What to do? Befriend the new editor as you had the former editor. Take the time to educate her about your book. Don't assume any knowledge has been passed on from your former editor. No matter who your editor is, you need her. As your primary advocate at the publishing house, your editor is your single most important contact there. It's a relationship you must both guard and nurture.

Writers who do manage to develop strong and happy working relationships with their editors are loath to let them go. Many follow them (contracts permitting) from house to house. Of course, if you become a best-selling author, you can always do what John Grisham did—hire your favorite editor to be your editor/agent!

The Least You Need to Know

- Your editor is your primary advocate at the publishing house. Befriend him or her ASAP.
- Your second most important contact is your editor's assistant. Befriend him or her as well.
- Respect your editor's time; she's busier than you imagine.
- Give your editor time to read your manuscript. Remember that she does most of her reading at home.
- When you have bad news, deliver it early so your editor can look for solutions.
- Editors come and go, so try to make as many friends as you can among the in-house staff.

So How Does My Book Get into Stores?

In This Chapter

- An overview of how sales works
- Sales conferences: do I get to go?
- Why won't that big bookstore take a display?
- At the printer and warehouse
- Should I go to the BEA?

When your book comes off the printing press, where does it go? The finished books are sent directly to your publisher's warehouse and from there (many, you hope) go directly to the shelves of bookstores around the country and the warehouses of online booksellers. (Your e-book version is available right away. But you know that already because you checked online and got your brother to download a copy to juice your sales rank, didn't you?)

How did that happen? When did those bookstores learn about your book? How did they know to order it? And how did they decide how many to order?

Good questions, all. What follows is a brief lesson in the sales process as practiced by the book publishing industry. The more you know about it, the less frustrated you will be later. Writers have a vested interest in how the sales process works, so here's your chance to get educated.

A Short Course in the Sales Process

As you know, the book publishing business was once a quaint pursuit, and the sales process is still more than a little quaint. The two critical elements in this process are the publisher's catalog and the publisher's sales representatives.

The Dynamic Duo: Catalogs and Sales Reps

You've read about the sales catalog in earlier chapters, so you know how important it is that your book be well represented in the catalog description. But you haven't heard much about sales representatives yet. Let's take a look at how these two critical elements—catalog and rep—come together.

Several times a year, the sales representatives make appointments with the bookstore accounts for which they're responsible. Some sales reps have large geographic territories (all the Pacific Northwest, say, or all the Midwestern states), and some sales reps have large-volume national accounts (for example, all the Barnes & Noble stores or all the Target stores).

EXPERTS SAY

Sales reps are so important that when Lewis Buzbee was putting together his proposal for a book about the pleasures of bookstores, he gathered and included letters of support both from publishers' reps as well as booksellers. How did he manage to do that? He had a bit of an in: Lewis himself is the former sales rep for Chronicle Books.

Most large publishing houses have their own full-time sales force. Many medium and small publishing houses use commissioned reps—sales reps who handle the sales for many publishers at once and receive commissions on the sales they create.

Are You Free on Tuesday?

The sales rep makes an appointment with a book buyer to either meet in person or on a phone call. The book buyer is responsible for deciding which of all the new books published the bookstore will carry and in what quantities.

In small, independent bookstores, the book buyer is often also the owner or the manager who buys books for the store in every category. These folks not only make buying decisions, but they also work on the bookstore floor and are in close contact with their customers' needs. With the large national chains, however, the book buyer is a staff position based at headquarters, far from the selling floor. These national book buyers also may specialize by topic area such as health and fitness or business and personal finance. Reps meet with individual buyers depending on what topics their books cover.

The actual sales call might be either a leisurely affair over lunch or coffee (with smaller stores) or just a hurried appointment in a national buyer's cubicle. Or it might be just a really, really long phone call in which the rep and the buyer go through the catalog page by page by page, discussing each one the same way they would if meeting face to face.

Let Me Show You ...

During the sales call, the publisher's sales rep presents the titles that will be published in the next few months (or in the next season). With the catalog between them, the sales rep and the buyer move through page by page. The rep gives a short (very short) presentation on each book using a tip sheet or sales sheet. The tip sheet includes the editor's vision, book contents, market statistics, and other data that isn't included in the catalog. The presentation includes these points:

- A description of the book and its contents
- The publisher's plans to promote, market, and publicize the book
- The author's credentials, other books he or she has written, and sales by the account

Sound familiar? Except for the publisher's publicity and marketing plans, these are essentially the same pieces of information you needed to give the publisher to show that the world needed your book. Now it's your publisher's turn (through the rep) to convince the bookstores that the world needs your book.

You can see how important the material you provided is. The sales rep has just a few minutes to convince the book buyer to buy your book, and he or she needs the best and most compelling information possible.

You can also see, we hope, once again how important it is not to exaggerate or lie in your proposal (particularly about your credentials or your past book sales) because that information gets used over and over and over again throughout the process. If you didn't tell the truth, it will eventually be discovered. Booksellers can instantly access their accounts' previous sales on a book, and editors and booksellers have access to services such as BookScan that reveal the overall sales numbers of books in the marketplace. It will kill your book's chances for success if the rep discovers incorrect information in the middle of a sales call.

The Numbers Game

If the book buyer likes your book, how many will he or she order? Small stores buy in quantities ranging from just 1 copy to 10 or 20 or more for a potential best-seller. Large chains or a big online retailer like Amazon.com follow pretty much this same formula per store, but the total order for the entire chain might be several thousand copies.

Just-in-Time Inventory

Bookstores used to order what they thought they could sell in the first 30 days. With the rise of "just-in-time" inventory management, most stores now order only what they think they can sell in the first 10 days. When those copies sell, bookstores either turn to wholesale distributors (rather than the publisher) for fast reorders or ask the publisher to begin sending them the amount they need automatically each month.

The theory is that less of the bookstore's money is tied up in inventory that way—and fewer copies of your book are sitting in either your publisher's or the bookseller's warehouse. This allows publishers to better control their print quantities, inventories, and—better for you—their returns.

Make-or-Break Comparative Sales

What was for generations a business of hunches and guesses about what books might sell now comes down to computerized records. Book buyers rely on them to help with all buying decisions. Imagine the rep has just presented a cookbook on vegetarian pasta. The book buyer turns to his computer and brings up the sales figures for other cookbooks on vegetarian pasta. If the sales look good, the buyer might order this new title, too. But if the sales look slow, chances are he might buy very few copies or—worse—completely pass on it.

Can that really be true? All the hard work you and your publisher put into writing and publishing your book, and the book buyer won't even put it on the shelf because of the recent slow sales of a similar book? Sad, but all too true. This is a business, and the book buyer just made what he thinks is a sound business decision based on his knowledge of his customers' needs.

> **EXPERTS SAY**
>
> Just a handful of accounts (Barnes & Noble, Amazon, Ingram, Walmart, Target, and a few others) make up most of a book's advance orders. So if one of these passes on your title, it can affect the initial print run. If several of them pass, the publisher may reconsider publishing the book at all. On the other hand, if they really like your book, it can be an almost instant success.

Imagine another sales pitch, this one by an author who's been published before. "This is his second novel?" the buyer notes. "Let me see how well his first book sold for us." The book buyer punches in the ISBN from the author's first book, and the buy for the author's second book is based in large part on the success of the first. Also frightening, but also true.

Hard Sell Hardcovers

Here is another reality check from bookselling: "It is really hard nowadays to publish in hardcover," one publisher told us. "You just don't get the big buys from the chains, it is harder to get the print runs to where they make sense economically, and it is just too risky."

The part of the retail book business that's fading the fastest is in the adult hardcover category, down a whopping 43 percent from February 2010 to February 2011. That's a reality in this business.

The Sales Conference

The amount of time the book buyer listens to the sales rep talk about your book is frighteningly brief—sometimes less than a minute per title. Does the sales rep base this critical sales pitch only on what he learned from reading the catalog? Not exactly. The rep also heard about your book at the sales conference he attended.

The traditional sales conference is a face-to-face meeting between the sales staff (who are based all around the country in their respective sales territories) and the editors, publicity, and marketing folk. The purpose of the sales conference is to introduce the new books for that publishing season and educate the sales reps on how to best sell them.

These meetings, sometimes held over the course of several days for the larger publishing houses, unfold like this:

- Each editor gives a 3- to 5-minute presentation on the books he's acquired (with longer presentations for the major titles).

- A large color slide of the front cover for the book is shown and maybe some inside art as well, if it's a heavily illustrated book.

- The sales reps ask questions during the presentation.

- The sales reps break up into smaller groups with the sales and marketing managers to work out how to best present each book.

- The editors are alerted to any potential problems with individual titles the sales reps anticipate.

How They've Changed!

In past years, the larger sales conferences were more like big parties than business meetings, often in resort areas such as Florida or even Puerto Rico. The conferences were seen as an opportunity to reward the tired sales staff with a little vacation treat before the next season began. Jennifer remembers fondly her trips to the Ritz-Carlton on Amelia Island in those halcyon days. But as the publishing industry has changed, so have the sales conferences.

Some publishing companies have even cut the face-to-face aspect of these conferences. They use videotaped presentations of the books, with each editor talking about the titles as though sitting up at the dais in a conference room.

Some large publishers such as Random House have even tested the idea of using the occasional huge conference call in place of a live sales conference to keep costs down. Hundreds of folks around the country—sales reps, editors, marketing folk, and so on—all sitting and listening in to the same phone call to hear the book presentations.

Random House also supplies its sales reps with audio recordings the editors make describing their books. This way they can develop greater knowledge of each individual title and be able to craft their own fresh-sounding way to pitch it to their customers.

Other publishers are forgoing creating these kinds of in-house materials and instead are focusing the money on social media campaigns to create word-of-mouth buzz prior to a book releasing.

Do Authors Go?

Occasionally, authors are asked to attend the sales presentation. Celebrity books and other types of books driven by the author's personality are the likeliest candidates for this. When this happens and the author has charisma, it does make a difference. Having met the author, and having heard the author's own take on his or her book, the sales reps are often more enthusiastic about selling the book.

> **SLUSH PILE**
>
> Sales reps are very nice people, but do not attempt to call them. They (and your editor) will not be amused if you track them down and chat them up about sales for your book. There have been many instances in which overzealous authors have soured the publisher's sales reps on pushing their books.

Should you offer to attend the sales conference? If you're a dynamite public speaker and are comfortable addressing large audiences, sure. It never hurts to ask. But don't take it personally if you're given a polite "no, thanks." Author presentations are rare these days.

Short of attending in person, is there anything you can do to try to jazz up the sales reps? Over the years, many authors have tried many things. Cookbook authors have endeared themselves by sending along sweet things based on recipes in their books. Natural health authors have sent along herbal supplements. T-shirts, CDs, and all sorts of little freebies are generally welcome, but they should tie in with your book somehow. Ask your editor how he or she feels about the idea before you rush out to the store to buy gifts.

Dumps, Store Exposure, and Other Promo Ideas

While the sales rep is working to convince the book buyer to order your book, he's also trying to convince her to take more than just a few copies. One of the best ways to do this is to package several copies of the book together in a display pack and offer it at a higher discount: "Order 12, get an extra copy," or "Order 8 copies and get this attractive *counter display*."

The days of *dumps* and displays are fading, however. The large chains seldom buy them because space in their stores is at a premium, and the publishers don't get enough orders to justify producing them. But savvy publishers continue to offer multiple-copy *prepacks* to encourage larger orders.

Booksellers are just as anxious to make money as publishers are. One of the more ingenious ways for them to make money is to charge publishers for special placement or displays. This is a part of the book business every writer needs to understand. We all want to see our books on the tables in the front of the store, and many a disappointed writer has called his publisher to complain when he didn't see his books displayed there. The bottom line is that prominent display costs money.

Let's say Valentine's Day is approaching, and bookstore chain X is planning to build special Valentine's Day–themed displays in all 500 stores. But it won't just wander around the stores pulling romance novels, sex books, and books with red or pink covers to use in the display.

DEFINITION

Several copies of the book placed in a cardboard holder can be called either a **counter display, prepack,** or **counter pack.** Larger displays that stand on the floor and display eight or more copies are called **dumps.** The **endcap** is the shelf at the end of an aisle, a prime place for bookstore browsers to see your book. Publishers can sometimes pay booksellers for the chance to have a display of their books on the endcap.

These stores sell positioning. For a fee, a publisher can buy a place in the holiday display. Sometimes the display is on the *endcap*, the small area on the end of each aisle; sometimes it's on a table. Keep in mind that almost all of the special display space you see in a bookstore is paid placement by the publisher. In many cases, publishers can't even purchase the space unless the bookstore has already decided it would like an extra-large order.

Remember those free bookstore gift catalogs we urged you to collect for research? The publishers of the books featured in those catalogs paid for them to be there. The cost to be included in these catalogs can run to several thousand dollars per title.

Ask your editor about all these things. You, as the author, have no control over whether your publisher decides to offer a counter display or pay for an endcap display for your book. Depending on the subject of your book, it might not be appropriate at all. But it never hurts to ask your editor if there are any special plans for displays or in-store promotions.

Printing and Shipping Your Baby (and Warehousing the Rest)

After leaving the account with orders in hand (or in the laptop, as the case may be), the sales rep transmits these orders to the main office. When all the accounts have been seen and all the advance orders for your book are in, these numbers are then used to set the size of your book's first print run, or *first printing*.

DEFINITION

Just before a book is shipped to the printers, the publisher takes a close look at the advance orders received from bookstores and uses this information to decide the book's **first printing,** or the number of books to be printed the first time out.

When the printer has printed and bound all your books (this takes 4 to 6 weeks, on average), the book is ready to be sent out. Large bookstore orders are sometimes shipped directly from the printer to the store's main warehouse, bypassing the publisher's warehouse and distribution system. Other orders may be filled from the publisher's warehouse.

When all advance orders have been shipped, the rest of your books are stored in the publisher's warehouse. There they wait, hoping to be sent out to fill other orders and reorders. Depending on the size of your book's print run, the publisher may have anywhere from 500 to several thousand copies of your book in the warehouse. Smaller, more frequent printings are now the rule. The publisher hopes that demand for your book will soon deplete the stock on hand and that the book will go into a second, third, and fourth printing—and beyond! Reprints happen quickly, don't worry. Actually, they don't happen quickly if your book has been printed overseas, but that's a different story ....

Why such small numbers of extra copies? Because the publisher's best chance to make money is by not overprinting. Many a profit has been squandered on an unnecessarily large second printing.

If any of your books are returned unsold by the bookseller, those copies probably will rejoin the others in the warehouse. If they are in good enough condition, they might be reshipped to fill other orders. If not, they are classified as damaged and head for the recycling center. Returns affect the inventory levels and are always taken into account when a new print run is under consideration.

Book Shows

No description of the book sales process would be complete without at least mentioning the annual booksellers' shows and conventions. Book shows come in all sizes and shapes and may cover more than just books (such as the Christian Booksellers Association show in the summer that includes music and gifts).

Book Expo America

While the smaller shows can be of interest, the biggest of them all is Book Expo America, or BEA. Held once a year in late May or early June, this is *the* trade show for the publishing industry. The location used to vary around the country from year to year, but it's now such a big show that it only happens in New York and once in a great while Los Angeles. (If this interests you, check bookexpoamerica.com to see when it's coming to LA.)

Publishers take large booths and display glossy blow-ups of the covers of their top titles. Their booths are stocked with catalogs for the fall list, and many publishers have freebies to pass out to booksellers: posters, advance reading copies, pins, jelly beans, T-shirts—you name it. Some of the larger publishers hold parties to fete their big clients and their big authors.

Yearly, publishers debate the value versus the cost of this show, which was designed to cater directly to independent booksellers buying books for the year but has increasingly become simply an industry gathering place. Agents actively sell rights for titles, editors set up meetings, and publishers prowl the floor looking at what the competition's offering.

Do Authors Go?

Yes, some authors do go to the Book Expo. Should you go? It depends on why you want to go. Unless you're a big celebrity author, no one will make a fuss over you. It can be quite a humbling experience to be an unknown author at this big event. Long lines form for free, autographed books from well-known authors. Not-so-long lines form for authors whose books are little known. Your publisher may not be willing to invest the money or the time in having you there.

One thing to ask about, though, is whether your book will be featured at your publisher's booth. If your book is just a few months away from being published and if it's a key title on the list, your publisher might decorate its booth with large posters of the book cover or pass out galley copies to book buyers and media folks to generate buzz.

> **SLUSH PILE**
>
> Understand that the books featured at BEA are from the fall list; the books are scheduled to be published in the autumn after BEA is held. Many an author whose book has just been published prior to BEA has been crushed to learn that his book won't be featured or that his publishing house may not even have a booth. But this isn't the kiss of death by any means. You can ask your editor what the presence will be, but don't be discouraged if your book isn't a key title. Being featured at BEA may help a few books, but the vast majority do just fine without it.

If you want to go to the Book Expo on your own as a visitor to learn more about the book business, go ahead. This is a great opportunity to pick up catalogs from many other publishers and learn about new books coming out. (Your publisher may be able to get you a free convention badge; just ask.) Check out the information for this year's show at bookexpoamerica.com. This site should also fill you in on the cost to register as a guest. You can also learn about special programs that happen just before the show itself and are geared to writers or indie publishers, like the Big Ideas at BEA conference. Check out ibpapublishinguniversity.com.

Smaller, regional booksellers' conventions also are held around the country. Ask your editor if there is a regional show in your area. Shows like the New England Booksellers Association or the Northern California Independent Booksellers Association are more likely to feature local authors, and they are a great way to meet book sellers, local media, and publishers' reps.

The Least You Need to Know

- Bookstores order books up to 6 months before the book is actually available.
- The size of a book order depends on the popularity of the topic, the popularity of the author, and the publisher's publicity plans.
- With so much sales data available, the order process is very formulaic and takes into account the actual sales history of other books on the topic, as well as the author's previous book sales.
- Celebrity authors might be invited to a sales conference or a bookseller's convention, but most authors are not.

Maximum Publicity for Maximum Sales

Chapter 21

In This Chapter

- What publicity can do for your book sales
- What to expect from the publicity department
- How two big promoters became mega-best-selling authors
- Tips on generating your own publicity
- The beauty of radio

"Publicity? But I landed a big-time publisher," you say. "Why should I have to learn about publicity?" Your publisher has a whole department that does publicity. Isn't that its job?

Yes, it is the publisher's job. But it's also your job. You should learn about publicity, and you should start learning about it the minute you sign the contract with the publisher. Publicity is a critical element in the success of your book. As the author, you need to be publicity savvy, just as knowledgeable about this part of publishing as you've become about all the other steps thus far.

Sheree and Jennifer meet other published writers all the time, and though all writers grouse about the high turnover for editors at big houses, the number-one gripe is in the area of promotion. Many authors feel their publishers don't live up to the promises made in the sales catalog and that promotional efforts are quickly abandoned if the book doesn't take off immediately. So learn what you can, because it will be important later.

On the other hand, big publishers work hard to stretch already-thin budgets across many books and authors. They have to balance expensive advertising and marketing materials, doing less with more.

It's never too soon to begin thinking about publicity for your book. By starting early, you can make media contacts now that you can call on in the future. You can send out copies of your proposal or manuscript-in-progress to writers and celebrities in the hopes that they'll give you an endorsement. You can even watch more television, listen to more radio, and spend more time online cruising blogs and websites so you have a better sense of which media outlets would be best for your book. Get started acting and thinking like a book publicist right away.

Publicity: Then and Now

The role of the author has changed dramatically over the years. In times past (or so we hear), an author could turn in a completed manuscript, dust off her writerly hands, and allow the publisher to take it from there. Authors didn't sully themselves with commerce. The in-house publicity staff would handle all the details about the book's publicity, sending sweet and gentle notes to the author to let her know the details on the many upcoming reviews, book signings, and publicity appearances.

Today, the publisher expects the author to take a very active role in publicizing the book, possibly even taking the lead (depending on how large the publisher's publicity staff is). Remember, "Does this author have a *platform?*" is the question asked over and over in all editorial meetings today. When evaluating the feasibility of your nonfiction project, the publisher places a great deal of weight on what you're already doing and how hard you plan to work on the book's behalf, with speeches, newspaper editorials, local appearances, magazine columns, social media presence, and the like. The publisher took all this into consideration on that fateful day in the editorial meeting when your book received the go-ahead.

DEFINITION

All publishers are looking for authors who have a **platform,** an existing audience for the book. Your platform might include lectures, a radio or television show, or a widely read blog. These aren't the planks that hold up your platform? Better start building a bigger platform now! Become an expert somewhere, if only in your local newspaper. Don't put it on hold while you write your book.

If you don't have an obvious platform, talk to your editor or marketing manager anyway. You may have contacts that are useful. No one pays for author tours anymore (it's nothing personal, it's just how it is these days), but they can work to schedule signings and media appearances if the author is traveling to a city anyway for another event. If you speak at seminars or conferences, travel for business, or are going to visit your great aunt in San Francisco, let your publisher know—it may be able to capitalize on your schedule.

Novelists? How do they ever build a platform? They can and they do. Garth Stein, best-selling author of *The Art of Racing in the Rain* has a well-read online newsletter that he sends to everyone who has attended one of his readings (and signs up for it, of course). Check it out at garthstein.com.

Just What Is Publicity, Anyway?

According to the dictionary, *publicity* is defined as "the process of drawing attention to a person or thing." You should know, however, that in the world of publishing, publicity refers more correctly to "the process of drawing attention to a person or thing for free." Publicity is not an ad in *People* magazine; it's an article in *USA Today*. Publicity is not a direct mail piece sent to a million homes; it's your voice on a radio station broadcast to a million homes. Publicity is not a small ad on a big website; it's an author interview on the website.

DEFINITION

Books become known to the reading public through **publicity:** reviews, articles, and mentions of the book and its contents in all forms of media. As media changes, so, too, do the opportunities for free publicity.

Print and television advertising is seldom done in the book business. Why? It has to do with the economics of advertising, the huge cost of the ad compared with the retail price of what's being advertised. General Motors buys lots of ads to sell cars, but remember how much a car costs. If just 10 or 20 cars sell, that pays for the ad. But if a publisher bought the same ad for your book, imagine how many books he'd have to sell at $22.95 to come close to breaking even. So don't tell your publisher your book would be a best-seller if only the publishing house would advertise on the *Today Show*.

The exception is targeted advertising (placing an ad for a massage book in a massage magazine) or paying for the book to be featured in the catalogs published and distributed by large bookstore chains. Okay, another exception is James Patterson, a former advertising executive who sells in such huge numbers that, yes, his publisher does indeed buy print ads for his books.

Publicity is the stronger way to sell a book. Articles and interviews make you appear to be an expert and give an independent endorsement to your book.

What the Publicity Department Can Do

As dazzling as the idea of glamorous television appearances and a late-night interview with Conan or Jimmy Kimmel might be, it seldom happens with most books. Let's take a clear-eyed look at what you, as a first-time author, can reasonably expect from your publisher's publicity department.

The actual legwork to publicize your new book begins in the publicist's office some 3 or so months before your book is scheduled to be released. Publicists might send out bound galleys or *review copies* to reviewers, work on setting up local book signings and local media tours, and try to be sure your book gets into the hands of the right media people. The publicists also make follow-up calls to be sure the information arrived, to gauge interest, and to arrange for book interviews. Publicist Arielle Ford calls this part of the publicity process "smiling and dialing."

DEFINITION

The publisher might send out free **review copies** of your book to anyone who might help promote it. Books might get sent to book reviewers, celebrities, bloggers, television and radio producers, online columnists, and the like. Sometimes these folks' mail is so heavy with free books that they need help lugging the sack inside.

Although all authors dream of a nationwide book tour, we've warned you that it's becoming a very rare thing indeed. To avoid disappointment later, ask your editor several months before your pub date if there are plans for any kind of tour. You might as well find out now. If there *are* plans for a tour, you'll need the advance warning to rearrange your schedule.

The Publicity Department's Full Plate

If you think the publisher's publicity department is going to work 24 hours a day to drive your book onto the best-seller list, guess again. The folks in publicity are responsible for doing what they can for as many as 10 or 15 books at a time. Understand that there's nothing for you as an author to gain by complaining about this situation.

Instead, you can use this opportunity to take your book's fate into your own hands. To avoid duplication of effort and some bad feelings all around, it's best to let the publicity department have a clear shot at your book for the first few months after it's released. When the people in the publicity department have let you know it's time for them to turn their attention to other books (and they will be honest with you, if you ask), that's the green light you need to roll up your sleeves and take it from there.

> **SLUSH PILE**
>
> Feel the need to call the publicity department for daily check-ups on what's going on with your book? Don't. Frustrated by what you view as a lack of effort and interest? Be careful how you communicate those feelings. Maybe your agent should place the call. A cranky author can turn off the staff—and once you're viewed as a problem, people in the publicity department may do even less for your book. Remember what your grandmother told you: you can catch more flies with honey ….

"We are thrilled to work with authors who have taken the time to learn the ropes about publicity and can take an active role in it," says a longtime industry publicist. Don't worry that the interest will have disappeared because the book has been out for a few months. If your book is well written, well researched, and well targeted, you can promote it for years to come.

Novel Approaches

Publicizing fiction is a challenge. With fiction (particularly first-time fiction), a publicist can't do too much beyond sending out review copies to well-known authors in the hope of creating a stir, targeting literary review sources such as *The Bloomsbury Review*, and trying to arrange for profile pieces in an author's local newspaper. "We also try to arrange readings at well-known literary bookstores such as Elliot Bay Booksellers in Seattle or Tattered Cover in Denver," a fiction publicist explains.

Targeting the nation's many active book groups is another way to publicize new fiction. Some publicists maintain lists of contacts for the bigger clubs and know which bookstores have large groups registered with them. At one time more than 400 book groups were registered with Denver bookstore Tattered Cover.

Novels can also be promoted through magazine excerpts or serialization. This is arranged not by the publicity department, but rather by the rights department. If you retained first serial rights in your contract, it's your responsibility (or your agent's) to sell these rights. No matter who's selling them, this has to happen many months before the book actually is published.

A recent trend has developed toward glossy and glamorous lifestyle articles about young novelists. These articles seem to talk more about the loft apartments they live in, where they hang out with friends, or an intriguing story behind the writing of their book than about the work itself. If you think there might be a cool lifestyle (as opposed to literary) angle your publicist could use, by all means tell him about it.

Jeff Kleinman of FolioLit, the agent for Robert Hicks's best-selling *The Widow of the South*, feels that the fact that Hicks's book was set in a real place helped publicity. "A producer could read the scene about young boys dying in the halls, then send a crew out to film those same halls to show their viewers. You could create a story about something real." The Hicks book was also the focus of lifestyle pieces that featured his own quirky home and his involvement in the successful attempt to preserve the mansion that serves as the centerpiece in his novel. Be creative about what in your life as a writer could translate well to a visual medium like television or a glossy lifestyle magazine.

Chicken Soup for Everyone!

Mark Victor Hansen and Jack Canfield are the well-known authors of the best-selling series *Chicken Soup for the Soul*, with a mind-boggling 140 million copies in print. But were they always best-selling authors? Did their publisher (Health Communications) have a superhuman publicity department that did all the work for them? Not by a long shot. Let's see how Mark and Jack did it.

Ask the Experts

The two friends decided they wanted their first book, *Chicken Soup for the Soul*, to be a best-seller. But instead of sitting back and waiting passively for a publisher to make that happen, these two took active steps to achieve their goal.

Long before their book was even published, they set out on a mission. They interviewed best-selling authors from the 1980s and 1990s, people like John Gray of *Men Are from Mars, Women Are from Venus* and M. Scott Peck of *The Road Less Traveled*. Mark and Jack asked each of these longtime best-selling authors a very simple question: "How did you become a best-selling author?" Makes sense, doesn't it?

The Secret Formula

So what did they learn on their fact-finding mission? The key to a best-seller truly is publicity—and lots of it! M. Scott Peck told Hansen and Canfield he gives one interview a day to any radio station, regardless of its size. His approach seems to have worked in a big way: *The Road Less Traveled* was on *The New York Times* best-seller list for 12 years—not 12 weeks or even 12 months, mind you, but *12 years!*

Hansen and Canfield have taken Peck's advice to heart. They not only gave an interview a day for years and years, but they also let producers around the country know they were always available as last-minute guests to fill in for a cancellation (a little trick they learned from best-selling sex advice author Dr. Ruth).

Although their books were best-sellers for more than a decade, they both still regularly do media appearances now for their various projects. No media outlet is too small for them to appear.

It's worth noting that Hansen and Canfield paid for most of their publicity efforts themselves. They worked with their publisher's publicity department, of course, and kept the staff informed of everything they did. But they firmly believe it's the author's responsibility to create demand for a book.

The Complete Idiot's Guide to Publicity

So how can you put what the mega-best-selling authors of *Chicken Soup for the Soul* learned into action? Here are ideas and suggestions to get you started planning your publicity campaign.

> **HOT OFF THE PRESS**
>
> Start now to gather things for your electronic press kit. Make a file in which you keep a bio, a professional picture of yourself in jpeg format, clips of your appearances or audio tapes of your speeches, and newspaper and magazine links to articles about you or the topic of your book. The earlier you start to build this file, the more you will have to choose from when the time comes to assemble your press kit. You can e-mail it quickly to any producer or media person who displays an interest.

Press Release Basics

A press release is a one-page announcement sent to various members of the media. Like the queries you now know how to write, a press release serves to catch the interest of the person reading it. Press releases start out with a catchy headline. Often these same headlines will be used in the newspaper or magazine articles that result, so choose carefully! Here are a few sample press release headlines.

- Authors Reveal Stunning Reasons for Juvenile Crime

- Rock Musicians Share Their Vegetarian Recipes in *Food Without Faces*

- Secrets to Surviving Your Husband's Midlife Crisis

Each of these was crafted to convince a jaded press person (who has seen and heard it all) to keep reading and to learn more about you and your book. A press release needs to deliver the basics of who, what, when, why, and where. It also needs to have a clear purpose: are you trying to interest the media in writing a feature article, announcing a press conference, or just hoping for reviews? To learn more about writing an effective press release, we recommend Marcia Yudkin's book, *Six Steps to Free Publicity*, *Third Edition*. She also has lots of free tips and an e-mail newsletter on publicity ideas you can get weekly. Check her out at yudkin.com.

A Sample Press Release

Cindy Bailey and her husband Pierre are the authors of *The Fertile Kitchen Cookbook* and have devoted countless hours to publicity. Here's an example of a compelling press release that will catch the eye of a producer or print editor.

NATIONALLY TELEVISED AUTHORS INSPIRE NEW HOPE FOR COUPLES BATTLING FERTILITY ISSUES

The Fertile Kitchen® Cookbook: Simple Recipes for Optimizing Your Fertility reveals the secrets to changing your diet and increasing your chances of conceiving.

San Jose, CA. September 20, 2012. Are you one of the millions of couples challenged with fertility issues and desperately trying to conceive a baby? Do you understand the importance of diet in conception and what foods you can eat to optimize fertility? The recently released cookbook, an Amazon top seller, unlocks the secrets to a "fertility diet" and is endorsed by Philip E. Chenette, M.D., and Medical Director of Pacific Fertility Center. *The Fertile Kitchen® Cookbook* teaches the importance of diet, what foods you can and cannot eat, how to shop healthy, and most importantly includes full color, easy-to-follow recipes that are simple and flavorful.

"I was devastated when I was told by a leading reproductive endocrinologist I had a 2 percent chance of becoming pregnant," says Cindy Bailey, co-author of *The Fertile Kitchen*® *Cookbook*. "As a now proud mother, I am excited to share with other women and couples how they can increase their chances of becoming pregnant just by changing their diet."

The Fertile Kitchen® *Cookbook* is not your typical cookbook. It offers simple recipes that make rigid dietary guidelines easy to follow. The cookbook additionally includes expert advice, dietary guidelines, tips on lifestyle factors for conception, cooking tips, and flexible recipes to accommodate substitutions. It is an all-in-one resource for women trying to conceive. This book is also for men experiencing fertility issues, men who want to support their partners, and cooks and noncooks alike.

"With these recipes, you can't tell they contain no sugar, dairy, or wheat, and that's the point!" says Pierre Giauque, Ph.D., co-author of *The Fertile Kitchen*® *Cookbook*. "We don't want you to feel like you're on a diet."

Cindy Bailey and Pierre Giauque, Ph.D., will be doing a cooking demonstration and book signing at DOMUS, the cooking store in Willow Glen at 1395 Lincoln Ave., San Jose, CA, on Saturday, October 20, 2012, from 1:00 P.M. to 2:00 P.M. Books will be available for purchase at the store.

About *The Fertile Kitchen*® *Cookbook*

The Fertile Kitchen® *Cookbook* includes a variety of simple-to-make, tasty dishes that make the "fertility diet" easy to follow. In this cookbook, the authors share flavorful recipes along with the dietary guidelines that helped them succeed in bringing home a baby. Readers will learn the importance of diet in conception and pregnancy, what foods you can and cannot eat to enhance fertility, how to identify and shop for healthy ingredients and food items, and how to prepare and cook the nutritious and fertility-enhancing recipes included. The Fertile Kitchen® doesn't guarantee success for every couple, but the cookbook does put you on a wholesome, healthful diet that is at the very least good for you. For more information, please visit fertilekitchen.com or e-mail info@fertilekitchen.com.

Useful Contacts, Bookstores, Websites, and Other Media

Draw up a list of media contacts you have now (and ask your friends who they know), and work hard to expand this list by joining organizations or attending events where you might meet members of the media.

Talk to your local bookstores about the fact that you have a book coming out, and ask for advice on how to promote it in their stores. Make it a point to attend events in many bookstores to learn what kind of event draws a crowd and what draws only the author's family members. An event in a bookstore described as a "book signing" is a flat-sounding event and only draws a crowd for a celeb who has many die-hard fans content to just stand in line for a chance to gaze upon him or her briefly while waiting for a signature. We know one author who is usually so worried that no one will show up that he sends e-mails and flyers to all his friends and family. His signings are usually well attended, but he doesn't sell many books.

HOT OFF THE PRESS

The cub reporter you befriend today may be the editor of the business section by the time your book is published!

Read papers, magazines, and websites, and take note of who writes articles on topics that relate to your book. Jot down not just the book reviewer but also the names of reporters whom you can try to interest in writing a feature-length piece about you and your book. One author sent a note to a woman at *USA Today* years ago to let her know how much he enjoyed one of her articles; now she is in regular contact with him as an expert in that field.

Here are some great tips from BookTour.com's Pressfinder to keep in mind when dealing on your own with the media:

- Don't spam.
- Don't brag.
- Don't harass.
- Don't give up.

Promotional Items

When your publisher has the finished artwork for your front cover, have a printed postcard made with the book's cover, publication, and ordering information. They make great thank you cards or note cards and help keep the name of your book in front of everyone's eyes. (On a similar note, co-author Jennifer and her co-authors on *Christmas Miracles* had ink stamps made that said "I Believe in Christmas Miracles" and used them on the outside of all their correspondence.) Other great, inexpensive promotional items can include bookmarks, sticky notes, and bookplates.

With these promo items, you can circulate the image of your book long before it appears on bookstore shelves. Of course, be sure to send out a whole bunch when your book is published to remind people to buy it.

"And Our Next Guest Is ..."

Among the best ways authors can help publicize their book when it's available in bookstores is to arrange radio interviews. Radio is still a tremendous medium for books; of all the different types of media, it sparks the quickest response. How does it work?

HOT OFF THE PRESS

Steve Harrison of Bradley Communications has published his *Radio-TV Interview Report* for years and has seen countless success stories of huge publicity bookings. He decided to take it all one step further and get top radio and TV producers together in a room with the authors and experts who want to pitch them. The National Publicity Summit in New York has become a great place to go to make face-to-face media contacts and pick up great information. Check out nationalpublicitysummit.com for details.

Radio Still Sells

If you see an ad for something on television, you file that impression away in your mind and perhaps act on it in the future. But countless advertising studies have shown that the information we hear on the radio sparks an immediate response. If you hear something on the radio about a book that interests you, you think to yourself, *Hey, I'm going to stop off at the bookstore on the way home tonight and pick that up!* Or *I'm going to order this on my Kindle right away!* Radio is a powerful way to sell books.

"Radio listeners just fire up their computers and order the book they just heard about," one author told us. "Which means that after every big radio interview nowadays, I check my sales figures on Amazon.com and can literally see the books selling from the earlier interview. It's a secret thrill!"

All those folks trapped in their cars on the roadways have nothing else to do but listen to you explain to them how much better their lives will be and how much more money (or love, or sex, or jobs) they will have if they will only rush out right now and buy a copy of your book. Make it your goal to become an expert radio talk show guest, and your book sales will shoot through the roof.

Selling Yourself to Radio

But how can you get yourself booked as a guest on the radio? There are two ways to become a guest on radio shows. The first is to call and try to get someone interested in you. The second is to let someone get interested and call you!

All the information you need to research radio stations across the country (from the size of the station to the phone numbers and addresses of the hosts and producers) is available online nowadays. Many of the services are quite costly and are geared to professionals, but at BookTour.com, you can sign up for their "Pressfinder" function for only $29.99 per year.

Which Stations, Which Shows?

How do you decide which stations in which markets to approach? Ask friends and relatives across the country for advice about which radio stations in their area are the most popular and which ones have live talk shows. Make it a point when you travel to listen to the local radio stations, station-hopping along the dial until you've identified a few that seem appropriate. Ask other authors you might know which stations have worked for them.

Be on the lookout for the largest stations in the area, those with the greatest broadcast area. Radio shows with syndicated programs (programs that play on more than one station) are gems you should always dig for. Giving one interview to a syndicated host helps you reach several media markets and millions of people at once.

Smiling and Dialing, E-Mailing and Pleading

When you've identified the likely stations, you're ready to begin your campaign. Call the station first to confirm that the information listed in Pressfinder is still current; stations can change their format at any time. It's very important that you have the correct name for the producer because it's the producer's responsibility to put together an interesting show.

Spend time and effort in creating your "pitch," your 30-second speech about why this particular producer should book you as a guest. (Likewise, if you're e-mailing, the subject line needs to be intriguing.) Don't start your pitch by saying, "I wrote a book on …," but instead say confidently, "I'm an expert on … and your listeners will be interested in the topic." If you don't come across well in those 30 seconds on the phone, the producer won't have high hopes for how you'll handle yourself once you get on the air. When you're confident that your pitch is compelling, pick up the phone and call (or compose your winning e-mail)! Follow up a successful pitch with a copy of your book and that press kit you've put together.

EXPERTS SAY

"We don't care about authors as authors and books as books. Authors as experts who can talk knowledgeably about topical issues, that is what we want on the radio," says Joel Roberts, morning talk show host turned media trainer. No producer for radio or television is really booking you to talk about your book, why you wrote it, and what's inside. She's trying to put together a show that will interest her audience, a lively and topical show that will grab and hold its attention. See more of what Joel Roberts has to say about how to get a producer's attention at joelroberts.com.

Longtime radio and television producer turned media trainer Michelle Anton (who, for 5 years, produced the *Dr. Laura Show*) believes that to get booked on big shows, you need to work hard to be sure you look and sound different from the other experts already out there. "There is hardly anything new on the planet, and chances are good that the producer will have heard similar pitches from other experts and may have already had those experts on the show. Visit the show website and check into past guests. If they have had someone recently in your field, figure out how to change your angle to be dramatically different."

Michelle warns authors that you need to work hard before you pick up the phone or hit "Send" to pitch a producer. "Create a real sense of value in your message for the producer of the radio show. What problem are you solving for their audience? Be sure you can convey that in seconds."

Jess Todtfelt, a media trainer and former television producer for FOX News, holds the *Guinness Book of World Records* for the most radio interviews in one day. How many? 112. That's right—112 5-minute interviews to promote his book! You can learn how he did it at prmarketinginsider.com.

Get Them to Come to You

Is there an easier way to get booked? Do the producers ever call authors instead of authors calling them? Yes. Each month, *Radio-TV Interview Report* is sent to radio and television producers around the country to alert them to possible guests. Instead of calling producers around the country, you can simply buy yourself an ad in this magazine and let producers know about you and your expertise.

HOT OFF THE PRESS

On most radio programs, the producer is responsible for coming up with a lively show that sounds good on the air. Producers are always on the lookout for good guests. If you can present yourself and your topic in a way that sounds like it will make a good show, it won't be long before you hear the words "You're on the air!"

Not sure how to advertise yourself in a jazzy way to make producers call? Don't worry, the magazine staff folks can help you position yourself and your topic to appeal to producers. For more information on *Radio-TV Interview Report* rates and scheduling, visit rtir.com.

A Cross-Country Whirlwind Radio Tour

One way to hit a great many stations and markets in one short period of time is to arrange a satellite tour. Satellite radio tours are prearranged interviews with a large number of stations, all done in a single morning. You can sit at home in your bathrobe and give the same short interview over and over and over again to stations from coast to coast.

This type of interview is expensive (several thousand dollars) and needs to be professionally arranged; it's not something you can do on your own. Planned Television Arts in New York (plannedtvarts.com; 212-593-5820) is the best-known firm for satellite tours. "Radio is still gold," Rick Frishman told us, "You can do hundreds of shows from home."

Should You Be Media Trained?

Not everyone makes a natural radio guest. But learning how to get your point across quickly, deal with questions, and work the title of your book into every other sentence are all skills that can be acquired. You can do it yourself by listening carefully to radio shows and analyzing what works (for example, practice talking in short sentences that will stick in people's minds), or you can have someone teach you. Media trainers specialize in helping you with your communications skills and your ability to field questions and think on your feet.

If you're serious about being effective on the radio, media training can be money well spent. Training boosts your confidence and lessens your fears, and it increases your ability to sell your book on the air. You can find the names of media trainers online, by asking other authors, or even by asking radio producers for recommendations.

EXPERTS SAY

When first-time author Heather King hit the road to promote her book *Parched* about her life as "a down-and-dirty barfly," she quickly learned a valuable lesson: she had to be prepared to talk to folks live on the air who don't know the first thing about what you wrote. Over and over she had to deal with interviewers who hadn't actually read her book. She tells other authors, "It's a good idea to have some stock stories and anecdotes on hand … and make sure you always carry a copy of your book."

Media training isn't cheap. A less-expensive way to hone your off-the-cuff speaking skills and fashion your book promotion patter is by joining your local Toastmasters club (toastmasters.org). Don't wait until the last minute to do this, though. Although media training can be done in a day, giving speech after speech at Toastmasters to feel comfortable is a much longer undertaking.

Three Key Points

To get your point across on the air, you must always have two or three key points at your fingertips. Write them down on index cards and have them handy while you're being interviewed.

And don't forget that great politicians' trick: no matter what the question is, you can always turn it to your advantage by saying, "I'm so glad you asked that, it reminds me of something I point out in my book ...." Then you're off and running with your own agenda!

Touring Libraries

A quieter way to get the word out on your book is to arrange a tour of your regional library system. In the same way you thought up an "event" for your local bookstore rather than a dull book signing, think of a lecture topic or presentation that would interest library patrons. For example, co-author Jennifer spent a Saturday morning once driving to three different libraries in the Seattle area, giving talks to writers gathered there.

Libraries are happy to host novelists—sometimes more eager than bookstores, in fact. Call and ask for the head librarian and ask whether that location has author events. If they don't, ask which libraries do! Some libraries even have a small budget for honorariums.

Libraries also sometimes organize or host writers' conferences or other author events. Be sure your local library knows about you and your book so you'll be asked to participate as a speaker.

Reality Check

Editors love authors who see the reality of the situation and are willing to contribute to their own promotional platform—that is, bring in a publicist or PR firm to help promote them, their speaking circuit or seminars, and the book along the way. However, we've also had bad experiences with this approach. PR firms and publicists sell the author on what they can do (book them on big, big shows and pitch them to big, big magazines) and all too often authors sign up to pay for the full PR treatment. In the meantime, though, your editor has seen the actual advance sales numbers from various accounts and knows the industry isn't responding in an encouraging way.

When the book comes out, the publicity folks pitch your book and … nothing happens, or perhaps just a few small hits that don't really get much of a sales response. The sad truth is that you can't make a best-seller happen by sheer force of will and money alone.

Maybe the lesson here is that as an author, you can do everything right and the publisher can do everything right and the book just doesn't pop. No one has a magic formula, but you can increase your chances of success by doing extra publicity on your own.

Publicity Pays Off

Publicity can sell books, and lots of publicity can sometimes sell lots of books. You've learned that you may have to do much of the publicity for your book yourself and that it really isn't such a hard thing to do after all. If you believe in your book and can craft a message that appeals to producers, you'll be on the air in no time. In Chapter 22, we explore two other avenues for book publicity: television and online.

The Least You Need to Know

- Publicity sells books better than anything else.
- Your publisher will do some publicity, but a more sustained effort is your responsibility as the author.
- Publicity techniques can be learned, and persistence is the key.
- Radio producers decide which guests will be booked on a show. Your press kits should be targeted to them instead of the host.
- It is possible to advertise your availability as a radio and television guest.
- The longer you publicize your book, the longer it sells.

Television and Online Publicity

Chapter 222

In This Chapter

- Ways to get on television
- Pack your bags: satellite TV tours
- Tips for getting on the big shows
- Dressing the part
- Publicity on the Internet

You've learned all about radio interviews, but how do you get yourself on TV to talk about your book? The short answer is: you don't. You don't get yourself on television to talk about your book; you get yourself on television because you have something to say of interest to television viewers.

Gonna Make You a Star!

Remember the advice from Joel Roberts, the longtime radio guy turned media trainer, in Chapter 21? He said, "We don't care about authors as authors and books as books." What he meant was that a producer's main concern (both on the radio and on television) is putting together an interesting show viewers will enjoy. If viewers enjoy the show, more viewers will watch, so the channel can charge more for advertising, and the producer gets to keep his job. Got it?

"So," the interviewer begins, "why did you write this book?" And the viewer reaches for the remote control. An author sitting in a chair being interviewed about his book makes for flat TV. But someone sitting in a chair being interviewed about dramatic current events, or sharing information that viewers could use, or sharing a heartfelt story that moves the audience—*that* makes for good television. The fact that the person in the chair wrote a book is secondary.

So how do you get yourself booked on television to talk about your book? By convincing the television producer that what you have to say is of interest to her viewers and will make a lively show.

What You Need to Get Booked

The process of getting booked on a television show is basically the same as for a radio show:

1. Find the show you want.

2. Learn the producer's name.

3. Send information to the producer.

4. Follow up with an e-mail to make your pitch.

The standards for press materials for TV are quite a bit higher, however. Your press materials have to be more extensive. Instead of just the pitch letter and sample book that sufficed for a radio producer, your press kit for television should contain these items:

- A press release

- Suggested interview questions

- An author bio sheet

- A professional-quality author photo

- Suggestions for shows based on your book

- A copy of your book

- Ideas for how your book could be featured on their website (chapter excerpt, recipes, how-to hints, etc.)

Sending along a list of sample questions in your press kit is a great way for you to help the producer see how lively and thought-provoking your segment can be. If the producer ends up using those questions in the interview, you will be totally prepared and sound impressive.

"I've Got an Idea for a Show …"

Also send a list of sample show ideas. This is your chance to help the producer envision just how he could build a show around you. Help make his job easy by describing as best you can a segment that features you and your book. But remember, your show ideas must be timely, informative, provocative, and/or amusing—not just you sitting around being interviewed about your book.

EXPERTS SAY

Tina Macuha has been working in morning television for 15 years. "We've seen everything, and the pitches can seem so clichéd. You really need to come up with a fresh idea, a fresh angle." For local TV, anytime you can tie your expertise and your book's topic into a local event, all the better. If there's a bullying problem at a local school and you're an expert, pick up the phone and call a producer.

Perhaps you've written a book about dating. You can suggest to the producer that you'll find several single people and counsel them on the air about the perils of being single and then the cameras can follow them out on an actual date. That's much more interesting to watch than just you and an interviewer.

Pay attention to the news. Can you somehow tie a current event to your book? Authors of relationship books can comment on celebrity couples, authors of health books can tie into recent health studies, and authors of parenting books can comment on juvenile crime sprees. You get the idea. From now on, you must watch the news with an eye toward your own publicity.

Sample TV Pitch

Here is a sample television pitch to give you an idea how to craft these materials.

Dear Producer,

In need of great ideas for interesting holiday segments? Look no further! *Green Christmas: How to Have an Eco-Friendly Holiday* (Adams Media) is filled with ideas that will educate your viewers on how to tread lighter on the planet this December.

Possible news segments include:

Christmas trees: chop down a live tree or get a fake tree you can reuse year after year—which is better? Could film in a Sierra foothills Christmas tree farm and discuss the issue with the growers. Could also film in SF with

Friends of the Urban Forest, who deliver live trees and then pick them up after the holiday. Could film a mulching operation and discuss where the mulched Christmas trees go—for trail restoration.

Holiday atmosphere: build a cozy fire with wood or a fire log? Film in Stockton at the headquarters and factory of Duraflame, which recycles 50,000 tons of wood shavings a year into nontoxic firelogs that burn cleaner than actual wood logs. Great visuals of factory interior.

Gifts under the tree: how to not create extra waste. (Americans create 25 percent more garbage than usual during the holidays.) Film in SF with a business that sells compostable wrapping paper and recycled cards. Focus on gifts made from recycled materials. Lots of great visuals.

Green holiday entertaining: emphasis on organic and local. Film at Frey Vineyards, the oldest organic winery in the country (Napa). Interview local caterers about ways to cut down on wasted food while entertaining.

Do any of these sound like they would work for you? I'd be happy to discuss it further and will call next week to talk.

Sincerely,

Jenny Publicist

Getting on Regional Shows

Sure, you know which local television shows you'd like to be on in your area, but how can you find the regional shows across the country? And is it worth your time to try to get booked on regional shows?

The very same reference books and websites that list radio stations across the nation also list television shows. And don't forget to ask your friends and family across the country what they watch in their area.

Does regional television make a difference? "Regional TV is valuable," a California-based book publicist told us. "You reach a smaller market, but if you do enough regional TV, it can really add up. A great example of a strong regional show is *Good Day Atlanta*. They do lots of authors on that show." It also gives you a *video clip* you can use to pitch a larger show.

DEFINITION

A producer might ask you for a **video clip,** a tape of an appearance you've made on another television show.

When you've targeted the television show—and the producer—you want to reach, send off an e-mail with your press kit attached. Then wait. A good rule of thumb is to give your press kit a week's head start before you send a follow-up. If you're feeling bold, call the show and ask for the producer. Tell him you're following up on a press kit you sent—did he receive it? And does he have any questions? Practice your 30-second phone pitch; the producer won't give you much time, so try to hook him quickly.

Satellite Television Tours

As with satellite radio tours, it's also possible to sit in one place and do television interview after television interview. You're simply the talking head shown on the screen while the host asks questions (the same questions the last host asked). These satellite television tours must be professionally arranged. Again, the best known firm is Planned Television Arts in New York.

With a satellite television tour, you spend a few hours in a studio doing television interviews across the country, one station at a time. "In 2½ hours, you can do 22 interviews," says Rick Frishman of Planned Television Arts. Most of the shows you're hitting are the local noon-hour broadcasts on affiliate stations for NBC, ABC, CBS, and FOX.

How much is a satellite television tour? To do the whole country costs in the $12,000 to $15,000 range. It's an expensive undertaking, but it can hit many markets all at once. And it's reasonable compared with the cost of actually going on tour, which could be $1,500 to $2,000 per city in travel costs alone.

EXPERTS SAY

Rick Frishman of Planned Television Arts says, "To succeed in publicity, you've always got to think of new ways to reach people faster, cheaper, smarter. Think of a satellite television tour as the ultimate armchair publicity tour."

Life Without Oprah

These small stations are all well and good, but what author isn't dazzled by the prospect of the big time: a nationally syndicated talk show like *The View*. It used to be that all authors, regardless of what kind of book they'd written, harbored hopes of appearing on *Oprah*.

There are two kinds of shows—*live* shows and *taped* shows. Live shows are really and truly shot in front of an audience and aired immediately. When you appear on a taped show, you have to ask the producers when the episode will air.

DEFINITION

Shows that are aired as they are being filmed are **live.** Shows that are filmed and then shown sometime later are **taped.** Barbara Walters's ABC show *The View* is live. *Dr. Phil* is taped. *The Daily Show with Jon Stewart* is taped.

Am I the Main Attraction?

Did an appearance on *Oprah* ever guarantee a best-seller? No. Although the show certainly built many best-sellers, many other authors appeared on *Oprah* and saw little effect on book sales. What makes the difference? On *Oprah*, as on any other television talk show, the theme of the show itself makes a difference.

If you're booked on any TV show, be sure to ask how you and your book fit in with the theme. Be sure you've been asked to appear in a positive way, not used as a foil to make some sort of point. Understand that on some shows you might be made to look foolish, in a good-natured sort of way. Morning television is sometimes like that, particularly the local morning shows.

Will It Sell Books?

Be sure to ask the producer if you and your book's topic are the sole focus of the show. If so, and if the host holds up your book on the air and says, "This book is incredible. Everyone should buy a copy," that could make a dramatic difference in sales.

But if you're on the stage as a part of a *panel* of experts (each with a different viewpoint), there'll probably be little impact on book sales. But what the heck, you got a free trip to New York (or Chicago or Los Angeles). And all the producers from all the shows are watching, so you might get a call from another show. At the very least, you'll have a tape of your appearance you can now send to other television producers as proof of your knowledge and charisma.

DEFINITION

On television, featured guests are those who are central to the show. **Panel** members are those who make up a roster of experts on a topic.

Do the Producer's Work for Him

"I've learned from countless talk show appearances that producers love it when their guests can help put a show together," Bill Adler Jr. says. He made the rounds for many years with his book on how to keep squirrels out of your backyard bird feeder.

"Anything you can do to make it easier for the show will make it easier for you to get on the show. Producers are typically juggling a dozen or more shows at a time, and they appreciate the help."

Hands Off (for Now)

With the top national talk shows, let your publisher's publicity staff handle the bookings. If your book has been out for several months and nothing is forthcoming, ask as politely as you can if you can take a crack at it. Remember, be diplomatic. Thank them for all the efforts the publicity department has made on behalf of your book. Then take it from there.

How do you pitch these big talk shows? The same way you pitch your local noon news: with an e-mailed pitch, a press kit, and a follow-up phone call.

SLUSH PILE

Don't go to the trouble of getting booked on television without also taking steps to be prepared when you step in front of the camera. Practice, practice, and practice again. Write down your key points, and memorize them. Develop short "sound bites," or talking points, with the information you want viewers to remember.

About That Plaid Jacket …

Going on television? Hey, great! Now what are you going to wear? This seems like a silly question, but it really isn't.

Here's your chance to watch a great deal of television and call it "work." Turn on the set and watch closely. Study what the news anchors wear, how reporters are dressed in the field, and what the characters on your favorite sitcom are wearing. Take notes.

Does the woman on the 11 P.M. news wear a bright white sweater? No, she knows it would create problems with the camera. And her co-anchor, is he wearing a loud plaid jacket and a paisley tie? Nope. He's decked out in a dark navy jacket and a light shirt, with a tie that has a medium-size print on it.

Dress for (TV) Success

There's a real science to dressing for television. You need to consider not only the way your clothes look on screen—especially the colors and patterns—but also what your clothes say about you. Are you trying to position yourself as an expert on a scientific topic? Better dress like a scientific expert. Are you a romance novelist? Go ahead and let your outfit show it.

One great way to check how your clothes (and you, too) look on camera is to do a practice run with a video camera. Have a friend or family member tape you in a few different outfits and then look at them all with a critical eye. Choose the outfit that both looks the best and presents you in the proper mode.

Different Looks for Different Books

Once during a two-week period, co-author Jennifer was featured on several different television shows for several different books. So she had several different looks.

She appeared on a network show as a small-business expert with her book *101 Best Extra Income Opportunities for Women*. She wasn't there as a big-business expert in a dark blue suit, but as a small-business expert in a light turtleneck sweater and a camel-hair jacket. The effect was very friendly and approachable.

The next week, she appeared on a local television show for her *Christmas Miracles* book. Same outfit? No. She needed to look like the author of a Christmas book, not a business book. And although she did have an off-white suit embroidered with gold thread and decorated with sequins and bugle beads she wore to bookstore readings (and you know a thrift store has it now!), she knew it wouldn't work for a minute on a television screen. So she appeared on camera in a bright blue, fuzzy sweater.

She made yet one more appearance that same month for an earlier edition of the very book you hold in your hands, this time as a publishing expert on C-Span's *Book TV*. Was she in the fuzzy sweater? You guessed right, she wasn't. That time the dark blue business suit was the appropriate choice for the topic and the show.

What Really Works Online?

A nice thing about the Internet is that you don't have to worry about what you're wearing! Unlike other types of media, such as newspapers, radio, and television, the idea behind web marketing is to "fish where the fish are." You can find highly specialized user groups that are most interested in your book. These aren't mass audiences made up of people who may or may not be interested in you and your book; they're highly targeted groups of people.

To properly promote your book on the web, you must first get a domain name that features your book's title, such as mybooktitle.com. If you can't afford a full-on professionally designed website, get a free blog from blogspot.com and then "point" your domain name at your blog.

 EXPERTS SAY

Joining newsgroup discussions related to your topic can be a great way to promote your book. But don't be a jerk about it. "The most subtle way is to make sure that your book's title is embedded in your online signature," says author and agent Bill Adler Jr. So if your book is called *My Story,* try to get author@mystory. com as your e-mail address.

Fully exploit Amazon.com's Author Page function. Upload a flattering picture and your professional bio, link your blog and your website, and list all your events. You can even add videos.

Be a social media maven. Start a Facebook page for your book and ask everyone you know to friend you, like you, share your page with their friends, and so on. Give people a reason, of course; make them want to friend, like, or share your page for an interesting reason.

Be sure to tweet in your field, too. Best-selling author Susan Orlean likes to think of Twitter as "an ongoing book tour" that keeps readers aware of what she's up to.

Should I Create a Website?

The short answer is "yes." Creating a website can be free (many e-mail services let their customers create free websites) or quite costly (if you hire an expert to do it for you).

Creating a website can promote—as well as sell—your book. When you're promoting your book in an interview, you can tell folks that it's available from your website at mybooktitle.com. To actually sell books to the people who visit your website, you can partner with Barnes & Noble online or Amazon.com as an affiliate. Simply register with either site, and it'll handle the sales from your site.

If your website is just a vanity site about your book, don't expect to be flooded with visitors. If there isn't anything in it for them—excerpts, quizzes, interactive functions, links to related sites, or other jazzy tools—why would they stay? Ask yourself that question as you're planning your site.

Also understand that not only do you have to get people interested in reading your book, you now have the added task of getting them to come to your website. No one really will stumble across you by accident. You will have to drag each and every visitor there by your own marketing efforts.

EXPERTS SAY

At the bare minimum, you should have a Facebook page for your book. It's free, simple, and frankly, your publisher expects you to do it.

Read All About Me!

Another great aspect of the web is that more journalists are poking around there. Why? They're looking for story ideas, for experts, and for ways to legitimize trends.

The easiest way to reach such journalists is by signing up for the Help a Reporter Out (HARO) list. HARO is an e-mail blast sent several times throughout the day with requests from journalists and producers about the exact kind of people they want to interview/book. Sign up for free at helpareporter.com.

Here are a few sample requests from a recent issue:

Media Outlet: MSNBC.com

Query: Looking for hiring manager and HR experts who can discuss whether job candidates are expected to wear suits to interviews these days, or whether they're seeing more men wearing suits. Also looking for male job seekers, or those who have recently landed jobs, who can discuss whether what they wore impacted their interviews.

Media Outlet: *Des Moines Register*

Query: Looking for an expert (author? medical expert? psychologist?) to comment on how to deal with spring fever.

Media Outlet: *Real Simple*

Query: I am reporting a road test on hand sanitizers/antibacterial wipes, focusing on whether hand sanitizers are necessary or not. I.e., is Purell only for emergencies, like when you're changing a diaper and can't wash your hands? Will using hand sanitizers breed a bacterial superstrain that will kill us off along with our young? And if so, what is the hygienic thing to use instead when we need to clean our hands and can't get to a sink? Ideally, I would like to talk to health-care providers (especially pediatricians), infectious-disease experts, people from the hand-sanitizer industry, and alternative-healing practitioners. Thank you!

So writers from the MSNBC website, the *Des Moines Register*, and *Real Simple* magazine were looking for experts to interview and quote in stories. This beats all the work that an expert on men's attire, spring fever, or hand sanitizer would have gone through in order to catch their attention. Sign up, start reading the queries, and respond only to the ones for which you're genuinely suited. If you answer with off-target pitches (answer the request for a hand sanitizer expert as an etiquette expert, say), you'll quickly be banned from the site.

In Today's Newsletter ...

Another great way to get folks to read about you and your book online is by creating your own e-mail newsletter. Try to capture the names and e-mail addresses of friends, fans, and visitors to your website, and send out a regular e-mail newsletter in which you can tastefully promote both yourself and your books to your readers. One way to build a readership is by having a "sign up for my newsletter" link on your website, blog, or Facebook page.

E-mail newsletters can generate tremendous book sales almost instantly. Best-selling financial author David Bach has successfully increased sales this way, as did Mark Victor Hansen not long after *The One Minute Millionaire* was published. Hansen sent e-mail messages to his thousands of fans on his newsletter list asking them to help him become the number-one book on Amazon.com that day. By including a link to Amazon so readers could respond instantly, his book shot up quickly to that very spot!

The Least You Need to Know

- You can book TV publicity directly with the show's producer by sending a press kit and an e-mailed pitch letter and then following up with a phone call a week later.

- TV shows aren't looking for authors per se, but rather for timely, topical, and interesting guests. So send them a list of great show ideas based on *you!*

- An appearance on a national talk show does not an automatic best-seller make.

- You can hit many TV markets in one day with a satellite television tour. It's an expensive option, but it's cheaper than touring many cities one at a time.

- Publishers will expect you to master the ins and outs of online social media marketing such as Facebook and Twitter and whatever else emerges.

Real-Life Publicity and Marketing Ideas

23

In This Chapter

- Tips for building media interest in your book
- Secrets of the great book promoters
- Ways to make your bookstore event a success
- What it really takes to be a best-selling author

Radio publicity, television publicity, Facebook and Twitter fans and followers, endless promotion—what does this all really mean for you and your book? It seems so unreal. Could you and your book really end up media stars?

Sure. From major *media markets* like New York to small markets like Lubbock, Texas, the media need programming 24 hours a day. Hundreds of newspapers are still published around the country every single day of the week. Just think of how many stories need to be generated to fill that space, and those stories can't all be about Charlie Sheen or Kate Middleton. Many of them could be about you and the book you wrote. Your book could be getting *placement* somewhere in the news every day of the week!

Yes, P. T. Barnum would be proud. No, not because of his famous quote, "There's a sucker born every minute." Barnum was the original publicity hound, creating media events out of thin air to draw attention to his circus. You also need to learn to create events. You need to learn how to get the media to come looking for you!

Creating Media Events

Some of what you read in the newspaper or hear about on radio and television is the result of publicity efforts. It's a staged media event, a press release, a *press conference*, or a story idea suggested by a public relations professional on behalf of a client.

> **DEFINITION**
>
> A **media market** is a geographic area covered by a particular station or newspaper. Some markets, such as New York, are large media markets; others, such as Omaha, are small. A **placement** is a story or a mention of an author or book that's been placed in the media due to PR efforts. A **press conference** is a meeting to share something newsworthy with members of the media.

A media event is an artificially created event staged solely for the benefit of the radio microphones, television cameras, and reporters' notepads. After the media event is over, these members of the press return to the studio or newsroom and write about what just happened.

You can learn to create media events to promote yourself and your book. A successful media event is one that draws a great deal of press attendance. Events that create a draw usually have one (or more) of the following characteristics:

- Timeliness
- Visually interesting activities or backgrounds
- Controversial content
- Humorous subjects or backgrounds

The Timely Event

Is there a way to tie your book and its topic into what's happening in the news right this minute? You learned to think about how to do this when crafting a press release in Chapter 21.

Let's imagine you've written a book on sexual addiction and a major political figure has just been caught in the act. This is the perfect moment for you to create a media event by calling a press conference. Alert the media (via a press release) to the fact that, at the press conference, you will reveal the number-one reason politicians are likely to cheat on their spouses—a topic radio producers will think is just perfect for *drive-time* talk radio! Will anyone show up to your press conference? Oh yes ... and you will be instantly booked on radio and TV.

> **DEFINITION**
>
> Radio shows that play between 6 A.M. and 9 A.M. are morning **drive-time** shows. They're ideal for book promotions. Listenership is high during these hours, and many stations feature live hosts who do interviews.

As an exercise, sit down with the morning newspaper and circle the major national news stories. Study them, and see if you can tie your book or your book's topic to them in any way. If you're at a loss with the national news, flip to your local news section and see if there's anything happening locally you can tie into. If there is, redo your press release to build up that angle and start e-mailing your new pitch to producers and reporters.

You should also spend time trying to think of seasonal angles for your book. Every year at Christmas, Jennifer gets booked on major television shows. Sure, producers want her for her Christmas books, but also for her gift books *Wear More Cashmere* and *The Martini Diet.* She sends out press releases touting her picks for the best "affordable luxury gifts" of the year and also offers to appear on talk shows to give tips on how not to gain weight at holiday cocktail parties. Works every time.

She does not play up the books themselves, though, since none of them are new releases. Instead she uses them as a way to position herself as "America's Affordable Luxury Expert" and then the books are slipped into mentions while she talks. Remember, to a producer, it isn't about you and your books; it's about what you can deliver for the audience (while still promoting as much as you can!).

Seasonal angles work for bookstore appearances, too. "Identify a theme in your book that you can hook to a holiday," Judith Horstman recommends. Her latest is *The Scientific American Book of Love, Sex, and Your Brain,* and yes, it is perfect for Valentine's Day.

A Visually Interesting Event

We live in a visual world, and the press will come if you can supply a good visual image. You know the type—those large newspaper pictures of a cute child frolicking on the banks of a lake on a sunny Sunday or dogs playing in the sprinklers—that sort of thing.

While managing a bookstore many years ago, co-author Jennifer created a media event on a sunny day by alerting TV stations to the fact that employees would be standing on a street corner blowing giant bubbles with wands. She was promoting a bubble book that came packaged with a plastic bubble wand. She was also promoting the bookstore. Did the television crews come? Yes. Those giant bubbles floating through the air made a wonderful visual image to show on the evening news.

So what can you do that's visual for your book? Deb Sharp wears an oversized bridal veil to events to promote her most recent mystery book, *Mama Gets Hitched*. "The veil is hard to miss. I get lots of attention when I wear that hideous veil."

Gretchen Anderson, author of *The Backyard Chicken Fight*, brings baby chicks to events at outdoor gardening stores, and it always draws a crowd of book buyers and television cameras.

Can you create a YouTube video from your event? Not the whole thing, of course, just a few memorable scenes that might draw viewers and (you hope) go viral. Anything that will make an interesting picture stands a chance of drawing media coverage. Keep this in mind when you're creating an event. Always include a visual element to ensure that footage will air or photos will run.

SLUSH PILE

You've heard it before: practice before you go on the air! Practice before you stand at the podium facing a sea of television cameras. Practice before you call a newspaper reporter on the phone to discuss a story idea. If you don't practice and you get it wrong the first time, there may not be a second time. To get over your stage fright, join a local Toastmasters speaking group and work on your skills. Check out toastmasters.org to find a chapter near you.

A Controversial Event

Is the topic of your book controversial? Can you create an event in which hundreds of angry people waving signs appear in front of a courthouse or a state capitol building? Then do it, because controversy sells. So does a surprise announcement or an amazing revelation.

If you plan to stage this kind of event, be sure you're prepared to verbally defend yourself and your beliefs.

A Humorous Event

Can you create an amusing event around your book? Perhaps design a silly contest or create an attention-getting award you'll bestow on some public figure.

These kinds of events are ideal for radio, particularly the kind of silliness that goes on during the morning radio shows. Producers of these shows are always on the lookout for something funny (or someone they can make fun of) and something that's outrageous.

Be warned, though: wear a thick skin because this sort of event could backfire. When Jennifer does radio and TV appearances as the author of *The Martini Diet*, she knows full well that the hosts will make all kinds of jokes and doesn't take offense. Because, hey, it sells books!

What Good Did That Do?

You staged an event and the media came. But when you turned on the TV that night, you heard the newsman say everything but the name of your book. And the lengthy newspaper article didn't even mention your book. So what good did that do?

Quite a bit. Even if your book didn't get any exposure, you did. You now have more experience in dealing with the media. You now have a newspaper article you can send out or a video or audio tape of you on the air. Keep trying. You'll soon learn how to be sure your book gets as much coverage as you do.

Use this story to generate more. Make a link to the television spot or media story on your webpage. Send the link along with a note in an e-mail to a producer or reporter you've been courting. Media exposure breeds media exposure.

EXPERTS SAY

In addition to all of this, we writers should be constantly tweeting and Facebook-ing, right? Maybe not, is what some writers are starting to realize. M. J. Rose, a longtime advocate of online marketing, said this recently: "Twitter or Facebook aren't the devil's spawn … the issue is just to decide how the return on the effort is working for you and if it's not—then don't beat yourself up." Check out her blog at mjroseblog.typepad.com/buzz_balls_hype.

In-Home Private Events

Want to meet your readers up close and personal and hand-sell a case or two of books? Maybe your book and its topic or theme will lend itself to an in-home event with friends. Rather than trying to get everyone to come to a static bookstore event (read on to learn how to make those less static), some authors put together entire evenings where the talk and the wine flow—and the book sales do, too. You can buy copies of your book from your publisher at your author's discount and sell them at retail price for a nice profit.

"Passion Parties, that is what we call them," Elaine Ambrose told us. "Not a sex toy party, mind you, but a classy one!" Elaine and several friends wrote *Daily Erotica: 366 Poems of Passion*, a book of poetry targeted to middle-age women, and that's who turned out in force for these events. "Instead of just selling one book at a time, we put together baskets that had books, wine with custom labels that said Menopause Chardonnay, and chocolate, of course. We made a 200 percent profit off the chocolate part!" The authors wore black dresses, red feather boas, red shoes, and sold their book all night long. They market their availability for in-home parties at their website, mydailyerotica.com.

Some novels can be promoted this way, too. Dawn Lairamore's YA novel *Ivy's Ever After* served as the basis for several home parties where moms brought their daughters dressed as princesses! Of course, every one of those little girls dressed in pink chiffon wanted a signed copy of Dawn's book.

How can you decide if your book will work for an in-home event? Be realistic, and realize not every book will. Sit down with an honest friend and brainstorm.

HOT OFF THE PRESS

Women love to go to home parties in private houses. Instead of a Tupperware party or The Pampered Chef, if your book will be of interest to middle-age women, design an entire evening around it. Include not just your book but other vendors, too, and make it an even bigger event when the other participants advertise it to their followers.

Can a successful in-home event lead to any kind of media coverage? Sure, if you invite a reporter or a news crew. And encourage everyone who came to Facebook about it to help spread the word.

Effective Bookstore Events

Okay, so maybe you're not quite ready for primetime TV or an in-home event. But what about an appearance at your local bookstore? That sounds easy enough, and it's simpler than getting on TV. But to have an effective in-store event still takes quite a bit of planning.

Many bookstores have a staff member whose primary function is to coordinate in-store activities. These folks are called *community relations coordinators* or *events coordinators*. In smaller stores, they're called "the owner."

> **DEFINITION**
>
> Many bookstores have an **events coordinator** on staff. This person's primary function is to arrange author appearances and other kinds of bookstore events. Sometimes this position is called a **community relations coordinator.**

The book business is quite competitive nowadays, what with all the online bookselling competition, and every bookstore tries hard to become a community center of sorts, the type of place where you head on a Friday night just to see what's happening. Music, poetry readings, author signings, appearances by children's book characters— all kinds of activities go on both at chain bookstores as well as at the independently owned stores.

You need to know this though: few experiences in life are as disappointing as an author appearance that flops. To sit at a desk surrounded by a stack of books, looking hopefully at people as they walk past without stopping … it's pretty awful. Many authors have been there. Read on to learn how to create a successful bookstore appearance.

An Event Is Better Than a Signing

An author book signing is a pretty dull event, especially if the author is unknown. So anything you can do to turn a bookstore appearance into an event helps create excitement and a crowd. An in-store class led by a how-to author is an event. A debate you've arranged between other writers with similar books is an event. A joint reading with local musicians, actors, and dancers is an event.

Don't sit behind a table and expect strangers to approach you. They won't. Give them a reason to come over and see what's happening for themselves.

"Always have food," Elaine Ambrose of *Daily Erotica* advises. "If you are going to sit there at a table in a bookstore at least have something tasty to draw strangers over to your table."

Elaine once used the "daily" aspect of her book to go around and approach browsers in the bookstore and read aloud to them the poem from their birthday. She sold more than one book that way!

HOT OFF THE PRESS

Invite everyone you know. A crowd builds a crowd. If bookstore customers see a crowd of people in a corner, curiosity will draw them over, too. For the author, it's always better to look out and see friendly and familiar faces. Just to play it safe, ask everyone you invite to bring a friend.

Don't Rely on the Bookstore for Publicity

Ask the bookstore what its standard procedure is for publicity and then do more. Much more. Don't make the retailer angry, but don't assume the bookstore will do it all for you.

This is a perfect time to approach a reporter for a feature article on you and your book. Bookstore appearances that are preceded by a newspaper story (and are mentioned in the story) are always more successful than those that haven't received any coverage.

Appearing on local television shows a few days before the event is also a way to build attendance. Ask the producer to flash the information about your event on the screen while you're talking.

Be creative about where you try to get publicity; try to get the message out to whatever group you believe will be interested in your book. Facebook the info to all your "friends," tweet some teasers about what might happen at the event, build curiosity, and give people a solid reason—other than loyalty or the fact that they're related to you—to show up.

Ask for a Display

Even if your appearance is a disappointment in terms of audience and sales, you might make some gains if your book is on display. Many stores have a special area where they display the books whose authors are coming. Many stores also make large posters for your book or display a poster you make. If your book is on display for a week or two, that's a victory in itself.

If all else fails, bring food. Yes, like Elaine Ambrose says, a plate of cookies can sometimes make a difference. Anyone who comes by for a bite will feel obligated to stop and listen to you for a moment anyway.

> **SLUSH PILE**
>
> Every author has a tale of a disastrous bookstore signing. If no one comes, use this as an opportunity to learn how to do the next one better. While giving in-store readings from her book, *Christmas Miracles,* Jennifer spent several hours one weekend afternoon at two different San Francisco bookstores sitting alone on a chair reading Christmas stories into a microphone. Embarrassing, but true. Even an ex-boyfriend who happened by unexpectedly wouldn't stay and listen! So if it happens to you, don't feel alone. You are now a bona fide member of a very, very large club.

Can You Really Afford a Best-Seller?

After all the information we've shared about publicity and how to get it, why would we ask you if you really can afford a best-seller? It may seem like an odd question, but it's worth thinking about.

Becoming a best-selling author is a job that requires work 24 hours a day, 7 days a week. Do you have that drive? Can you afford it emotionally, physically, or even financially?

Are you willing to spend less time with your family? Many best-selling authors tour constantly, living in hotel rooms across the country and sleeping on overnight flights. More than one marriage has been strained as a result of this lifestyle.

Do you have the stamina to be on the go all day long, from early morning interviews through to late-night talk shows? It can be a physically demanding job. Effectively maintaining a website, a Facebook fan page, or a constant Twitter presence is also a huge time commitment.

Some authors pay for constant promotion of their books. Richard Paul Evans of *The Christmas Box* and countless other seasonal best-sellers runs (and pays for) an elaborate publicity network that employs four people. Jack Canfield and Mark Victor Hansen paid for much of their own publicity during their long run with the *Chicken Soup for the Soul* books. It's a costly undertaking, one few publishers are willing to fund forever. (Of course, if your book makes it big and makes big bucks, you'll recoup your investment.)

Before you take the plunge and dedicate yourself to building a best-seller, stop and consider the effect your decision will have on others in your life. This is a major lifestyle change, and once undertaken, it's hard to turn back.

> **HOT OFF THE PRESS**
>
> Yes, really, some people do complain about success. It seems odd to work so hard to achieve something and then gripe about it when it works, but it happens. Listen in sometime to idle chatter among best-selling authors, and don't be surprised if you hear about how hard it is to get up in the morning for those early TV shows, that your hand really is designed to sign only so many books in one evening, and that they never see their children anymore ....

The Least You Need to Know

- The media is in constant need of new and interesting stories. Learn how to exploit this for your book's benefit.
- Creating media events that receive coverage can be a powerful way to spread the word about your book.
- To catch the media's eye, your event should be timely, controversial, visual, and/ or humorous.
- Anything you can do to make a producer's job easier increases your chances of getting a good spot on TV.
- Bookstore events need lots of promotion and publicity to really work.
- Having a best-selling book can extract a heavy toll emotionally, physically, and financially.

Continuing Your Career as an Author

Your book is on the bookstore shelves, but for how long? The more you understand what happens in the stores and what it means to you, the better you can make decisions about your future.

And is the life of an author really for you? How do you decide if your book is a success? Do you want to do it again? In Part 5, we help you make the decision where to go from here, and we give you ideas for other ways you can make money with your writing talents.

And after all this information on the publishing world, have you decided to do it yourself? Everyone is talking about how easy indie publishing is, and who made a ton of dough doing it, but does that mean it's the right path for you and your book? We help you decide.

After the Party Is Over

In This Chapter

- The shelf life of a book
- Dealing with returns
- Another chance as a paperback, new edition, or sequel
- How did you do?
- Getting better all the time
- What's next?

Both you and your publisher are working as hard as you can to let the world know your book exists. You're working yourself through every social media technique available.

Meanwhile, back at the bookstore, what's happening with your book? What happens to books after the box is unpacked and the book is placed on the shelf, after the page appears in an online bookstore and you hope someone stumbles across it?

There was a time when books sat on bookstore shelves for years, growing ever dustier. Once or twice a year, a bespectacled bookseller would comb the shelves for the oldest-looking books and return them to the publisher. The average life span of a published book was fairly long. But today, it's a different story.

You may remember from the beginning of this book that the retail book business is 100 percent returnable. Books that are ordered from the publisher, placed on the bookstore shelf, and then remain unsold may be returned to the publisher for full credit.

Will that happen with your book?

Sold Once ... and Then Again

One of the more peculiar aspects of publishing is that books essentially have to be sold twice. The first time, the sales rep sells them to the bookstore. Then the bookstore has to sell them to customers. Until that second sale occurs, you haven't really sold a single book.

SLUSH PILE

It strikes fear in the hearts of publishers and authors: several times a year the large chains thin their stock and send back large returns. The chains analyze which titles have been moving and which ones haven't, and the "haven't" books are boxed up and returned for credit. Yet another reason to constantly promote your book so there's always steady movement on it.

Will a customer be able to find your book when she goes into a bookstore looking for it? Does that major online retailer show it in stock? If your publicity creates demand, will there be supply to meet that demand? If someone goes into a bookstore or cruises online looking for your title, both you and your publisher hope she can easily find a copy. And if she can't find the book (and a bookstore employee can't find it either), she can order it just as easily.

Remember when we learned about how brick-and-mortar bookstores buy and reorder books? In today's bookstore, you hope your book is moving off the shelf. That is, if the bookstore has ordered multiple copies and week after week those multiple copies remain on the shelf, that means excess inventory is stacking up in its distribution center as a result of the automatic ordering it set up with the publisher. This inventory eventually comes back—as returns.

If one day there are three copies of your book on the shelf and four days later there are none, don't despair! That means the book is *selling through* or moving from the publisher through to the customer. The bookstore will restock (hopefully), and books will be on the shelf again in a few days. Online booksellers use the same methods, stocking up their warehouses and reordering from the publisher or a wholesaler only as needed.

Your Book's Inventory: It's Gotta Move

In this fast-paced, high-tech world in which we all now dwell, the shelf life of a new book has shortened considerably. Some industry experts believe the window of opportunity for a new book is as short as 6 weeks. The clock begins ticking the minute a book is placed on the store shelf. As the author, you hope it's placed on the shelf faced out with the cover showing, but all too often, books are put on the shelf sideways with only the *spine out*.

> **DEFINITION**
>
> In the long run, how many books were shipped out to bookstores doesn't matter. What matters is the number of books that **sell through.** Books that sell through are books customers bought. Books placed on the shelf with the cover facing out catch a customer's eye better than books that are **spine out,** or placed sideways on the shelf so only the slim edge of the book shows. Publishers and design teams spend a great deal of time designing the spine to make it as eye-catching as possible.

Bookstores know exactly when an individual book arrived in their warehouse and when (and where) it was placed on the bookstore shelf. Unless the computer notes that it has sold, the book will someday be hunted down for return.

Why? As far as the bookstores are concerned, an unsold book is money sitting there on the shelf. And money tied up in a book that isn't moving could be freed up and spent on buying another newer, hotter book—one that might sell quicker!

Extending Your Book's Shelf Life

What keeps your book on the shelf? Steady sales. Publicity. Customer requests. Bookstore appearances. Constant tweets and Facebook hype. It has happened before (and will happen again) that an expensive publicity and marketing campaign has gone for naught because the book had already been returned by bookstores.

Do you, the author, have any control or input in this process? Not really. You might be able to convince bookstores in your area that you're an aggressive marketer who will send in an endless stream of customers looking for your book. But with the rest of the country, you just have to cross your fingers. This is where your own commitment to continually publicizing your book nationwide can make a big difference. Every interview on a small radio station somewhere in the country could be sending in someone to his or her local bookstore asking for your book. Day in and day out, these kinds of requests do help.

> **EXPERTS SAY**
>
> Small, independent bookstores seldom return unsold books as aggressively as their larger cousins. "It is a dying habit, but we will give a new hardcover book 6 months or more before pulling it," one old-school bookseller told us. "We'd much rather sell it than return it."

Dwayne Raymond, the longtime literary assistant to the late Norman Mailer, still posts favorable reviews of his book *Mornings with Mailer* as his status on Facebook now and again. "I just like to get the word out every month or so that the book is still quite viable and available," he says. Worried that your Facebook friends might tire of hearing about your book? Get over it. Not only should you follow Dwayne's example, but you should also read his charming book for insight into the work habits of one of America's great literary lions.

Returns to Sender

Returns not only make your book disappear from the shelf, but they also make dollars disappear from your royalty account. When books are returned to the publisher, that's noted in the publisher's inventory system. When the publisher's royalty department factors in that information, your account could slowly dwindle.

Remember, if you have received an advance, you're already in the hole. Your book must sell enough to earn back the advance and move into the black before you make any more money. Books returned unsold can easily drag you back into the red, delaying the long-awaited day you do earn back your advance and begin to accrue more royalties. That's another reason to cross your fingers, say your prayers, and send out another press release or two.

For many years, publishers have accused bookstores, both large and small, of returning books in lieu of paying bills. That may be the case. Streamlined ordering practices can lessen that problem, but this has also lessened the size of publisher's print runs.

The End of the Line

One day you get a letter in the mail from your publisher. Your book is being taken *out of print* (*OP*). What does that mean? What will happen to the rest of your books? And what happens to the e-book version of your book? Well, that part of the equation is still up in the air and is one of the reasons agents and authors and publishers have been fighting so hard the last few years.

DEFINITION

A book that's currently available from a publisher is in print. A book that's no longer available from a publisher is **out of print** or **OP.**

Coming Out Again?

If your book was published first in hardcover, you might have something else to look forward to: a paperback edition, either in a trade paperback size or as a mass market paperback.

If an e-book was going to be done, it was most likely done at the same time the first version of your book (hardcover or original trade paperback) was released.

The path from hardcover to paperback used to be quite routine but is now reconsidered with every book based on sales. Do the sales figures justify bringing it out again? They might, if the total figure is somewhere north of 10,000 copies and the information in your book is still current. A book on a topic that was timely in hardcover might not be a candidate for a paperback, though, if interest in that topic has flagged.

If your book meets these criteria, get ready for another round of cover design, copywriting, and publicity. If not, let's consider what else might lie ahead.

A Rose by Any Other Name …

If your book dies a slow death on the shelf, or even if it succeeds and sells for many years, is that all there is? You worked so hard for many months—and, in some cases, many years—to produce this book! Is it time to move on to the next thing?

Not necessarily. With a novel, yes, you'll have to take what you've learned from this first experience and get busy with another book. In fact, you've probably finished another novel in the time it took to see the first one published.

With nonfiction books, a few other options are left:

- A revised and expanded second edition
- A renamed and repackaged book
- Electronic publishing in various forms
- Series and sequels
- Indie publishing

Revised and Expanded!

If your nonfiction book sold in respectable numbers the first time around—respectable being solely determined by your publisher—you can certainly discuss with your publisher the opportunity to revise, update, and expand the material for a new edition, provided, of course, that it's a topic that still has an audience. Almost any nonfiction book can go through this phase—health books, travel books, reference books, and even cookbooks can be revised and expanded. If the second edition succeeds, you can look forward to a third, fourth, fifth, sixth edition, and so on.

It never hurts to go into a book project with an eye on developing long-term income, and annual editions or a frequently revised book is a great way to go.

Renamed and Repackaged

So your book didn't sell well, and the book has gone out of print. Check your contract to see what the publisher's process is for reverting the rights to you. This is where the POD and e-book stuff in the contract can trip you up because the publisher can still claim it's "available" and hang on to the rights rather than reverting.

You might also be able to buy the remaining copies of the book for a fraction of the original price. If you do want a supply of your books, you have to buy them quickly. The publisher offers any unsold stock to a remaindering company that, in turn, sells it to booksellers for a small price for their bargain tables.

Is it over? Again, if the topic is still timely, it doesn't have to be. But you need to completely change your book. To dust it off and make it salable to another publisher, your book needs to undergo quite a face-lift as well as a name change. Your book could be reborn with a better title, a different editorial focus, or a changed format.

If you do decide to work to improve your book and resell it, you need to be up-front about it. Tell your agent, as well as any publisher that expresses an interest, that you once published a similar book under a different title. They'll probably find out later anyway, and that could spell trouble.

HOT OFF THE PRESS

Sometimes a title is changed between the hardcover and paperback editions to give the paperback a fresh start and a better, more tightly focused title. A recent memoir from Ruth Reichl was called *Not Becoming My Mother* in hardcover, but by the time the trade paperback arrived, it had morphed into *For You Mom, Finally*.

After the rights have officially reverted, you could also bring it out again in an edition you publish yourself. Indie publishing is all the rage nowadays, and we will devote the next chapter to giving you a quick seminar on how (and why) to do it.

If you're overwhelmed by the idea of doing it all yourself, Ellen Reid, the "Book Shepherd" (indiebookexpert.com), works with clients to shepherd them gently through the process of self-publishing and has seen more than one book given a second life. "You can change the name to give it a tighter focus the second time around," she suggests. "Or you can redo the body of the book to broaden the focus."

If you decide to go this route, revisit the first three chapters of this book to remind yourself how to find a healthy niche audience. Spend time thinking about how your book can be repositioned for a new and healthy life.

Sell a Small Monograph?

Best-selling author Jim Collins—whose book *Good to Great* spent more than 4 solid years on the best-seller list—wanted to put out information targeted to nonprofits so they, too, could learn how to apply the success principles he'd uncovered. He didn't want to muddy the market for his next book, though, and decided on a radical approach. He self-published a 35-page book called *Good to Great and the Social Sectors.* An article in *Newsweek* helped get the word out, and his self-published booklet quickly ranked among Amazon's fastest-selling books. Five years later, it still sells and sells.

Is this a technique you could use? If your first book has found its audience and you aren't yet ready for another big book effort, why not a smaller, self-published book for a specific audience? Or why not skip the print world entirely and remake your book into a small and inexpensive e-book?

E-Book It

We've discussed electronic publishing in several different parts of this book, and we bring it up yet again because it's something to consider for the future of your book (also because it's a topic that will never go away). If the rights to your book have reverted to you, you can take what you've written and do several things with it.

You could turn it into an e-book, or break it up into a series of "special reports" that you market through your own website or through social media. Or you could sign up with one of the POD services such as Xlibris (xlibris.com) or Lulu (lulu.com) so your book is always available somewhere, somehow.

Although electronic publishing possibilities are thrilling, that still leaves you, the author, with a basic problem: how to create sales for your book. It's up to you to create demand, a critical part of the POD equation.

Here's how author Joe Vitale thinks it can work: "After 10 years of being published by mainstream publishers and never making enough to pay the rent, I came out with my first e-book and tasted blood. In 24 hours I sold 600 e-books of *Hypnotic Writing* for $29 each. The secret is a dedicated website with powerhouse sales copy on it, a strong guarantee, bonuses to encourage action now, a tested price, secure ordering, and oh yeah, a good book focused on a specific theme for a specific audience helps." You can learn more about what Joe does and how he did it at his website, mrfire.com.

Series and Sequels

Are the sales of your book strong enough to warrant more of the same? Has your editor hinted that she'd like to see you do another similar book? Welcome to the world of series and sequels where, if one book sells, another just like it should do fine, too!

Deciding whether to pursue a sequel to a book or to build it into a series is strictly the publisher's call. If you aren't sure whether your publisher is interested in a series or a sequel, ask your editor. She'll be honest about the chances it might happen.

Evaluating Your Success

How do you know if your book is a success? How many books sold are enough? Or worse yet, how many are too few? Evaluating your book's success strictly by the numbers is relatively easy. Evaluating your book's success in other ways is a little harder.

Show Me the Money!

How many books need to sell to make it a success? That question needs to be considered in relationship to the size of your book's first print run:

- If your book had a modest first printing of 7,500 and sold at least 5,000 copies, you did fine.
- If your book had a first printing of 10,000 and sold 5,000, you didn't do as well.
- If the publisher printed aggressively (more than 25,000 for a first-time author) and you didn't sell through more than 50 percent, you didn't do well.

Remember, the size of the print run was determined by the advance orders. The advance orders were determined by how well the bookstores thought your book would sell. So if a book with a small print run (a book with modest sales expectations) sold well, that's a heck of a victory. But if a book with a large print run (big sales expectations) didn't do well, that's a disappointment.

Even a book that goes into a second printing can be considered a flop if suddenly sales hit a dead end and the publisher still has most of that print run on hand.

Was It a Personal Best?

Was the book a personal success for you, the author? You wrote a book; you published a book. That sets you apart from most other people on the planet. Instead of just talking about how someday you plan to write a book, you did it!

Let's return to the reasons to write. In Chapter 1, you looked at a list of reasons:

- I'm compelled to write.
- I want the personal satisfaction of being published.
- I hope to advance my cause.
- I want to share my knowledge.
- I'd like to advance my career.
- I'd like to achieve fame.
- I'd like to earn a fortune.
- All of the above.

Which reason (or reasons) was yours? Did your book help you achieve it? Even a book with modest sales can easily achieve many of the reasons on the list.

Are you compelled to write? You wrote. Did you seek the personal satisfaction of being published? You have it. Did you want to advance your cause or share your knowledge? Everyone who bought a copy of your book, read about you in the newspaper, visited your website, friended you on Facebook, follows you on Twitter, or heard you talk on the radio is now aware of both your cause and your knowledge.

Has your career been advanced? You now have the prestige and distinction of being published. And regardless of how well your book has done in bookstores, it's on your resumé in black and white. That means you have the opportunity to speak around the country and sell books to clients and your professional audience. If you want, you could keep your book in print forever in a self-published edition. (Chapter 25 is entirely devoted to helping you assess the indie publishing world, so help is very nearby if you want it.)

> **EXPERTS SAY**
>
> Many folks on the professional speaking circuit make money with "back of the room" sales. If a roomful of people have already paid to come and hear you speak, they're primed to buy your book. They won't look to see which New York publisher is behind your book; they just want to take a little of you home with them. A speaking career is a great way to promote and prolong the life of your book. Buy copies in bulk with your author's discount from your publisher to sell from the back of the room at retail. When those run out and the rights have reverted, publish it yourself. Bonus: when you publish it yourself, you make almost twice as much as you did before.

But Really, Show Me the Money!

Did you achieve fame or fortune? Ah, here's the tricky one. As you learned in Chapter 1, it *is* possible to achieve fame without fortune and vice versa.

Fame may still be achieved. If you continue to promote and sell your book on your own long enough, you can achieve a measure of fame.

Fortune is not always elusive either. The mere fact that you published a book may someday spawn other opportunities. Other opportunities may have occurred to you during this long, long ride as well. Or maybe fortune will come with the next book.

Maybe this will cheer you up: Ian Fleming, the creator of the James Bond franchise, didn't start to make real money until his fourth or fifth book. Recently he topped the list (ahead of Agatha Christie) of richest dead British authors.

But This Book Was Perfect!

The publisher screwed up.

Ask most authors why their books didn't sell, and that's the reason you'll hear: the publisher screwed up, not me.

The book didn't get to the stores in time. The cover (or the title) was awful. They didn't do any publicity. They never cared about my book. The staff was incompetent. My editor left. The sales reps didn't sell it. The stores returned it too soon. We've heard those laments over and over again, and sometimes there really is a measure of truth in them.

Perhaps. But indulging in that sort of thinking won't further your career as a writer. A better way to spend your time postbook is to do some follow-up work:

- Continue to work on your writing.

- Sharpen your ability to create a book large numbers of people will buy.

And remember, if you feel this way about your first publishing experience, keep it to yourself. Grouse to your friends and family all you want, but button your lip when talking to industry folks or hanging out at writers' conferences and the like. Agents and editors know full well from years of experience that someone who complains about his or her first publisher will sooner or later complain about the second publisher. They take it as a sure sign to steer clear.

Work on My Writing?

Yes, work on your writing. Continue to take classes, attend conferences, and seek out other writers. Build your own community of writers around you. A group of published authors in northern California meets twice a month as "The Rich and Famous Writers' Club" to share ideas, contacts, and inspiration with each other. Every writer benefits when he continues to practice and polish his craft.

Another group we know of meets socially as Writers Who Wine in order to hang out and prosper together. There's a chapter in northern California and one in Idaho. Check them out on Facebook, or make your own group of like-minded writers and see where it can take you.

EXPERTS SAY

Why continue to go to writers' conferences after you've already been published? Other unpublished writers will look at you with awe. It can be a nice little ego boost. You also will make new contacts with agents and editors, sharpen your skills, and come away reinvigorated.

You have been published. Now take that accolade and build on it. Write more. Get better.

What Book Will Large Numbers of People Buy?

Hopefully, they'll buy your next one. Again, take what you've learned with this first book and build on it. If that's your goal, work on developing novels and nonfiction books that have the potential to affect large numbers of readers.

Chapter 3 might not have interested you when you began reading this book. After all, you already knew what you wanted to write. Is it time to go back and reread that chapter? It gives you a clear-eyed view of how book professionals try to develop book ideas with big potential. Reread that chapter, and try out a few of the exercises. It will help you begin to think like a publisher.

Co-author Jennifer's favorite writing success story holds great encouragement for anyone whose first published book didn't quite set the world on fire. Some years ago, she discovered a wonderful food writer named Marlena de Blasi. Marlena wrote a delightful cookbook called *Regional Foods of Northern Italy*, which Jennifer published at Prima. Despite its beauty and charm, the book was not a terrific success.

Marlena did find terrific writing success, but it wasn't as a cookbook writer, which was how she originally perceived herself. She wrote the lyrical story of her midlife romance with an Italian man who swept her off her feet and convinced her to move on a whim to Venice, leaving her familiar American world behind.

Marlena's book, *A Thousand Days in Venice*, became a literary travel best-seller in the vein of *A Year in Provence* and *Under the Tuscan Sun*. And a scant 2 years later she wrote a sequel, *A Thousand Days in Tuscany*. Then came *That Summer in Sicily* and *Amandine*. Marlena lives and writes in Italy year after year, including recipes in her books but never again trying to be just a cookbook author.

Moving On to the Next Phase

So what's your next move? Will you try to write another book, or will you try to return to your life as it was before you embarked on all this?

If you're returning to your previous life, be proud of what you've achieved. You now have a lasting symbol of a great and unusual accomplishment: a published book.

The Least You Need to Know

- The life span of a new book can be short, but steady sales, constant publicity, and customer demand combine to keep a book available and in print for a long time.
- Between special orders placed with distributors and the rise of online book-selling, while your book is in print it is almost always in stock and available somewhere.

- If the sales were satisfactory, a hardcover book will come out in paperback, and a paperback might someday come out again as a revised and updated second edition. An e-book version might never go out of print.

- Sometimes a book is renamed during the transition from hardcover to paperback to give it a better chance for better sales.

- To be considered a sales success, a book must sell through a majority of its print run.

- Even if your book has not been a sales success, you might have achieved your reasons for writing.

Going Indie, the Pros and Cons

In This Chapter

- What's all the fuss about indie?
- Major benefits of DIY publishing
- Major pitfalls of DIY publishing
- Deciding what's right for you and your book

Indie is the new black. Or so it seems, with the topic on the minds of every writer, agent, and publisher we talk to. So if everyone is talking and thinking about self-publishing the indie way, should you, too?

Everyone Is Going Indie—Shouldn't You?

Indie. Doesn't that sound cool? Independent, brave, hip, entrepreneurial, modern, self-reliant. So much cooler than the words *self-publishing* or, worst of all, *vanity publishing.* The latter conjures up uncomfortable images of a lonely pallet of dusty books taking up space in a garage, the sad remnants of a dashed dream.

That garage full of unsold books from the olden days of vanity presses couldn't happen in these days of POD, e-books, and powerful online marketing, right? Alas, it does. You might not have the actual printed books stacked in a corner to remind you of what you'd hoped to achieve, but you could still experience disappointment.

So with that realistic idea in mind, let's take a look at how this all could work (or not).

> **DEFINITION**
>
> **Indies** have long been small, privately owned publishing companies like Workman or Pelican. The term has now morphed into being the new and glossier-sounding term for someone who self-publishes.

Success on the Best-Seller List

Books, writers, and booksellers are all over the news nowadays. Sometimes it's a story about the imminent demise of a bookstore or a publisher, sometimes it's a muckraking story about what did or did not happen in a best-selling memoir, and sometimes it's about a young woman sitting alone in her house at her keyboard, banging away on her stories and selling millions of e-books on her own. Ah yes, Amanda Hocking. The 26-year-old creator of the *Trylle* trilogy.

In fact, self-published e-books have done so well in the marketplace that the stalwart *New York Times* and the more nimble *USA Today* both had to make changes in their best-seller rankings to reflect what was really happening in e-books rather than just focus on sales of electronic books from major publishers.

Seth Godin Suggests ...

Seth Godin, who got his start decades ago as a book packager before morphing into an online marketing guru, has now declared that he has moved beyond ever being published by anyone else ever again.

Teaming up with Amazon to form The Domino Project (thedominoproject.com), he now goes directly to readers, selling his work at prices that can fluctuate according to how many people preorder, or giving away copies that have been "sponsored" by major corporations like GE.

Smart business model, but will it work for you?

The Biggest Benefits

Yes, there are some real, solid benefits and advantages to doing it all yourself. There are also some big pitfalls, however, so don't just read this section; please also read the "The Biggest Pitfalls" section that follows.

It's Way Fast

Way fast. Did we say way fast? We mean way, *way* fast. The time it takes to get from book idea to book on the market is lightning speed in the indie world, and it's all controlled by you.

You've read through all the chapters about editing, book production, and the sales process, and yes, it can be like watching ice form. But if you decide on a Tuesday that you want to make all your grandmother's homemade pie recipes available to the world, you can type up those old tattered index cards on Wednesday, format them on Thursday, upload the file to a publishing site on Friday, and be selling (you hope) by Friday afternoon.

Wine educator Roxanne Langer had a speech coming up in New York, and her client asked to order 250 copies of *The 60 Minute Wine MBA* she'd mentioned in her marketing materials. Great, but … Roxanne hadn't yet produced the book. It took just 3 short weeks to go from her finished manuscript (she did have that part done), to a beautiful cover and interior design from designer Vanessa Perez, to having finished and printed books from the Espresso Book Machine. She happily delivered the 250 books to her client before the speech.

A Bigger Slice of the Pie

A standard royalty deal with a traditional publisher will pay you a percentage for each book sold. How much varies, but it's roughly around a little more than $1 for a book that retails for $20.

But if you've published a book yourself that sells for $20, and you're selling them in the back of the room when you give speeches on the topic, you're making the publisher's profit rather than the author's royalty.

HOT OFF THE PRESS

Years ago, Jennifer self-published a small travel booklet that she sold for $10. It cost her $2 to produce and send off to her mail-order customers. An $8 profit off each one? Not too shabby—and she wishes she still had that income stream today!

The Hip Factor (Way, Way Cooler)

Just like in the music business, it's now way cooler to say you're an indie publisher than to say you're published by some faceless New York firm. You get to be perceived instead as this scrappy do-it-yourselfer who doesn't take "no" for an answer and is pursuing your dreams. You'll impress at parties.

Total Control

As we warned you earlier in the book, once you sign with a publisher, many of the things that mean so much to you—the title of your book, the way it looks, how much of what you wrote gets used—are now totally out of your control.

Not so if you're in charge of your own project. The title you choose is the title that will appear on the book. The picture your daughter drew of you is indeed the author picture on the back cover. Every word you love is in there—no cuts, no edits you don't like. Your words are there the way you want the world to see them.

The Biggest Pitfalls

All those benefits of indie publishing sound great! So why not be an indie publisher and bypass all the agita of trying to get an agent and a book deal?

Well, as we've not-so-gently pointed out, there are pitfalls indeed to indie publishing, and you could end up regretting the experience. How? Let's take a look.

You Could Flop

Here's the truth: what makes a book sell makes a book sell regardless of who the publisher is. Could be Random House, could be you, but the elements for success are the same. They don't change. What's the fundamental element for success? An audience who cares. Readers.

That means there are plenty of books—from Random House as well as from DIY self-publishers—that won't sell in significant numbers beyond the burst of friends and family support.

Nonfiction is easier to find an audience for than fiction—that's true for everyone who publishes. With much nonfiction, you can identify an audience for your book (fishermen, left-handed people, visitors to Cape Cod) and then directly target those folks for sales.

With fiction, you have to hope your writing and the book's theme resonate with large numbers of people and that they tell everyone they know how great your book is. How often does that happen with indie fiction? Not all that often. You need to know going in how hard it is to make a novel sell.

> **SLUSH PILE**
>
> "It wasn't as easy as I thought it would be," said one indie author who uploaded her story on Smashwords (smashwords.com). "Uploading it was easy, sure, but then once I'd Facebooked it and put it on my blog, I ran out of places to link to and the sales just stopped."

Jennifer tells this tale to all would-be indie publishers: she knew three lawyers, all very successful and distinguished in their fields, who self-published in the 1980s. One, an estate lawyer, wrote and published a book on how to avoid probate. Another, a water lawyer, published a book on the history of a water district. The third one wrote a mystery novel.

The result? The probate book and the water book were big successes, and clients and the interested public embraced them. The mystery novel mostly stayed in the boxes the printer sent to the author. Would it be different today with all the cool self-publishing tools? Not really. The water book and the probate book would again find their niche audiences, and the general mystery novel, unrelated to the lawyer's specialty and built-in network, would find it hard to get noticed.

It's Hard to Keep Up

Why did Amanda Hocking decide to sign a four-book deal with St. Martin's Press after raking it in as an indie publisher of her YA e-books? Because she was exhausted. Because she wanted to just be a writer rather than the person who had to be in charge of everything from cover design and interior formatting to dealing with the money end of things. She wanted to be able to focus on storytelling rather than being a full-time businessperson with a writing hobby on the side.

Think about it. Are you prepared to do it all from now until forever? It can be a ton of work, something not all writers are well suited to.

So Many Ways to Mess It Up

Sure, you can type like no one else, you can use your cell phone to do cool things, and hey, once you even put a home video on YouTube. But have you ever tried to get the layout to work properly on the copyright page of an e-book? Ever uploaded a file to a public site and then tried desperately to take it down after you noticed a major error? More than one indie publisher has proudly opened a box of books from the printer, only to notice right away a big typo on the back cover.

In a publishing house, an entire staff is devoted to all the technical things, as well as keeping an eye out for errors everywhere. Can you be that entire staff, spotting problems and fixing them as they occur?

EXPERTS SAY

Not everyone is happy that the word *indie* has been co-opted by the folks who want to sell you the tools to publish your own work. For many years, it's been applied to small and nimble publishing houses, as one publisher writes on her blog: "How and when did 'indie publishing' become the definition for doing it yourself, and why did I not get the memo? *Indie publishing* used to mean a small trade press who was independent—that they weren't part of a conglomerate. They acted just like their big brothers in New York, assuming all costs of production, marketing, promotion, and distribution—but their balance sheets lacked the same number of zeros."

What's Right for You?

So should you go out on your own and publish? What determines who does well and who does not? How do you know what kinds of self-published books sell and what kind don't? How can you ensure that, if you do go indie, you don't kick yourself later?

Let's go back to some of the same questions we asked you to consider in Chapter 1 and help you decide.

Back to Basics—What Do You Want?

Remember the different reasons to write—you are compelled to write, you want the personal satisfaction of being published, you hope to advance a cause, further your career, achieve fame, earn a fortune, or all of the above? Depending on which one drives you, self-publishing might be right for you.

You are compelled to write? Then write and self-publish if you want. You want the satisfaction of being published? Go ahead and go indie if—and that's a big *if*—you won't forever torture yourself for not having been published by a big New York house.

You hope to advance a cause? Then DIY publishing might be best of all because you can quickly get your message out via all sorts of ways without the lag time of trying to get someone else to publish it.

Further your career? Sure. We've mentioned this before: one of the best candidates for self-publishing is a professional speaker who can sell from the back of the room. If you're self-publishing, though, and you hope it will move you up a rank in your world, you owe it to your career to hire the best designers and advisers so you have a very professional-looking product at the end. A cheap and shoddy-looking book will only backfire.

Fame or fortune? If those are your goals, well … you might end up disappointed if you go the DIY route. Why? Because ours is a selective world, and the most prestige and attention still go to books from big publishing houses. Hardly ever do self-published books end up being reviewed in important places, and despite some high-profile cases like Amanda Hocking, thousands and thousands of self-published books hardly sell at all. Sorry to be blunt, but we want you to know the reality.

Do You Have the Skills?

It all seems so easy to do, and in some ways it is. It takes minutes to upload a file, create an e-book, and have it available for sale online.

But does that e-book you just created look anything like an e-book from a publisher? No. They use the same interior designers and layout people for what gets read on the screen as they do for what gets printed on a page. And if you want to do it all right, there are some technical things you need to learn. Fortunately, most of the e-book companies like Smashwords (smashwords.com) and CreateSpace (createspace.com) have online tutorials to walk you through it.

Winding your way through the POD world can be bewildering. No one is a natural-born editor, designer, and publicity department all rolled into one.

Can You *Buy* the Skills?

Sure, you can buy the expertise if you don't have it. With so many cutbacks in the publishing world, a plethora of publishing professionals are available to help you get through this process and ensure your book ends up looking like something you and your family can be proud of, not something that will make others blush on your behalf.

HOT OFF THE PRESS

As an experiment, Jennifer uploaded to Smashwords a free e-book she and a friend wrote called *The Writer's Secret*. She posted about it on Facebook, she tweeted, her friends in the writing business reposted and retweeted, and it was seen by several thousand writers in a few short days. Instant success? No. It took over a month for the first hundred free copies to be downloaded. *Free,* mind you. Had she charged, who knows how many would have sold. Check it out and download it yourself at smashwords.com.

Promote Your Hip, Indie Self

Okay, this really can be the fun part. You read the earlier chapters on publicity, and it can be quite a charge to be out there in the world promoting something that you made from start to finish.

Now if you're published by someone else, you can expect at least a short burst of activity on the publisher's part before you have to do some of it yourself. But if you're self-publishing, it's all on you from day one. Are you ready to write your own press releases, send them out to prospective shows and producers, make follow-up calls, and make more follow-up calls?

If you're not, or if this isn't something that comes naturally to you, you can hire publicity help.

What's Around the Corner?

Is indie publishing the way of the future? Maybe. Jennifer was recently at a writers' conference where many of the panelists were in some way involved in doing it themselves, and they were happily referring to the traditional publishing world as either *legacy publishing* or *dinosaurs*. Ouch. Sheree and Jennifer both love the publishing world.

We love writers. We love editors, agents, and book designers. We hope it doesn't dry up and go away, and we strongly believe it won't. Having said that though ….

Throughout the history of storytelling, and throughout the history of books, the form has changed and morphed over and over again, and it's still changing with us. What a book looks like and how it gets to a reader have both changed continually. Books have changed according to lifestyle—more people can read, so they're smaller, more available, and less expensive than back in the day when huge, hand-decorated books belonged only to a select few. Books also have changed according to technology as printing, papermaking, design, and production techniques all have evolved. They will continue to do so. There's no reason for this change to stop. End of story.

What never changes is the desire to learn, to discover a fascinating tale, to happen upon a fact you've never known before. That desire stays constant, and that's what's behind the longevity of the book business. Our desire as writers to share what we have to say never changes either.

Books as we know them right now won't be the same 10 or 20 years from now. The publishing business as it exists today won't be the same 10 or 20 years from now. Writers? We will all be the same, and the opportunities for us to share what we've written with the world will be even greater.

So hang in there. If what you want is to share what you've done with the world, share it. We applaud your bravery and your efforts. You are a writer, indeed.

The Least You Need to Know

- What makes a book sell—a receptive audience—is the same regardless of who the publisher is, you or Random House.
- To do it right, self-publishing takes enormous skill and drive.
- You can hire publishing experts to help you produce a professional-looking book if you don't possess those skills.
- The publishing scene is constantly changing, so get ready for more in the future.
- Books will change. The desire to write and publish will not.

Glossary

acquisitions editor   An editor responsible for bringing in new books to publish.

advance   The money a publisher pays an author to write a book. Usually half is paid upon signing a contract, and the remainder is paid upon delivery of an acceptable manuscript. This is an advance against future royalties earned, and the book must sell enough to earn back the advance before more royalty money will be paid out. *Advance* can also mean the number of copies sold by the sales reps for the first 2 months of the book's publication.

agent   A literary agent represents an author to the publisher and secures a publishing contract in exchange for an agreed-upon percentage, usually 15 percent.

assistants   The young, unsung folks who answer the phones, sort the mail, and otherwise keep publishing offices going. Also known as editorial assistants.

auction   A sale, usually conducted by an agent, that gives several publishers the opportunity to bid on the rights to publish a book. The book goes to the highest bidder.

audience   The part of the population that will be interested in buying a specific book. Also called readers.

author   The writer of a book or books; the term usually implies a published writer.

author guidelines   The set of guidelines a publishing house usually provides an author that details the way the submission should come in, formatting, and often the process and people involved.

author queries   A part of the editing process in which the editor and/or copy editor ask the author to further explain meaning, answer questions about accuracy or intent, or rewrite small sections.

backlist   The list of books the publisher has available for sale that are older than 12 months.

bar code   The coded digital information on the back of a book that is scanned when a book is purchased.

best-seller   A term used quite loosely in the publishing world. Strictly speaking, the term refers to a book that has appeared on a best-seller list somewhere. In reality, publishers and their publicity staff attach the term to almost any book they haven't lost money on.

blog   A web log, an online-based diary or postings on a particular topic.

bluelines   The cheap test proof of a book, usually in blue ink, the printer sends to the publisher for approval before printing the entire job.

boilerplate contract   A publisher's standard contract before the author or agent requests modifications.

book doctor   An outside editor who can be hired (increasingly by the author or agent) to rewrite or suggest major edits on a manuscript. *See also* proposal doctor.

Book Expo   The annual publishing industry trade show. It used to be called the American Booksellers' Association (ABA), but now it is the BEA, short for Book Expo America.

book packager   Packagers (also called producers) create books for publishers, providing them with finished manuscripts, finished books, or anything in between.

book proposal   A packet of information about the writer's book idea. A proposal typically contains a solid description of the book's content, the potential market for the book, the competition, and the author's credentials. It also contains a table of contents, an extensive book outline, and at least one sample chapter.

book trailer   A video to promote a book. Many are simply the author talking, but some are highly produced mini-movies.

BookScan   The subscription-only retail tracking system in place to monitor reported books sales.

bound galley   Often a paperback version of the book (sometimes unproofread) marketing may have produced four months before the book's publication date to enable reviewers to read the work and review for publication.

buyer   The bookstore employee who meets with publishers' sales representatives to decide how many copies of a book to order.

buzz   The word-of-mouth excitement created in the publishing community before a book is released.

camera-ready art   The finished artwork that's ready to be photographed, without alteration, for reproduction.

chain   The large chain stores that sell books. Barnes & Noble is a chain bookstore.

chapter book   A category of children's books that have longer stories and are written for the intermediate reader.

chick lit   A style of novel that is targeted to women in their 20s and 30s and revolves around a young woman main character.

clip art   Artwork specifically designed to be used by anyone without needing to obtain any permission.

commercial publisher   A publishing company that assumes the full cost of producing, printing, and distributing a literary work and pays the author a percentage of the proceeds.

commission   The percentage of the advance and subsequent royalties an agent receives as his or her fee after selling your work to a publisher. This can run anywhere from 10 to 25 percent. (The larger percentages are for subrights.)

community coordinator   *See* events coordinator.

compositor   A person who designs and typesets manuscripts and prepares and sends formatted discs or final files to the printer. Also called a layout tech.

copyright   "The right of authors to control the reproduction and use of their creative expressions that have been fixed in tangible form," according to *The Associated Press Style Book and Briefing on Media Law.*

counter display   Several copies of a book in a cardboard holder for display in a bookstore. Also called a counter pack or dump.

deadline   The due date for the completed manuscript as specified in the publishing contract.

demographics   Population statistics, age groups, buying habits, personal income levels, and other categories that can be used to estimate a book's potential success.

distributor   A business that calls on bookstores and takes orders for the publishers it represents.

dump   Publishing industry slang for a counter display. Dumps are usually the larger cardboard displays that stand on the floor.

e-book A book available in an electronic file format. E-books can be downloaded (and sometimes printed out) and read on an e-book reader like a Kindle or iPad or on a computer.

easy readers A category of children's books with short, simple sentences designed for beginning readers.

editorial board The group of people who collectively make the decision to publish a book. Acquisitions editors present book proposals to the editorial board for its approval. Also sometimes called a pub board.

electronic publishing Paperless publishing as e-books.

electronic rights Refers to a variety of digital rights.

endcap The shelves at the end of an aisle in the bookstore. Publishers pay booksellers for the chance to display their books on the endcap.

English cozy A type of mystery book set in England that often features a quaint English atmosphere.

events coordinator A bookstore employee who is responsible for arranging author signings, author appearances, and in-store events. May also be called a community coordinator.

exclusive submission When only one agent or editor is considering your proposal.

F&Gs Sheets of paper that have been "folded and gathered" in preparation for printing. This is another test step the publisher can review and approve before seeing finished, bound books.

face out Books that are placed on the shelf with the cover facing out toward the customer.

fact checker A publishing employee who checks the veracity of an author's claims. More often used in magazine and newspaper publishing than in the book industry.

featured guest A guest who is central to a television or radio show's segment. If a number of experts are used on the same show, the guest is a panel member rather than the focus of the show.

fiction A work of the imagination.

first printing The number of books printed in the initial print run.

first serial An excerpt that appears in a newspaper or magazine before the book's publication and actual release.

floor The minimum bid in an auction.

foreign rights The right to publish a book in another country or language.

formatting The way the printed words appear on the page, including things such as margins, indentations, type size, and type font.

front matter The first several pages of a book that typically contain the half-title page, the title page, copyright information, the dedication, acknowledgments, table of contents, introduction, and a prelude or foreword. Front matter pages are numbered i, ii, iii, iv, and so forth.

frontlist The publisher's current list of books just published; typically any book fewer than 12 months old.

galley (or **loose galleys**) *See* page proofs; bound galley.

genre fiction A term applied to Western, romance, sci-fi, horror, thriller, and fantasy novels.

ghostwriter A professional writer who writes a book without getting author credit for it.

head The title introducing a chapter or subdivision of the text.

hen lit Women's fiction aimed at the 35-and-up crowd.

illustrated books A category of children's books with lots of pictures and few words.

in print Books currently available from the publisher. If a publisher decides to discontinue publishing a title, the book goes *out of print* and rights are reverted to the author.

independent booksellers Locally owned and operated bookstores, not affiliated with a large chain such as Barnes & Noble.

indie publishing Another term for self-publishing.

instant book A book that appears on bookstore shelves just weeks after the event about which the book is written, like the e-book *Tweets from Tahrir*.

intellectual property   According to *Random House Legal Dictionary*, this consists of "copyrights, patents, and other rights in creations of the mind; also, the creations themselves, such as a literary work, painting, or computer program."

ISBN (International Standard Book Number)   The unique 13-digit number each book is assigned that identifies it.

list   A publisher's list of forthcoming titles; the books it plans to publish in the coming season or year. *See also* frontlist.

literary agent   *See* agent.

live show   A television or radio show broadcast at the same moment it's happening.

manuscript guidelines   A publisher's rules regarding the proper way to prepare a manuscript for submission. *See also* author guidelines.

mass market paperback   A 4×7-inch softcover book often found in book racks in airports, drugstores, and supermarkets as well as in bookstores. It's sometimes called a pocket book.

masthead   The section of a book or magazine that lists the editors and publishers.

mechanicals   Finished laid-out pages ready to be sent to the printer.

media market   A geographic area covered by a particular radio station, TV channel, or newspaper. Some markets, such as New York, are large media markets; others are small.

memoir   An account of the events in the author's own life.

midlist   Books that are acquired for modest advances, given modest print runs, and have a relatively short shelf life.

morning drive-time shows   Radio shows that broadcast between 6 A.M. and 9 A.M. while commuters are headed to work.

multiple queries   When more than one agent or editor is approached at once about a book idea. *See also* exclusive submission.

nonfiction   A work that contains true information or observations.

option clause   A clause typically found in publishing contracts that requires the author to give the publisher the first chance to buy his or her next book. Also called a next work clause.

out of print   *See* in print.

overview   A Hollywood term now leaking into the book world that refers to a one-sentence description of a book and its audience.

P&L   A profit and loss statement an editor prepares in advance of acquiring a book.

page count   The number of book pages. Sometimes the minimum (or maximum) number of pages in a completed manuscript is stipulated in the book contract.

page proofs   The stage at which the printer sends sample pages to the publisher/editor/author for one final check before the entire press run is done.

panel member   *See* featured guest.

parody   A comic imitation of a well-known literary work.

payment on publication   A term meaning the writer is not paid until the work actually appears in print. This is the policy of many magazine publishers and some book publishers.

PDF file   An electronic file that contains camera-ready images of book pages that cannot be manipulated. These are traditionally the final files sent to the printer. The initials stand for "portable document format."

peer review   A method in academic publishing whereby a manuscript is circulated for comment to a number of the author's peers; most often the peers comment anonymously.

permission   The legal right to use someone else's material in a book. The writer must get a permission form signed by the copyright holder.

pitch   An attempt to create interest in a project.

placements   Stories or mentions of the author or book in the media resulting from the efforts of publicity. Can also refer to the location of a book in the bookstore and/or the placement of a book in a promotional position in the store.

platform   The author's proven ability to promote and sell his or her book through public speaking, a television or radio show, or a newspaper column.

podcast   A broadcast that can be downloaded and played on an MP3 player.

prepack   Several copies of a book offered at a special discount and packaged together in a cardboard display. *See also* dump.

press conference   A meeting to which members of the press are invited to hear something newsworthy.

press release   A 1-page announcement to the press about the new release of a book or an author's planned event.

print on demand   Short-run printing from an electronic file.

print run   The number of books printed each time a book goes to press.

production   The production department in a publishing house designs and prepares manuscript for the printer.

promotion   Free publicity methods and/or paid advertising for a book or its author to create public awareness and stimulate sales. Can also be any paid placement in a bookstore paid for by the publisher to showcase a book, or a marketing/sales discount program to give bookstores incentive to buy more product from publishers, sometimes offering discounts back to the reader ("buy one get one free" or "buy one, get the second at 50 percent off").

proposal doctor   Experienced editors and writers who help others whip their proposals into shape.

public domain   Creative works, such as writings and artwork, that are no longer protected by copyright laws. Anyone can use works in the public domain without asking permission or paying royalties or fees.

publicist   The person who attempts to get publicity for a book.

publicity   Attention directed to a book or its author. Publicity is usually free and includes book reviews, feature articles, television and radio appearances or interviews, and online mentions.

query   The initial contact between a writer and an agent or editor. This short letter or e-mail is meant to spark interest in the writer's project.

readers   The method by which university presses evaluate projects. Readers, or "referees," are experts in that field and are paid to read and pass judgment on the scholarship of a proposed work.

reading fees   A fee requested by an agent to pay for the time he spends reading a writer's project to decide whether it's worth representing.

rejection letter   A formal "no, thanks" letter or e-mail from an agent or an editor, passing on a project.

remainder   Books that have been sold by the publisher to a discounter for a fraction of their worth. These books end up on the bargain tables at bookstores.

retail price   The price a retail store charges its customers for a book. Unlike other types of products, most books have the retail price printed on the cover.

review copies   Free copies of a book sent out to media people in the hopes they will review the book or mention it in an article.

royalty   The percentage the publisher pays the author for each book sold.

SASE   Shorthand for a self-addressed, stamped envelope. A SASE must accompany unsolicited material sent through the mail if you want to hear back regarding your submission.

seasons   Publishers put together their lists of books and their catalogs according to two or three seasons, usually fall, winter, and spring/summer.

second serial   Excerpts from a book published after the book is published and available.

self-published   A book the author himself has paid to have edited, produced, printed, and distributed.

sell-through   Books that have actually been purchased by customers at the bookstore and are not going to be returned unsold to the publisher.

sequel   A second book that features many of the same characters as the first book by the same author.

series   Books linked by a brand-name identity or by theme, purpose, or content. You're reading a series book right now.

shtick lit   A book based on a gimmick, usually an oddball goal or task that takes a year to complete.

sidebar   Text set apart in a box, margin, or shaded area or set in smaller type to distinguish it from the rest of the text on the page.

slush pile   The to-be-read stack of unsolicited manuscripts. They're usually read by an assistant instead of an editor.

small publisher   A general term applied to publishing houses with revenues of less than $10 million a year. Such publishers are also sometimes called small presses.

spine out   A book that's placed on a bookstore shelf with only the spine showing.

submission   The process by which a writer or agent submits a book proposal or manuscript to a publisher. If the author isn't using an agent, it's called an unagented submission.

subrights   A wide variety of rights, including book clubs, electronic, video or movie, dramatic, and merchandising.

syndicated   Used to refer to a column or show packaged and sold to more than one radio or television station or published in more than one newspaper.

synopsis   A 10-page summary of a novel, written in third-person present tense. It spells out the plot of the novel in an effective and readable way. A synopsis is included in a proposal to an agent or editor.

taped show   A television or radio show not broadcast immediately but recorded and played at a later date.

text   Words on a page. This distinguishes them from artwork.

trade paperback   A paperback book of any size other than the 4×7-inch mass market–size books.

type solution   Design term for a book cover that contains only typography with no pictures.

video clip   A video of an author's television appearance, sent as an electronic attachment, on a DVD, or on a flash drive.

vook   A video book, an electronic book that includes embedded video.

word count   The number of words on a page or in a book. This is often used in a book contract to stipulate the minimum or maximum number of words a manuscript should contain.

work for hire   An arrangement in which a writer is paid one time for his or her work. Under a work-for-hire agreement, the writer does not own the copyright and receives no royalties.

writers' conference   An organized gathering of writers; editors and agents also attend.

YA (Young Adult)   Books targeted at the 10- to 16-year-old market. The YA market is dominated by mass market paperback series publishing.

Great Books and Blogs for Writers

B

Books

Beard, Julie. *The Complete Idiot's Guide to Getting Your Romance Published*. Indianapolis: Alpha Books, 2000.

The Chicago Manual of Style: The Essential Guide for Writers, Editors, and Publishers, 16th Edition. Chicago: University of Chicago Press, 2010.

Children's Writer's and Illustrator's Market. Cincinnati: Writer's Digest Books (updated annually).

Hamilton, April. *The Indie Author's Guide*. Cincinnati: Writer's Digest Books, 2010.

Jassin, Lloyd, and Steve C. Schecter. *The Copyright Permission and Libel Handbook: A Step-by-Step Guide for Writers, Editors, and Publishers*. New York: Wiley, 1998.

Kirsch, Jonathan. *Kirsch's Guide to the Book Contract: For Authors, Publishers, Editors and Agents*. Venice, California: Acrobat Books, 1998.

Lamott, Anne. *Bird by Bird: Some Instructions on Writing and Life*. New York: Anchor/ Doubleday, 1995.

Levine, Mark. *Negotiating a Book Contract: A Guide for Authors, Agents, and Lawyers, Revised and Expanded Edition*. Massachusetts: Asphodel Press, 2009.

Levinson, Jay Conrad, Rick Frishman, and Michael Larsen. *Guerrilla Marketing for Writers: 100 Weapons for Selling Your Work, Revised and Expanded Edition*. New York: Morgan James Publishing, 2010.

Literary Market Place. New York: R. R. Bowker (updated annually).

Lott, Lynn, and Nancy Pickard. *Seven Steps on the Writer's Path*. New York: Ballantine Books, 2003.

Lukeman, Noah. *The Plot Thickens: 8 Ways to Bring Fiction to Life*. New York: St. Martin's Press, 2002.

Maass, Donald. *Writing the Breakout Novel Workbook: Hands-On Help for Making Your Novel Stand Out and Succeed*. Cincinnati: Writer's Digest Books, 2004.

Phillips, Brigitte M., Susan D. Klassen, and Doris Hall, eds. *The American Directory of Writer's Guidelines*. Sanger, California: Quill Driver Books/Word Dancer Press, 2004.

Poynter, Dan. *The Self-Publishing Manual: How to Write, Print, and Sell Your Own Book*. Santa Barbara, California: Para Publishing, 2007.

Rabiner, Susan, and Alfred Fortunato. *Thinking Like Your Editor: How to Write Serious Nonfiction—and Get It Published*. New York: W. W. Norton & Company, 2002.

Raymond, Dwayne. *Mornings with Mailer*. New York: HarperCollins, 2010.

Sambuchino, Chuck, and the editors of *Writer's Digest Books*. *Formatting and Submitting Your Manuscript*. Cincinnati: Writer's Digest Books, 2009.

Sexton, Adam. *Master Class in Fiction Writing: Techniques from Austen, Hemingway, and Other Greats*. New York: McGraw-Hill, 2006.

Shoup, Barbara, and Margaret Love Denman. *Novel Ideas: Contemporary Authors Share the Creative Process, Second Edition*. Athens: University of Georgia Press, 2009.

Sloane, Sarah Jane. *The I Ching for Writers: Finding the Page Inside You*. Novato, California: New World Library, 2005.

Strunk, William Jr., and E. B. White. *The Elements of Style*. New York: Macmillan, 1979.

Underdown, Harold. *The Complete Idiot's Guide to Publishing Children's Books, Third Edition*. Indianapolis: Alpha Books, 2008.

Walsh, Bill. *The Elephants of Style: A Trunkload of Tips on the Big Issues and Gray Areas of Contemporary American English*. New York: McGraw-Hill, 2004.

———. *Lapsing Into a Comma: A Curmudgeon's Guide to the Many Things That Can Go Wrong in Print—and How to Avoid Them*. New York: McGraw-Hill, 2000.

Writer's Market. Cincinnati: Writer's Digest Books (updated annually).

Zinsser, William. *On Writing Well: The Classic Guide to Writing Nonfiction: 25th Anniversary Edition*. New York: HarperResource, 2001.

Blogs

Blog Book Tours
blogbooktours.blogspot.com
Organized "tours" on blogs.

Blog of a Bookslut
bookslut.com/blog
Wonderful commentary on books and reading.

The Blood-Red Pencil
bloodredpencil.blogspot.com
A group of writers on writing.

Buzz, Balls and Hype
mjroseblog.typepad.com/buzz_balls_hype
M. J. Rose is a true pioneer when it comes to indie publishing and building online buzz.

GalleyCat
mediabistro.com/galleycat
Lots on publishing, deals, writers, and reviews.

Jane Friedman
janefriedman.com/blog/
For years, Jane was the publisher and editorial director of *Writer's Digest* magazine. Today, she teaches in the industry.

Nathan Bransford, Author
blog.nathanbransford.com
Nathan was a literary agent for many years and has much to say as a result.

Navigating the Slush Pile
navigatingtheslushpile.blogspot.com
Literary agent Vickie Motter shares the inside scoop.

Project Mayhem
project-middle-grade-mayhem.blogspot.com
A group of writers who specialize in middle grade and YA.

Publishers Weekly Columns and Blogs
publishersweekly.com/pw/by-topic/columns-and-blogs/index.html
Publishers Weekly hosts a number of writing- and publishing-related blogs.

More Good Resources

Professional Associations

For Agents

Association of Authors' Representatives
676-A 9th Avenue, Suite 312
New York, NY 10036
aaronline.org

For Freelance Editors

Editorial Freelancers Association
71 West 23rd Street, 4th Floor
New York, NY 10010-4102
212-929-5400 or 1-866-929-5425
the-efa.org

Kate Gilpin
wordsintoprint.com

For Self-Publishers

Independent Book Publishers Association (formerly PMA)
627 Aviation Way
Manhattan Beach, CA 90266
310-372-2732
pma-online.org

For Writers

The American Society of Journalists and Authors
1501 Broadway, Suite 403
New York, NY 10036
212-997-0947
asja.org

The Authors Guild
31 East 32nd Street, 7th Floor
New York, NY 10016
212-563-5904
authorsguild.org

National Writers Union
256 West 38th Street, Suite 703
New York, NY 10018
212-254-0279
nwu.org

North American Travel Journalists Association
3579 E. Foothill Boulevard, #744
Pasadena, CA 91107
310-836-8712
natja.org

Romance Writers of America
14615 Benfer Road
Houston, TX 77069
rwa.org

Sisters in Crime
PO Box 442124
Lawrence, KS 66044
785-842-1325
sistersincrime.org

Society of Children's Book Writers and Illustrators
8271 Beverly Boulevard
Los Angeles, CA 90048
323-782-1010
scbwi.org

Publicity Agencies

Book Publicists

Planned Television Arts
1110 Second Avenue
New York, NY 10022
212-593-5847
plannedtvarts.com

Marika Flatt
PR by the Book
prbythebook.com

Susan Harrow
Harrow Communications
1-888-839-4190
prsecrets.com

Annie Jennings
Annie Jennings PR
908-281-6201
annie@anniejenningspr.com
anniejenningspr.com

Sherri Rosen
Sherri Rosen Publicity
212-222-1183
sherri@sherrirosen.com
sherrirosen.com

Media Trainer

Jess Todtfeld (former producer, *FOX & Friends, The O'Reilly Factor*)
Success in Media
1-800-369-3421
jess@successinmedia.com
successinmedia.com

Publishing Consultants

Authornomics
authornomics.com
Full service consulting, packaging, and editorial services.

Big City Books Group
basyesander@yahoo.com
Former Random House editor and best-selling author Jennifer Basye Sander helps writers shape their work into marketable book ideas.

Breaking Books with Bridget Kinsella
510-465-3853
breakingbooks@gmail.com
breakingbooks.com
A one-stop shop for book consulting, editing, marketing, and publicity from a published author with nearly 20 years in the book business.

Jay Schaefer
415-362-0344
jay-schaefer-books.com
Former editor at Chronicle Books and Workman, Jay works with authors in all stages of writing and publishing.

Paul Dinas
dinas.paul@gmail.com
Independent editor/publishing consultant for all genres of commercial fiction and nonfiction.

Vanessa Perez
vlperez@sbcglobal.net
Former art director for a division of Crown Books, cover and interior design for print and e-books.

Short-Run and Print on Demand Book Printers

CreateSpace
createspace.com
POD owned by Amazon.com.

Dorrance Publishing
DorrancePublishing.com

Espresso Book Machine
ondemandbooks.com
Search for a location near you.

Infinity Publishing
infinitypublishing.com

Morris Publishing
morrispublishing.com

PrintOnDemand.com (owned by Lulu)
printondemand.com

Websites of Note

Backspace: The Writer's Place
bksp.org
Resources for writers.

Jenkins Group
bookpublishing.com
General publishing information for custom publishing and indie book publishing.

Publishers Marketplace
publishersmarketplace.com
Info about agents, packagers, industry news, and subscriptions to Publishers Lunch e-newsletter.

Poets & Writers
pw.org
Poets and writers, literary links, links to small presses, and writers' conferences.

Shaw Guides
writing.shawguides.com
Current info about writers' conferences.

Sheree Bykofsky Associates, Inc.
shereebee.com
Information for writers.

The Publishing School for Writers
thepublishingschoolforwriters.com
Jennifer Basye Sander's advice, info, and the inside scoop on how to get published and succeed in the new world of books.

Writing-World.com
writing-world.com
"A world of writing tips … for writers around the world."

Writer's Digest
writersdigest.com
Contact information for book publishers, information on conferences, and discussion forums.

Who You Should Follow on Twitter

@AAKnopf
Knopf publishers.

@bridgetkinsella
Bridget Kinsella, published writer, publishing consultant.

@janefriedman
Jane Friedman, writer/media professor, former publisher of *Writer's Digest*.

@Mikeshatzkin
Mike Shatzkin, publishing guru and industry observer.

@MJRose
M. J. Rose, novelist and creator of Authorbuzz.com.

@NaNoWriMo
The folks who do the National Novel Writing Month.

@NPRbooks.com
NPR book editor.

@publisherslunch
Industry news.

@thebookslut
Book and publishing commentary.

@VeryGoodGin
Jennifer Basye Sander, publishing consultant.

Writing Retreats

Jennifer Sander's Write by the Lake (Tahoe)
writebythelake.com

Joyce Maynard's retreats in Guatemala, Maine, and Marin County
joycemaynard.com

Norman Mailer Writers Colony
nmwcolony.org

Write at the Farm (Washington)
writeatthefarm.com

Sample Proposals

Sample Proposal 1

Why Did I Bother? Every Writer's Lament

A Somewhat Soothing Collection of Pithy Quotes, Shared Anxiety, Straight Talk, Scathing Reviews, and Amusing Anecdotes About the Business of Writing

New York Times best-selling author Jennifer Basye Sander, co-author, *The Complete Idiot's Guide to Getting Published*

Writers write. Oh, and they also complain. They complain about writing. They complain about publishing. They complain about other writers. Jennifer Basye Sander listens to those complaints, and once in a blue moon does it herself. As a former senior editor for Random House, she has listened to many a writer describe the many ways in which the publisher was to blame for the lackluster sales of a book. As the founder of a writers' retreat, she listens to frustrated writers vent about a wide variety of topics. As a writer herself, she has once or twice expressed mild frustration when the fates of the book world seemed to have turned against her.

Writers and their complaints are a fine and honorable tradition, one that stretches back to the first moment when the written word appeared. In a recent Huffington Post blog, writer Michael Wex observed:

> Writers in general don't seem to complain any more than musicians or painters or any other group of freelance workers, they just tend to do it better; they're often more articulate and virtually always have less in common as professionals than people who paint or play music. Where three musicians who play the same instrument can discuss mouthpieces, bows, or picks, even though one plays classical music, another jazz, and a third nothing but rock 'n roll, writers of different sorts—fiction and nonfiction, genre writers and

high-art types—don't seem to engage in too many spirited discussions of dot-matrix printers or innovative touch-typing techniques. Instead of tools, working writers have editors, publishers, agents, and almost any conversation among writers eventually ends up as a debate: Who has the most illiterate editor? Whose publisher is more clueless, whose agent more feckless?

"How do you make a writer *kvetch*?"
"Publish his book."

The Idea

There are plenty of books about writing (I wrote some of them myself), but the world needs a book about writers' complaints. Writers need to know that when they complain, they are part of a long literary tradition. Witness the first-century Roman poet Martial, who griped, "My book is thumbed by our soldiers posted overseas, and even in Britain people quote my words. What's the point? I don't make a penny."

Wannabe writers need to learn how to complain about their craft from the masters, authors like Hemingway and Fitzgerald, Parker and Capote.

Why Did I Bother? gathers together complaints from the past and combines them with juicy tidbits from the present.

The centerpiece is Jennifer's loose and pithy abridgement of Balzac's *Lost Illusions*, the greatest tale of author woe ever written—young, wet-behind-the-ears poet arrives in Paris, is quickly shunned by publishers, tries again, and succeeds, only to learn after the fact that his novel has been published (no one ever told him, they changed the title, he hates the cover) and then quickly remaindered. Sound like what everyone complains about now in cafés everywhere? You bet, but this all takes place in 1840. *Plus ça change ….*

Today's writers need to know that they are not alone in their frustration, not by any means. Take cheer in the bad reviews of well-known literary figures, in potshots they take at one another, at the petty complaints they indulge in. John Steinbeck didn't like his pencils, and Stephen King doesn't like Stephanie Meyer.

The Book

Intro—Jennifer the editor welcomes fledgling writers and warns them of the rocky shoals ahead …

Section 1—Famous Writers Complain—Hemingway, Twain, Fitzgerald, and many others unleash their disdain upon the world of writing and publishing. They also complain noisily about each other, academics knife each other's manuscripts during peer review, and critics eviscerate both the known and the unknown without mercy.

Section 2—*Lost Illusions*, Writ Small—Balzac's classic tale of woe, the young and talented Lucien arrives in Paris, ready to claim the praise he is due.

Section 3—This Could Happen to You—Cautionary Tales from Today—Tale after tale of instances of When Bad Things Happen to Good Writers. Your name is wrong on the cover, the author picture is of someone else, and *The Today Show* has changed its mind about booking you.

Section 4—Stern Words of Advice—What Every Writer Needs to Know—The voice of Jennifer the editor emerges from hiding (well, perhaps it has been there all along) to console writers about the business of writing. Some of it is encouraging; much of it is hard to hear; all of it is useful.

Sample Material

A Writer's Worst Enemy—Another Writer:

Maureen Dowd on Dan Brown's *The Lost Symbol:* "The author has gotten rich and famous without attaining a speck of subtlety."

Pete Dexter on successful writers: "Jealousy's the wrong word for what I usually feel," he said. "It's closer to hoping they get hit by a car."

Norman Mailer on Ernest Hemingway's *Old Man and the Sea:* "I think if he had written the story 20 years ago it would have been half as long and twice as good."

Norman Mailer on Arthur Miller, looking back to when they both lived in the same Brooklyn brownstone: "I know he was thinking what I was, which was, 'That other guy is never going to amount to anything.'"

Norman Mailer on Tom Wolfe's *A Man in Full:* "At certain points, reading the work can even be said to resemble the act of making love to a 300-pound woman. Once she gets on top, it's over. Fall in love, or be asphyxiated."

Gore Vidal on Norman Mailer (while lying on the ground after Mailer punched him): "Words fail Norman Mailer yet again."

John Updike on Tom Wolfe's *A Man in Full:* "… entertainment, not literature, even literature in a modest aspirant form."

John Irving on Tom Wolfe: "I can't read him because he's such a bad writer … He's a journalist … he can't create a character. He can't create a situation … If I were teaching fucking freshman English I couldn't read [one of Wolfe's sentences] and not just carve it up."

Tom Wolfe on John Irving: "Irving needs to get up off his bottom and leave that farm in Vermont or wherever it is he stays and start living again. It wouldn't be that hard. All he'd have to do is get out and take a deep breath and talk to people and see things and rediscover the fabulous and wonderfully bizarre country around him: America."

Stephen King on Stephanie Meyer's *Twilight* series: "… Stephanie Meyer can't write worth a damn. She's not very good."

Stephen King on James Patterson: "… I don't respect his books because every one is the same."

Gore Vidal after hearing of the death of William F. Buckley Jr.: "… hell is bound to be a livelier place, as he joins forever those whom he served in life, applauding their prejudices and fanning their hatred."

Ernest Hemingway on Ford Maddox Ford: "He is so goddam involved in being the dregs of an English country gentleman that you get no good out of him."

T. S. Eliot on all writers: "Good literature is produced by a few queer people in odd corners."

Norman Mailer on Saul Bellow: "It is not demanding to write about characters considerably more defeated than oneself."

Lynn Freed on teaching MFA student writers: "Had marriage been this bad? I tried to remember."

Philip Roth on James Patterson and Nora Roberts: "I don't know their books. They are entertainers. They aren't writers."

Robert B. Parker on everyone else: "Writer's block? That's just another word for lazy."

F. Scott Fitzgerald on writers in general: "I avoided writers carefully, because they can perpetuate trouble as no one else can."

Vladimir Nabokov on E. M. Forster: "My knowledge of Mr. Forster's works is limited to one novel, which I dislike …."

Nabokov on almost everyone else: "Many accepted authors simply do not exist for me. Their names are engraved on empty graves, their books are dummies, they are complete nonentities insofar as my taste in reading is concerned. Brecht, Faulkner, Camus, many others, mean absolutely nothing to me, and I must fight a suspicion of conspiracy against my brain when I see blandly accepted as 'great literature' by critics and fellow authors Lady Chatterley's copulations or the pretentious nonsense of Mr. Pound, that total fake. I note he has replaced Dr. Schweitzer in some homes."

Writers on Readers:

John Steinbeck: "I don't think the lovers of Hemingway will love this book. You may have noticed that young people in particular like only one kind of book."

Michel de Montaigne: "I am myself the matter of my book. You would be unreasonable to spend your leisure on so frivolous and vain a subject."

Audrey Niffenegger of *The Time Traveler's Wife* to her fans: "I do read all my e-mail. Then I resolve to answer it after I've had more coffee. Then I end up weeks and weeks behind, and it all starts to seem overwhelming. I am in awe of Jodi Picoult, who answers all her e-mail. You should write to her."

Critics on Writers:

Jonathan Yardley of *The Washington Post:* "… writers are rarely as nice, or as decent or as likeable, as the characters whom they bring to life."

Dwight Macdonald of *Playboy* on Carolyn See: "Carolyn See isn't half the writer she thinks she is."

Lawrence Leighton, *The Hound and the Horn* (1932): "I wish to consider the work of Messrs. Ernest Hemingway, John Dos Passos, and F. Scott Fitzgerald and to indicate my reasons for finding it repulsive, sterile, and dead."

Sven Birkerts, *The New York Observer:* "I'm talking now about Philip Roth, John Updike, Norman Mailer and, to a degree, Saul Bellow, though one wouldn't need a shoehorn to get a few others on to the list. [Their] latest novels … are weak, makeshift, and gravely disappointing to all who believed that these novelists had a special line on the truth(s) of late modernity. Not one of the books can stand in the vicinity of their author's finest work … the books flow forth yearly, whether they need to or not."

Writers Complain Some More:

Gay Talese: "Nonfiction writers are second-class citizens, the Ellis Island of literature. We just can't quite get in. And yes, it pisses me off."

Oscar Wilde: "I spent the morning putting in a comma, / And the afternoon taking it out."

John Steinbeck: "Before too long I am going to have to write Chapter One."

Samuel Beckett: "All of old. Nothing else ever. Ever tried. Ever failed. No matter. Try again. Fail again. Fail better."

Anonymous (for good reason): "I ran into Patty the day her ninth book became her first to hit the *Times* bestseller list. She grabbed me by the shoulders, looked deep into my eyes. 'It doesn't change anything,' she said grimly. 'My mother still doesn't approve of me. I still don't have a boyfriend. I still can't sleep at night. Don't let this be what you're waiting for.'"

John Steinbeck: "For years I have looked for the perfect pencil. I have found very good ones but never the perfect one. And all the time it was not the pencils but me. A pencil that is all right some days is no good another day."

Oscar Wilde: "The artistic life is one long, lovely suicide."

Ernest Hemingway on *A Farewell to Arms*: "All I got out of this book was disappointment. I'm a professional writer now … there isn't anything lower. I just hate the whole damn thing."

F. Scott Fitzgerald on the cover illustration for *The Beautiful and Damned*: "The more I think of the picture on the jacket the more I fail to understand his drawing that man. The girl is excellent, of course—it looks somewhat like Zelda, but the man, I suspect, is a sort of debauched edition of me. At any rate, the man is utterly unprepossessing, and I do not understand an artist of Hill's talent and carefulness going quite contrary to a detailed description of the hero in a book."

Philip Roth: "I don't expect anything from them [the Nobel Prize committee]. And they usually reward my expectation."

Truman Capote, after his glamorous friends realized he was writing about them and abandoned him: "What did they expect? I'm a writer, I use everything."

Michael Chabon: "A book itself repeatedly tries to kill its author during its composition."

Harper Lee: "When you are at the top there is only one way to go."

Stephen King: "Look, writing a novel is like paddling from Boston to London in a bathtub. Sometimes the damn thing sinks."

Academics with Long Knives:

From a peer review:

> The true scholarly meatiness of the book gets lost in verbal fat.

> An example of a study that undercuts its certainly significant contributions with a prose presentation that is often pedantic and wordy, repetitive and tiring.

Author's Haiku:

A few syllables with which to sum up a career:

> I hate the cover
> Publicity never called!
> My editor left

> At last! I got signed.
> Then the book was remaindered…
> My agent dropped me.

Writers and Their Money:

The Washington Post on Twain's hapless investing record: "One way to locate an unsafe investment is to find out whether or not Mark Twain has been permitted to get in on the ground floor."

End of sample material.

Marketing and Promotion

Jennifer has the opportunity and the ability to market *Why Did I Bother?* in many different ways. Her professional life is built around writers—she teaches them at UC Davis Extension, she takes them on writing retreats, she advises and consults with them on their projects, and she speaks and teaches at writers' conferences. In addition to face-to-face contact with hundreds of writers a year, Jennifer maintains online presence in the writing world as well. Between online marketing of her Write by the Lake seminars and retreats, the Writers Who Wine group, and the MasterMind Writers group, there are countless viral mentions of Jennifer and her books for writers—every time she mentions it on Facebook, it appears on the pages of her friends, where it is seen by their friends, and on it goes ….

Among the opportunities to promote the book are:

UC Davis Extension—Jennifer teaches three writing courses a year for the Arts and Humanities department and also develops and moderates their open-to-the-public literary speakers series. This book would be a required text in her courses and would be mentioned in the thousands of course catalogs that UC Davis produces.

Write by the Lake (writebythelake.com)—A writers' retreat weekend in Lake Tahoe attended by more than 50 women a year and heavily marketed online, as well as through brochures and speeches and articles to thousands more every year. *Why Did I Bother?* would be included in all press and marketing mentions. Write by the Lake has its own Facebook group, and the book will be included on the page.

Writers Who Wine—Monthly social get-togethers for writers. Conceived and organized by Jennifer, this group now meets in Sacramento, Boise, and Lake Tahoe and is attended by hundreds of writers a month. The organization maintains a blog presence and also a Facebook page to which the book will be added.

MasterMind Writers—An online support group for writers founded by Jennifer and J. T. Long, her co-author on the e-book *The Writer's Secret: MasterMind Your Way to Publishing Success.* A daily writing prompt is sent out to followers on Facebook and through Twitter. The book will be promoted every day to these followers.

Jennifer's speaking and teaching schedule, spring and summer 2011:

March 5, 2011—author appearance, Sacramento Library Authors on the Move dinner

April 1–3, 2011—three workshops and speeches at the Whidbey Island Writers Conference

April–June 2011—teaching a UC Davis Extension nonfiction writing workshop

April 16—publishing talk, California Writers Club, Marin chapter, Book Passage bookstore

April–June—four weekend writing retreat sessions at Lake Tahoe, Write by the Lake

May 3—"How to Write About Your Mother" talk to women's club in Auburn

June 15—Sierra Writers Club publishing talk, Grass Valley

July 23—Young Writers conference, Marin County, "How to Think Like a Publisher"

Jennifer Basye Sander

Jennifer Basye Sander has been creating successful book products since 1983, the day she published her first book, *The Sacramento Women's Yellow Pages*, as a way of escaping a failing career in California politics. Since that day, she has worked in all aspects of the book publishing business, everything from book retailing to book publicity, from authoring *New York Times* best-selling books herself to acquiring them for a large trade publisher. A graduate of Mills College in Oakland, California, she has also attended professional publishing programs at Stanford University and the University of Chicago.

Jennifer creates books that sell. The books that she has developed have achieved in excess of $40 million in retail sales. As the senior editor and chief book developer for Prima Publishing (a now-defunct division of Random House), she developed well over 70 new titles. Book developers (packagers) spot a need in the marketplace for a book on a topic, develop a marketable concept, hire a writer, and then supervise the completion of the manuscript. Her most successful book ideas on staff were the "Cozy Series" of gift-size cookbooks (over 500,000 copies in print) and the "101 Best Home-Based Businesses for Women" series (over 400,000 copies in print). Since starting her own book development company, Big City Books Group, her best-selling creation is the "Miracle Books" series for William Morrow, a *New York Times* best-selling series with five titles and combined sales of over 300,000. She is also the author, co-author, or ghostwriter of more than 30 books herself, including the recent gift book hits *Wear More Cashmere* and *The Martini Diet*. Along with the New York agent Sheree Bykofsky, Jennifer authored *The Complete Idiot's Guide to Getting Published*, which is now in its fifth revised edition and has over 100,000 copies in print.

Jennifer and her books have been featured on CNBC, CNNfn, *The View* with Barbara Walters, *American Journal*, C-Span's *Book TV*, *Fox News*, *Living It Up with Ali and Jack*, *It's a Miracle*, and *Soap Talk* on ABC's Soap Opera Channel. Articles about Jennifer have appeared in *People*, *USA Today*, *Investors Business Daily*, the *New York Post*, *New York Newsday*, *Chicago Sun-Times*, *Cosmopolitan* magazine, the *Boston Globe*, the *Los Angeles Times*, the *Sacramento Bee*, and many other magazines, newspapers, and television shows. Jennifer was recently featured in *The National Enquirer* (Sarah Palin was on the front cover, but it was Jennifer in the two-page centerfold story!) with her book on budget living. For three years she was a weekly online columnist writing about entrepreneurship for *USA Today* and *Fortune Small Business*. She speaks regularly on the topics of writing and publishing, small business, personal finance, and lifestyle topics like indulgence and affordable luxury.

Jennifer leads a women's writing retreat 12 weekends a year in South Lake Tahoe, called Write by the Lake, and maintains active MasterMind groups in northern California to support her retreat attendees with their writing goals. She also hosts monthly get-together for northern California writers, Writers Who Wine. Close to 300 writers get biweekly e-mails from Jennifer. She teaches the nonfiction writing workshop and getting published courses for UC Davis Extension.

Books by Jennifer Basye Sander and Big City Books Group

Hot Flash Haiku (Adams Media)

Faith, Hope, and Healing (with Bernie Siegel, Wiley)

Boyfriend University (Wiley)

Green Christmas (Adams Media)

Wear More Silk: 151 Luxurious Ways to Add Adventure, Spice, and Romance to Your Everyday Life (Fairwinds)

The Gross News: True (and Truly Gross) News Stories from Around the World (Andrews McMeel)

Raging Gracefully: Smart Women on Life, Love, and Coming into Your Own After 40 (Adams Media)

Why We Love Moms (Adams Media)

Why We Love Dads (Adams Media)

MomSpa: 75 Relaxing Ways to Pamper a Mother's Mind, Body, and Soul (Fairwinds)

The Weekend Entrepreneur (Entrepreneur Press)

Opening the Gifts of Christmas (Andrews McMeel)

The Complete Idiot's Guide to Self-Publishing (Alpha Books)

The Pocket Idiot's Guide to Living on a Budget, Second Edition (Alpha Books)

Wear More Cashmere: 151 Luxurious Ways to Pamper Your Inner Princess (Fairwinds Press)

The Martini Diet: The Self-Indulgent Way to a Thinner, More Fabulous You (Fairwinds Press)

Christmas Miracles (Wm. Morrow)

A Gift of Miracles (Wm. Morrow)

The Magic of Christmas Miracles (Wm. Morrow)

Heavenly Miracles (Wm. Morrow)

Mothers' Miracles (Wm. Morrow)

The Miracle of Boys: Heartwarming True Stories to Inspire Parents (Perigee)

The Complete Idiot's Guide to Getting Published (now in a fifth revised edition; Alpha Books)

The Millionairess Across the Street (Dearborn)

The Complete Idiot's Guide to Investing for Women (Alpha Books)

101 Best Extra Income Opportunities for Women (Prima)

The Complete Idiot's Guide to Day Trading (Alpha Books)

How to Become a Successful Weekend Entrepreneur (Prima)

The Sacramento Women's Yellow Pages (two revised editions, Big City Books)

The Air Courier's Handbook (six revised editions, Big City Books)

Creating Wealth on the Web (Adams)

The Complete Idiot's Guide to Publishing Magazine Articles (Alpha Books)

The Quotable Businesswoman (Andrews McMeel)

Love Stinks: A Collection of Romantic Writing on Jealousy, Envy, and Revenge (Andrews McMeel)

Niche and Grow Rich: How to Turn a Unique Idea into a Fortune (Entrepreneur Press)

Don't Sweat the Small Stuff Story Collection (Don't Sweat Press/Hyperion Publishing)

Ghostwritten books:

What's Your Net Worth? (Perseus Publishing)

Sample Proposal 2

Don't Swallow Your Gum! Mistakes, Half-Truths, and Outright Lies About Your Body and Health

A proposal by
Aaron E. Carroll, M.D., M.S., and Rachel C. Vreeman, M.D.
Represented by Sheree Bykofsky Associates, Inc.

Table of Contents

The Idea

The Authors

The Market

The Competition

The Promotion

Chapter Outline

Sample Material

Additional Materials

  Op-ed piece written by Dr. Carroll

  Press clippings on research by Dr. Carroll and Dr. Vreeman

  Links to radio and TV interviews by Dr. Carroll and Dr. Vreeman

The Idea

Have you ever walked past a cemetery and thought for just a moment about the growing, curling fingernails of the corpses underneath you? When you saw that man with enormous feet, did you wonder if other parts of him were just as large? Did the Thanksgiving turkey make you fall asleep before the football game? Have you considered switching to waxing your legs because shaving just makes the hair grow back faster and thicker? Are you worried that you'll never be able to drink the recommended 8 glasses of water a day? After working so hard to stick to your diet, do you get a little nervous at the thought of all those calories in semen—especially since eating at night makes you fat?

You were wrong. You believed a medical myth. Although everyone has more access to medical information than ever before, we still believe things about our body and health that are just wrong. Some of the things you hear are simply unproven. Many more of these ideas about your body and how to keep it healthy have actually been proven through scientific evidence to be untrue. And yet, we still see these things on TV, read about them in magazines, or hear them from our friends. *Don't Swallow Your Gum! Mistakes, Half-Truths, and Outright Lies About Your Body and Health* explains why so many of those weird and worrisome things we think about our bodies are mistaken.

In our professional lives, we spend a good deal of our time teaching people, from parents to other physicians, how to understand health research. You would be amazed at how often even doctors do not understand *why* we come to accept something as true. Doctors might tell you that you need to be worried about strangers poisoning your kid's Halloween candy or that adding a little cereal to your baby's bottle will help him or her sleep through the night. They might even secretly think that most people only use about 10 percent of their brains. But these doctors would all be wrong. They are relying on what they have heard and not on what the science really says.

We first started investigating health myths to remind doctors in a light-hearted way that they need to consider the research behind the things they believe. We will publish a very short version of this concept as an article in the prominent *British Medical Journal* in late 2007. However, doctors are certainly not the only people who might believe these things. From the health nut religiously taking vitamin C to the guy surreptitiously picking up the cookie off the floor before 5 seconds pass, people believe plenty of things about their bodies and health that are just not true. Readers of *Don't Swallow Your Gum!* will be amazed to discover how simple facts that they have read or heard again and again, even from "reputable sources," have absolutely no truth behind them.

Changing beliefs is no simple task. We have no wish to be one more expert opinion; in *Don't Swallow Your Gum!* we want to show you the science. All of the beliefs debunked in *Don't Swallow Your Gum!* will be accompanied by a discussion of the research done to disprove them. We want you to love the research, not to be confused by it. We enjoy nothing more than telling our friends and family members about these myths and hearing them yell, "What?" when they find out that yet another thing they believed is really a lie.

That's what we want to hear from our readers—the shocked "What?" or the sigh of relief about the question they never dared to ask. Every day, we explain complicated scientific research so that others can understand it. In *Don't Swallow Your Gum!* we combine a vernacular voice and authoritative research to show that evidence exists to disprove these myths, from the basic concerns about whether you are pooping enough to the complicated questions about whether vaccines are really safe. We will clarify exactly how the science leads to our conclusions, but we hope you'll forget we're doctors at least some of the time. We like to think of our book as an amalgam of *You: The Owners Manual* and *Why Do Men Have Nipples? Don't Swallow Your Gum!* not only includes myths from sources as disparate as locker rooms and your grandmother, but it also describes the research disproving them. Plus, *Don't Swallow Your Gum!* delves into more complicated or controversial areas, such as drug company tactics, what medical advice doesn't work, and things that cause cancer. Whether you are a teenager wondering if you should use two condoms, a parent wondering if your child's eyes will be permanently damaged from reading after lights out, a professional trying to avoid getting sick this winter, or a dedicated conspiracy theorist always on alert for how the establishment is out to get you, you will learn something new from our book.

Don't Swallow Your Gum!'s evidence-based approach will leave readers feeling that they really understand *why* the things they have heard are outright lies, even as they are shocked to learn these things aren't true. We envision this book as 60,000–70,000 words long with about 120 myths. One of the strengths inherent in our approach is the ease with which we can add or remove myths from this list to accommodate the needs of a publisher or editors.

The Authors

Aaron E. Carroll, M.D., M.S., is an assistant professor of pediatrics at the Indiana University School of Medicine. Although he wanted to be a doctor for as long as he can remember, he realized, even in college, that he was much more interested in understanding why things are true than in actually learning the things themselves. As a pediatric resident, Dr. Carroll earned a reputation as a bit of a troublemaker for continually questioning the beliefs and practices of his superiors; if anything, this reputation only solidified as his career progressed. Dr. Carroll has had remarkable training, earning a B.A. in chemistry from Amherst College, an M.D. from the University of Pennsylvania School of Medicine, and a M.S. in health services research from the University of Washington School of Public Health. He also spent two years as a Robert Wood Johnson Clinical Scholar, honing his skills as a Health Services researcher. Dr. Carroll serves on a number of committees for the American Academy of Pediatrics, the American Medical Informatics Association, and various government organizations at both the state and federal level. Dr. Carroll is a very accomplished young Health Services researcher, having authored over 30 publications in the medical literature. His research has been covered in magazines and newspapers all over the world and has been featured in many medical and legal blogs. He has also published opinion pieces in the *Indianapolis Star* and been interviewed about his work for radio shows and print media. Dr. Carroll's areas of interest are varied, but most of his work still centers on proving that what we often believe is not quite right; many of his publications are in controversial areas of health policy or professional practices.

Dr. Carroll has been a speaker at conferences across the United States and in Canada. He has also been an invited presenter to audiences of all types to speak on issues ranging from health-care reform to pharmaceutical company practices. He is an engaging speaker and takes great pride in his skill in convincing people to change their minds through his use of research and facts; he rarely loses an argument.

Rachel C. Vreeman, M.D., is currently a fellow in children's health services research at the Indiana University School of Medicine. Dr. Vreeman prepared for medical school by following the untraditional path of majoring in English literature at Cornell University where she received her B.A. While at Cornell, she also polished her practical writing skills working as the public relations coordinator for a nonprofit organization that runs educational programs in Nepal. Dr. Vreeman may be the only recipient of Cornell's award for the best honors thesis in English to earn an M.D. Little did she know that all of her essays and press releases would prepare her perfectly for the world of academic medicine, where the best medical research ideas constantly need translation into language that anyone can understand. After earning her M.D. at the Michigan State University College of Human Medicine and specialty training in pediatrics at the Indiana University School of Medicine, Dr. Vreeman became convinced that the best way to improve children's health is to invest time and energy in things that actually work. Out of the desire to determine what health services matter, she entered health services research and began pursuit of a Master's in clinical research science. Dr. Vreeman has developed and published a tool to assess physicians' compliance with guidelines for managing ADHD. She also investigated and published a critical review of bullying prevention methods. Now considered a national expert on bullying prevention, Dr. Vreeman is a member of the U.S. Department of Health and Human Services Bullying Prevention Working Group and has been interviewed for newspapers, magazines, websites, radio, and television about what schools can really do to decrease bullying.

After Dr. Vreeman served as a chief resident for pediatrics at Indiana University, she joined the quest to improve physician education in evidence-based medicine. She teamed with Dr. Carroll to study the interactions of pharmaceutical companies with medical trainees and then to investigate medical myths, leading to conference presentations, a medical journal article, and now to the creation of this book.

Dr. Vreeman's magazine and web interviews include articles in *The Times Educational Supplement, MedlinePlus,* and several articles on kaboose.com. Even her misfortunes seem to garner good publicity as the *Wall Street Journal* described the theft of her home's central air-conditioning unit. She has been interviewed by the NPR-affiliated radio show *Sound Medicine* on several occasions, including interviews on what home remedies really work for the common cold, what schools can actually do to prevent bullying, and orphans and HIV care for children in Africa. She has also been interviewed for television by the Indianapolis CBS affiliate, WISH-TV.

The Market

The market for our book is large and varied. We believe that tailoring specific campaigns to these markets would likely increase sales.

1) *Physicians*—There are currently over 800,000 physicians practicing in the United States. Our initial paper was pitched at this audience and was quickly accepted into the *British Medical Journal*, one of the most widely read medical journals in the world. Many physicians are asked about the beliefs contained in our book on a regular basis. Discovering where their own answers are wrong, or even learning *why* they are right, would be of interest to many of them.

2) *Parents*—Many of the beliefs we confront in our book specifically pertain to children. In our practices, we have been bombarded with many questions that would be answered by reading our book. Parents want to do what is right for their children and may be particularly susceptible to following "expert advice" without realizing when it's unfounded. All told, there are about 73 million children in the United States, all of whom have parents. There are approximately 24 million children under the age of 6, and an additional 24 million between 6 and 11. These would be the parents most interested in the book's material.

3) *"Mythbusters"*—Although this term specifically refers to a successful television show, and we would never use it without permission, a significant number of people are entertained by the concept of disproving accepted facts. Over a million of them regularly tune in to watch the television show. Call them curmudgeons, skeptics, or disbelievers, they would be drawn to a book such as ours.

4) *General interest*—We are sure that many authors believe their book will appeal to everyone, but there has traditionally been a large and long-standing interest in books about health. We would be remiss if we did not at least acknowledge this large audience. In fact, the success of many other books in similar areas is a testament to this population. Many people are fascinated by the weird and wonderful workings of the body.

Anecdotally, we have yet to tell someone a few of these myths and not have the person want to know what makes them untrue. From teenagers to educated professionals, almost everyone has wondered if one of these myths just might be true.

The Competition

Although no books currently exist that exactly duplicate our approach and content matter, there are, of course, some that share similarities with ours. As we have stated before, our methodology crosses a number of genres and combines the strengths of them.

Why Do Men Have Nipples? and *Why Do Men Fall Asleep After Sex?* by Mark Leyner and Billy Goldberg, M.D. (Three Rivers Press) are very successful books that answer many medical questions, often with a humorous bent. There is some overlap with some of the myths we propose to cover. However, they often rely on expert opinion for their answers, which has led to their inadvertently perpetuating a medical myth on at least one occasion. Even when they do mention studies that support their reasoning, they do not describe why the studies can be trusted or what the studies actually show. Moreover, these books are more focused on trivia and odd facts and are less likely to have useful, everyday applications.

Can a Guy Get Pregnant? by Bill Sones and Rich Sones, Ph.D. (Pi Press) is similar to the previous two in its content and format. It includes more myths about animals and nature, however, and fewer regarding our bodies or health.

You: The Owner's Manual by Michael F. Roizen, M.D., and Mehmet C. Oz, M.D. (Collins) is a comprehensive book that focuses on specifics about the body. Although it does overlap in some material with ours, it does not discuss any aspects of health outside of the body, nor does it focus on mistaken beliefs like ours does. Furthermore, this book remains much more serious in tone.

The Promotion

As we stated in the Market section, we believe that a varied approach to promotion, targeting the different audiences, would be the most successful. However, we would be remiss if we did not at least attempt to make use of the additional opportunities that will present themselves in the course of our promotion of our manuscript in the *British Medical Journal*. The paper is set for release at the end of December. We are quite experienced at promoting our research in the media and have the use of experts employed by our university to aid us.

We are planning press releases for wide distribution before the paper is released and have already scheduled some radio interviews which will be broadcast throughout the state and on our local National Public Radio affiliate. These would be perfect opportunities to begin to hype an upcoming book. Indeed, when we have talked to some of the radio hosts about this potential book, they expressed interest in having us back a number of times to delve into the topic more deeply. With that said, we still have a number of ideas through which we could gain publicity for this book.

We would be willing to coordinate the creation of a website about the book and would be happy to contribute to it regularly. Both of us are quite experienced with technology and would welcome this opportunity. Moreover, we have a good sense of how to spread awareness of such a website to other sites, blogs, and organizations.

We would also be excited to help organize a "virtual book tour." We could designate a specific month or two and query websites and blogs aligned with the book (including those related to health, trivia, and "mythbusting") about whether they would like to host us to answer questions about medical myths or to talk about the book's content. For example, Dr. Vreeman has previously consulted for a series of articles on bullying for the popular parenting site kaboose.com, and she could ask the site's editors if they would like to focus several segments on myths parents believe. With each of these virtual book tour sites, we could include direct links for readers to buy our book.

In addition, we believe a targeted approach to various market populations will be the most cost effective.

1) *Physicians*—Our first plan of attack would be to make use of our significant contacts all over the country to notify physicians about the book. We would also target professional publications with press releases as well as inquiries to review the book. We have done such reviews for other books for medical associations such as The Ambulatory Pediatrics Association, and we could ask for a review in turn. In addition, we are active members of large physician associations, including the American Academy of Pediatrics, the Ambulatory Pediatrics Association, the Society for Pediatric Research, and the International AIDS Society. We have access to listservs through these organizations, as well as to listservs of faculty members at several medical schools, chief residents around the country, and researchers in sexually transmitted diseases (who are always excited to debunk sex myths). We would also be happy to speak at "Grand Rounds," the customary talks given to hospital staff, in the Midwest and beyond as requested in order to discuss the work behind the book. We are experienced with describing our work in these settings.

2) *Parents*—Obviously, this is a larger demographic than physicians, and we therefore would recommend that more of the general publicity be targeted at this group. General press releases could highlight some of the myths more pertinent to parents, as could our radio interviews. In particular, the radio interviews for health-related radio could focus on parental worries. Selecting certain myths to hype at different times to different audiences could maximize interest. We would also direct press releases and books to parenting magazines, which often are receptive to physicians, particularly pediatricians, who are interested in speaking through them. We would also take advantage of contacts we have through schools and local groups and offer ourselves as speakers to interested parties. As previously mentioned, parenting websites could be an important component of our virtual book tour.

3) *Mythbusters*—This group will be most interested in some of our more controversial myths, as well as those that are often hyped in the media. We will make sure to prominently feature these in press releases and in interviews to attract interest from this dedicated demographic. Again, websites targeted at mythbusters are natural options for virtual book tour promotion.

4) *General interest*—We will, of course, make use of all other contacts as well. These will include our various alumni organizations and schools, which are interested in recognizing and promoting books written by their graduates. We will also appeal to our personal contacts, friends, and family to help promote the book. Although this is likely something that every author attempts, we have lived all over the country at various times and have contacts throughout the United States; moreover, these contacts are nearly all professionals and in positions of relative authority. Many would be willing to buy a book and talk about it with friends.

Chapter Outline

Introduction

PART I: "Look at the size of his feet!" Myths about your body.

1. Men with big feet have bigger penises.

2. You only use 10 percent of your brain.

3. Your hair and fingernails continue to grow after you die.

4. If you shave your hair, it will grow back faster, darker, and thicker.

5. If you read in the dark, you'll ruin your eyes.

6. The average person swallows eight spiders a year.

7. You should poop at least once a day.

8. You don't get thirsty until you're already dehydrated.

9. Your urine should be almost clear.

10. Virgins don't have an opening in their hymen.

11. You can tear your hymen if you ride horses or do gymnastics or …

12. Losing weight will make your penis bigger.

13. You can beat a breathalyzer by sucking on a penny.

14. If you don't shut your eyes while you sneeze, your eyeballs will pop out.

PART II: "Do you want to catch pneumonia out there?" Myths about how you get and treat diseases.

15. Cold or wet weather makes you sick.

16. You get a hernia from lifting something heavy.

17. You can catch poison ivy from someone else who has it.

18. Short-haired or nonshedding dogs are better for allergies.

19. A dog's mouth is cleaner than a human's mouth.

20. You should never wake up someone who's sleepwalking.

21. Mucus color matters.

22. Cell phones are a danger to patients in hospitals.

23. Don't take a hot shower if you're sick.

24. You should put butter on a burn.

25. Blisters heal faster if you pop them.

26. Flu shots sometimes cause the flu.

27. You need to stay awake if you've had a concussion.

28. If you agree to donate your organs, the doctors won't work as hard to save your life.

PART III: "You're going to get cancer!" Myths about cancer.

29. If I drink diet soda, if I don't eat enough fruit, if I eat food that's been grilled too long, I'll get cancer.

30. Reusing plastic water bottles is dangerous.

31. You are much more likely to die from cancer than you used to be.

32. Using deodorant causes breast cancer (prepare for BO).

33. If I drink alcohol, I'm going to get breast cancer.

34. Breast cancer is the most common killer of women.

35. When it comes to SPF, the higher the better.

PART IV: "Natural is safer." Myths about alternative therapies.

36. Herbs and natural medicines are safer than the drugs doctors prescribe.

37. Vitamin C can keep you from getting sick.

38. Echinacea cures colds.

39. If the echinacea doesn't work, you can try zinc.

40. If the zinc doesn't work, try Airborne®.

41. Breast milk can cure ear infections.

42. So will a clove of garlic.

43. Acupuncture doesn't really work.

44. Doctors hate alternative therapies.

PART V: "Every seven seconds!" Myths about sex.

45. Men think about sex every 7 seconds.

46. Condoms will protect you from all STDs.

47. Most women lose interest in sex after menopause.

48. Your orgasm gets weaker with age.

49. Semen is loaded with calories.

50. Sex is better if you're not circumcised.

51. Singles have much better sex lives than married people.

52. Geeks who play video games don't get laid much.

53. If you talk to kids about sex, it will make them want to do it.

54. Your doctor can tell if you're a virgin or not.

55. Your doctor can tell if you have had anal sex.

56. Don't have sex the night before a big game.

PART VI: "But I was on my period!" Myths about getting knocked up.

57. You can't get pregnant during your period.

58. You can't get pregnant if he pulls out before he comes.

59. You can't get pregnant while having sex standing up.

60. You can't get pregnant if you have sex in the water.

61. You can't get pregnant when you're on the pill.

62. It's better to use two condoms than to use just one.

63. Birth control pills don't work as well if you're on antibiotics.

64. If you really want a baby girl, you should have sex like this ….

65. You can tell if the baby is going to be a boy or a girl by seeing if the mother is carrying low or carrying high. Or if the heart rate is higher. Or by mixing the mother's urine with Drano. Or if you use a Chinese fertility chart. Or …

66. Twins skip a generation.

67. Flying on a plane will hurt your baby.

68. If you are pregnant, you better not eat feta cheese. Or sushi. Or …

69. Pregnant women need to avoid eating fish.

70. Bed rest prevents preterm labor.

PART VII: "He won't get into Harvard without Baby Einstein®." Myths about babies.

71. Baby Einstein® will make your baby smarter.

72. Adding cereal to your baby's bottle will make him or her sleep longer.

73. Teething can cause a fever.

74. Prop up your baby to stop the spitting up.

75. It's safe to have your baby sleep in your bed.

76. Babies who don't poop in a week are in big trouble.

77. Babies need water when it's hot outside.

78. You can spoil a baby.

79. It's okay to drink alcohol when you're breast-feeding.

80. Over-the-counter infant cold medicines are safe for babies.

81. Using a walker will teach your baby to walk earlier.

82. Formula with iron will constipate your baby.

PART VIII: "Get that kid to the doctor!" Myths about children's health.

83. If your kid gets a lot of sore throats, the doctor will take out his or her tonsils.

84. Video games make kids violent.

85. Sick kids need antibiotics.

86. Too many antibiotics will make your kid resistant.

87. Ritalin for ADHD will make your kid an addict.

88. Juice is healthy for kids.

89. Kids need to take vitamins.

90. If your kid gets diarrhea, he or she can only have bland foods.

91. Benadryl helps kids sleep on planes.

92. Cough medicines work for kids.

PART IX: "Don't you dare swallow your gum!" Myths about your food and drink.

93. Chewing gum stays in your stomach forever.

94. Eat your spinach to grow strong like Popeye.

95. I saw it on *Seinfeld*—eating turkey makes you sleepy!

96. Milk makes you phlegmy.

97. You just ate! You can't go in the pool yet.

98. You can burn fat by eating things like grapefruit and cabbage soup.

99. Drinking Coke or coffee will just dehydrate you.

100. Eating at night makes you fat.

101. You should drink at least 8 glasses of water a day.

102. Sugar makes kids hyper.

103. If you pick up food within 5 seconds of it hitting the floor, it's still safe to eat.

PART X: "Bad moon rising." Myths about certain times of the year.

104. The full moon makes people go crazy.

105. Strangers have poisoned kids' Halloween candy.

106. You should have your kids' Halloween candy x-rayed.

107. Holidays cause suicides.

108. More women get beaten on Super Bowl Sunday.

109. More babies are born during the full moon.

110. Hospitals are unsafe in July when the new doctors start.

PART XI: "Shots made my baby autistic." Myths that spark controversy and debate.

111. Vaccines cause autism.

112. You don't really need the chickenpox vaccine.

113. Teachers want kids on Ritalin to make their jobs easier.

114. Fluoride in your drinking water is bad for you.

115. Newer drugs are better.

116. Dental fillings cause mercury poisoning.

117. Doctors get sued because they make big mistakes.

Sample Material

Myth #3: Your hair and fingernails continue to grow after you die.

Have you ever walked across a cemetery and thought about the growing, curling fingernails of the corpses underneath you? This is an incredibly creepy idea, the kind of thing you might hear around a campfire as a kid when your friends take turns trying to scare one another. It has such a morbid appeal that artists have used this image in books and movies for a long time. In the 1929 novel *All Quiet on the Western Front*, the author describes the eerie image of a friend's fingernails growing in corkscrews after the burial. A character in the 1959 movie *The Tingler* claims that hair and nails continue to grow after one's death. Johnny Carson even joked, "For three days after death, hair and fingernails continue to grow, but phone calls taper off."

Despite the popularity, it's just not true. To quote the expert opinion of forensic anthropologist William R. Maples, "It is a powerful, disturbing image, but it is pure moonshine. No such thing occurs."

This myth does have a basis in the reality of what happens to your body in the grave. After you die, your body begins to dry out or become dehydrated. As the skin dries out, it shrinks. (This is a different kind of shrinkage than what happens to a man in cold water.) The shrinking or retracting of the skin around the hair and nails makes them look longer or more prominent compared to the shrunken skin. It's just an optical illusion, though; the nails and hair stay the same, it's the skin that pulls back and tightens a bit. To really keep growing, hair and nails require a complex mixture of hormones and hormone signaling that is just not going to happen after you die. Studies of the cellular regulation of hair growth confirm that a person would need to be alive for his or her hair to keep growing. So there's no need to book a haircut and manicure for your corpse, no matter how long it's been since the last one.

Index

Find us on
facebook®

facebook.com/completeidiotsguides

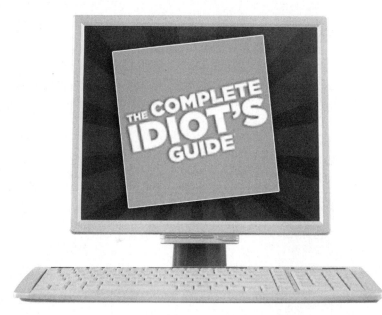

Become a fan and
get updates on upcoming
titles, author book
signing events, coupons,
and much more!

ALPHA